The
Six
Unsolved
Ciphers

The Six Unsolved Ciphers

Inside the Mysterious Codes That Have Confounded the World's Greatest Cryptographers

RICHARD BELFIELD

Ulysses Press

Published in the U.S. by
Ulysses Press
P.O. Box 3440
Berkeley, CA 94703
www.ulyssespress.com

First published in Great Britain in 2006 as *Can You Crack the Enigma Code?*
by Orion Books, an imprint of the Orion Publishing Group Ltd.

ISBN10: 1-56975-628-7
ISBN13: 978-1-56975-628-7
Library of Congress Control Number: 2007905465

Printed in the United States by Bang Printing

10 9 8 7 6 5 4 3 2 1

Editorial Associates: Amy Hough, Elyce Petker, Lauren Harrison
U.S. Proofreader: Tiffany Watson
Production: Judith Metzener, Lisa Kester, Tamara Kowalski
Index: Sayre Van Young
Cover design: Double R Design

Distributed by Publishers Group West

For George, Gloria and Lowell
As always

Contents

Acknowledgments

There is only one name on the cover of this book, but inevitably there are many people who help writers along the way—and one of the best things about being an author is that you can thank people publicly.

First off, a huge round of applause for Carlos Cid, Jason Crampton, Laurence O'Toole and Kenny Paterson at the Information Security Group, Royal Holloway, University of London, who set the code which underpins the title of this book. Being in a room with four enormous brains, all of whom think completely differently, has given me a huge buzz every time and I am eternally grateful for their wit, perception and great humor. A special thanks to Kenny and Jason, who very kindly read the manuscript and made lots of excellent suggestions.

My son George did the original research, having just completed a History Degree at Manchester University, and he has been a fine sounding board while I plowed on. As ever, my two other children, Gloria and Lowell, have been fantastic, always supportive, and the endless games of table tennis on the kitchen table have been a great relief when my head has been spinning with numbers and letters and other intractable problems.

Several people have given me invaluable insights throughout the writing: Andrew Baker, Nicholas Gibbs, Richard Kemp, Robert Noel and David Watkin all provided great help in trying to untangle the web of mystery at Shugborough. Ms. Christine Beauregard, the Senior Librarian in Manuscripts and Special Collections at the New York State Library in Albany, went out of her way to secure a copy of the Beale Papers. She is a model for librarians everywhere. Dave

Barclay gave me some very perceptive insights into the mind of the Zodiac killer. The staff at the British Library were helpful as always.

The staff at the publishers, Orion Books, have been brilliant. Ian Marshall, Lorraine Baxter and all others have been wonderful to work with, always enthusiastic, creative and supportive.

As ever, a small group of close friends helped refine my thinking and clarity of thought as I tried to explain the intricacies of the various stories. A big thanks to Jonathan Harris, Abdallah Homouda, John Hughes Wilson and Chrissy White. Catherine Cameron was a model of joyous efficiency throughout.

And finally—as they say in TV land ...

Having worked at both the BBC and ITV, I should follow the example of the truly ambitious and claim that the idea for this book was entirely my own, but it was not. It sprung from the ever creative brain of my agent, the excellent Robert Kirby at Peters, Fraser and Dunlop, when he had lunch with Nick Pritchard of the *Sunday Times*, who was originally going to write this book but then dropped out, giving me all the fun.

In the beginning
was the code ...
and the code
was good

"Few persons can be made to believe that it is not quite an easy thing to invent a method of secret writing which shall baffle investigation. Yet it may be roundly asserted that human ingenuity cannot concoct a cipher which human ingenuity cannot resolve."

Edgar Alan Poe,
a few words on secret writing, 1841

This book is a celebration
of those codes that have
defeated human ingenuity ...
and the creators of
the mysterious secrets
that lie within.

Introduction

> "Forty-two!" yelled Loonquawl. "Is that all you've got to show for seven and a half million years' work?"
>
> "I checked it very thoroughly," said the computer, "and that quite definitely is the answer. I think the problem, to be quite honest with you, is that you've never actually known what the question is."
>
> —Douglas Adams, the answer to the ultimate question of life, the universe and everything, *The Hitchhiker's Guide to the Galaxy*

January 1917

The war in Europe is locked in a mutually homicidal stalemate. The new industrialized warfare has reduced conflict to two matching conveyor belts: one to deliver soldiers to the Front, the other to take corpses to the nearest graveyard. It's the same for both sides, who are by now ground down in the shell-shocked mud of northern Europe and in a state of exhausted balance everywhere else—the Balkans, Eastern Europe and even parts of the Middle East. For the main protagonists—Britain and France on one side, and Germany on the other—there is only one real question: who will run out of young men first? The United States could make all the difference, but president Woodrow Wilson is firmly neutral, even though the Germans had sunk the cruise ship *Lusitania*, in May 1915, killing nearly twelve hundred passengers and crew, including more than one hundred and twenty American civilians.

1

Philosophically and emotionally, Wilson is a non-combatant, and he has a very good reason for staying out of the war: the continued armed struggle on the other side of the Atlantic is sensationally profitable for U.S. business.

At this stage of the war, jobs and prosperity at home are more valuable to the White House than the loss of a few dozen American lives. The *Lusitania* is an incident that can be spun and forgotten. The cruel fact is that both Britain and France are desperate for American goods: they require food to stay alive, as well as machinery to build the armaments needed to sustain the war in the killing fields of northern France. Both countries will pay whatever price is demanded, and the Americans know it.[2] The war would be even more profitable for the United States if they could only export to Germany as well, but the still-mighty British Navy maintains a firm blockade, stopping U.S. merchant shipping from getting anywhere near German harbors. The German response is to use their U-boat fleet to attack American merchant shipping as it crosses the Atlantic laden down with cargo.

Seeing Wilson's neutrality as weakness, the Germans come up with a plan to break the deadlock: they will build more U-boats, patrol the Atlantic far more effectively, sink the American merchant ships that are keeping Britain and France alive, and then starve their enemies to the negotiating table and a humiliating peace settlement. The time scheduled for this is just six months, after which follows the grand plan: once they sit astride a conquered Europe—and with much of the American merchant fleet at the bottom of the Atlantic—their thoughts can turn to the domination of the advanced commercial world, and that includes North America.

The view of the hawks in Berlin is that the United States is soft, not ready for conflict and therefore ripe for the taking. The German chancellor, Theobald von Bethmann-Hollweg, is opposed, describing the move as "*finis Germaniae*," meaning "the end of Germany." His vice-chancellor, Karl Helferrich, says, "Now Germany is lost for centuries."[3] But the prevailing mood in Berlin is that this is no time for caution. There is a war to be won, and global domination beckons the bold.

The first ever invasion of American soil by a foreign power would have followed but for the code-breaking skills of two men: the Reverend William Montgomery, a forty-five-year-old fluent-German-speaking divinity graduate, whose special area of interest is early Church history, and Nigel de Grey, a thirty-year-old former publisher, a lieutenant in the British Navy and already a cryptography veteran.

The Reverend William Montgomery has already impressed everyone who knows him. His translation from German of Albert Schweitzer's *The Quest of the Historical Jesus* is widely regarded as flawless, and he has a superbly fluid, lateral-thinking brain, solving puzzles that baffle everyone else, long before they become fashionable.

Sir Henry Jones, a professor of moral philosophy, receives a blank postcard from Turkey from his son who has been captured. The card is addressed to him, but not at his address, being sent instead to 184 Kings Road, Tighnabruaich, a tiny village in Scotland. It puzzles everyone, including Jones himself, who lectures on Christianity, but Montgomery cracks it straight away: "184 Kings Road" means "Chapter 18, Verse 4, the Book of Kings" from the Bible, which reads, "Obadiah took a hundred prophets and hid them by fifty in a cave, and fed them with bread and water." He is therefore able to tell Jones that his son is safe but living on a subsistence diet of bread and water.

The Reverend Montgomery's young sidekick is Lieutenant Nigel de Grey, who, with just two years' experience, is already one of Britain's most experienced wartime cryptographers.

They both work in Room 40, where a hastily assembled team of fluent-German-speakers and code-breakers are given the job of deciphering enemy communications. These brilliant men and women all share impeccable establishment credentials and are the quintessential ragtag army, which the British, above any other nation, specializes in assembling during wartime. They all come on personal recommendations, a cross-section of the flotsam of good "county and service families." There is an ancient historian, an expert on painted Greek ceramics and another who specializes in reading the fragments of bits of papyrus. Initially, they flounder, but after a few months, they get into their stride, the acquisition of three German naval code books giving them a good start. In a few months, they are running an effective operation cracking the bulk of naval traffic, though they quickly discover one of the more unpleasant facts of wartime code-breaking: having the intelligence and using it are two separate things, and some crucial intercepts are squandered. They discover that when the German admiral Reinhard Scheer is onboard ship in dock, he uses the code DK and then hands this over to someone else when he leaves. Shortly before the Battle of Jutland, they tell the director of British Naval Operations, Captain Thomas Jackson, that Scheer has already sailed, but he does not believe in cryptography and ignores them, an arrogant mistake.

Though much German naval traffic is relatively transparent, the crucial diplomatic traffic is a closed book, until they are gifted a huge stroke of luck. In 1915, a careless German diplomat, Wilhelm Wassmuss, leaves behind a code book called 13040 when he is transferred out of the Persian Gulf. But for this moment of rashness, Wassmuss would be something of a German hero. Regarded by the Germans as their Lawrence of Arabia, he organized an Iranian rebellion against the British, but the value of all his heroics in the Middle East is hugely outweighed by the value of the code book to the British, as it forms the basis for what will become the single most important piece of code-breaking of the twentieth century, an act that will turn the tide of modern history and affect the everyday lives of everyone on the planet.

Having the means to break key German communications is one thing; actually acquiring some messages to decrypt is another. As today, the international telegraph system in World War I is a system of interlocking national networks. The British try to find a weak spot, somewhere they can get in and siphon off the German messages without Berlin ever knowing. In theory, there should not be any. The key transatlantic cables are owned by Sweden, which has declared its neutral status, though it is clear that their impartiality is paper-thin and they secretly lean toward the Germans. But the British make a fabulous intelligence breakthrough: by a quirk of the system, the Swedish cables to the U.S. are routed through a relay station in Cornwall in southwest England. Now, British intelligence has a source of material—a tap into the German top-secret communications pipeline that goes via the Swedish cable to the U.S.—and the means to decipher it. They routinely collect a large slug of secret German communications, lulling them into a false sense of security.[4]

By now, the code-breakers in Room 40 are getting much better at breaking the German messages. The big breakthrough, in fact the single most important decrypt in modern history, starts on January 16, 1917, when the British code-breakers in Room 40 pick out what looks suspiciously like a major German telegram. It consists of about a thousand code groups and is addressed to the ambassador to the USA, Count Johann von Bernsdorff. Montgomery and de Grey have learned to attack the heading of the telegram first—as this often contains routine information, which is much easier to break—but like all smart military operators, the Germans change their encryption system and by 1917 are moving to a new code book, called 0075. For all nations, much diplomatic communication between headquarters and their local embassies round the world is relatively low grade, but not in this case. The telegram is reproduced on page 6.

The first British attack on the cipher text produces an intriguing insight into the darkest secret of the German high command. What they can decipher of the plain text—and translate into English—is enough to double the pulse-rate of even the most phlegmatic British heart. It reads:

> Most secret for Your Excellency's personal information and to be handed on to the imperial minister in (?) Mexico with ... by a safe route.
>
> Most secret. Decipher yourself.
>
> We propose to begin on 1 February unrestricted submarine warfare. In doing so, however, we shall endeavour to keep America neutral ... (?) If we should not (succeed in doing so) we propose to (Mexico) an alliance upon the following basis: (joint) conduct of the war, (joint) conduct of peace.
>
> Your Excellency should for the present inform the president secretly (that we expect) war with the USA (possibly) (... Japan) and at the same time to negotiate between us and Japan.

Though it was barely decipherable, the next sentence was a killer for the British:

> Please tell the president that ... our submarines ... will compel England to make peace in a few months.
>
> Acknowledge receipt
>
> Zimmermann.[5]

Having got this far, de Grey takes the partial decrypt to his boss, Captain William "Blinker" Hall, nicknamed "Blinker" due to his severe facial twitch. Hall tells them to work on the bits of the cipher they have not yet broken, and then addresses himself to the problem of how to release the contents to the Americans without revealing how they had come by it, as this would blow the leak in the communications pipeline in Cornwall forever.

The telegram had been sent from Berlin to Washington using code system 0075, where it was decrypted and re-encrypted using code system 13042, which was used by smaller embassies like Mexico City and which the British by now could break with ease. Using agents in Mexico City, they acquire a fresh copy of the telegram and immediately break the missing parts. A key previously undeciphered sentence is explosive. In return for their support, Germany is proposing to return to Mexico their lost territories of Texas, New Mexico and Arizona. I have italicized the crucial extra passage that they finally manage to break. The full telegram now reads:

> We intend to begin on 1 February unrestricted submarine warfare. We shall endeavor in spite of this to keep the United States of America neutral. In the event of this not succeeding, we make Mexico a proposal of alliance on the following basis: make war together, make peace together, *generous financial support and an understanding on our part that Mexico is to reconquer the lost territory in Texas, New Mexico, and Arizona. The settlement in detail is left to you.* You will inform the president of the above most secretly as soon as the outbreak of war with the United States of America is certain and add the suggestion that he should, on his own initiative, invite Japan to immediate adherence and at the same time mediate between Japan and ourselves. Please call the president's attention to the fact that the ruthless employment of our submarines now offers the prospect of compelling England in a few months to make peace.
>
> Signed, Zimmermann.

The British prepare a convincing cover story about how they have acquired the original telegram in Mexico City, and it is then given to President Woodrow Wilson via his ambassador in London on the evening of February 24. The British put a veiled threat in their telegram to Wilson, asking him to keep the source secret but saying that there is "no prohibition on the publication of Zimmermann's telegram itself," which is diplomatic language saying, "If you don't publish it, we will and then you will look really stupid."

Once tipped off, the U.S. State Department also get a copy of the original telegram and Wilson discovers that not only are the Germans planning to invade the United States in league with Mexico, but they have been planning it all along using the telegraph wires he had lent them for what he thought were peace negotiations. American neutrality is no longer possible. Woodrow Wilson is blown off the fence where he has perched so carefully since hostilities began on the other side of the Atlantic. The United States has no choice but to declare war less than two weeks later. Even though American troops do not fight in Europe until May the following year, their late arrival tips the balance.

The Armistice is signed six months later, in November 1918.

The two men most responsible for decrypting the Zimmermann telegram—the Reverend William Montgomery and Lieutenant Nigel de Grey—had started a chain reaction of events that broke the stalemate and ended World War I. However, the potency of their phenomenal achievement is barely recognized by mainstream historians; it is often airbrushed from history, as is the entire story of the Zimmermann telegram, yet they, and the rest of the gifted amateurs in Room 40, had as much impact on World War I as their successors at Bletchley Park did in World War II.

Wherever there are codes being broken in wartime there are conspiracy theories about what happens with the intelligence. What unites both Room 40 and Bletchley Park is a bizarre sense of historical déjà vu. Some historians argue that the sinking of the *Lusitania* in 1915 was an early attempt by the British to sacrifice American lives and so drag the United States into the war. The British were intercepting and breaking top-secret German naval traffic, and so the intelligence officers in Room 40 knew there was a U-boat lurking in the Channel but did not provide a British destroyer to protect the *Lusitania*. The conspiracy argument is that the perfidious British deliberately allowed the *Lusitania* to be an easy target for the Germans in order to lure an outraged American public into war in Europe. An alternative view is that the *Lusitania*, essentially a passenger ship, was carrying steel for the Allied cause and the British did not believe the Germans would dare sink a ship full of tourists, over a hundred of whom were American. Whether such a British plan existed or not, it changed nothing. The American president, Woodrow Wilson, refused to take the bait and remained firmly neutral, until the Zimmermann telegram gave him no option.

But the *Lusitania* looks—to some—like a bizarre pre-run of history. In World War II, there is the suspicion that exactly the same stunt was pulled by the British, though this time with the collusion of the American president. In the case of Pearl Harbor, many historians believe that the Japanese codes were broken and therefore senior members of the British and American government knew of the impending attack but did nothing to prevent it so that the American president, Franklin Roosevelt, could drag an unwilling nation into war.

In both cases, the same man plays a pivotal role. In the case of the *Lusitania*, the First Lord of the Admiralty was Winston Churchill. In the case of Pearl Harbor, the British prime minister was Winston Churchill.

***

On the face of it, it seems odd that a man of God, the Reverend William Montgomery, should be such a gifted cipher-breaker, compelled by the architecture of everyday military secrecy when he was—at least in theory—supposed to be driven by the spiritual realm. But one of the quirks of the history of cryptography is that it is peopled with men of God.

Roger Bacon, one of the founding fathers of British cryptography (and one of the country's greatest ever cryptographers), was a thirteenth-century Franciscan friar. Johannes Trithemius, regarded by the Germans as the "Father of Cryptography," was elected abbot of the Benedictine abbey of St. Martin in Spanheim, Germany, in 1483. Most of the great creators of Arabic cryptography were also clerics of one sort or another. Cryptography forms a strong current through the early history of the Church on both sides of the Protestant-Catholic divide, with leading Christians of all denominations recognizing the value of keeping their own communications secure, while reading everyone else's. Several popes were key in supporting and developing the talents of some of the greatest ever cryptographers.

The real founding architect of modern cryptography, Leone Battista Alberti, only gets into the business late in life. He is approached when he is in his early sixties by Leonardo Dato, the secretary to Pope Paul II, who takes him for a walk and casually drops the question of "decipherers" into the conversation, asking Alberti whether he thinks he can do better than the ones already on the Vatican payroll. Not only does he do better, he revolutionizes cryptography through the sheer power of his intellect.

Over the border, in France, Cardinal Richelieu, the ruthless and ambitious chief minister, also quickly realizes the importance of code-breaking, when the young cryptanalyst Antoine Rossignol deciphers a message that reveals just how desperate the opposition Protestant forces are. This crucial intelligence gives him victory and further secures his position in the French establishment. Richelieu immediately establishes Rossignol as France's first cryptologist, whose brilliance then makes him a major figure in French bourgeois society.

Across the English Channel, the Protestants also recognize the value of the gifted code-breaker. The Reverend William Montgomery has a noble predecessor, another minister who drifts into the business. John Wallis, a minister at Queens' College, Cambridge, is generally regarded as the greatest English mathematician before Sir Isaac Newton and easily possesses the most numerically fluent brain of his day. One evening, in 1643, he is head-hunted, like Alberti before him, by a man with a little local difficulty. The specifics of his problem are contained in an encrypted letter that had been found by the Parliamentary Army when they seized the town of Chichester. Wallis is an inspired choice. He is a Puritan sympathizer, opposed to the monarchy and an obsessive mathematician. From the moment he sees his first mathematics book, aged fifteen, his brain dances to the rhythms of numbers. He had never worked with codes before, so when the letter is left with him after supper, it is more as a slim hope than with any expectation: after all, it had already defeated the in-house Puritan code-breakers. The cipher is a series of symbols, "barely but a new Alphabet," notes Wallis. He starts work on it late in the evening, and within a few hours he has "overcome the difficulty" and has a clear plain text. So easy is it for him that he writes, "This good Successe upon an easy Cipher (for so it was) made me confident that I might with the like ease read any other, which was no more intricate than that."

The Puritans cannot believe their luck and immediately give him another cipher, one that had defeated their code-breakers for the previous two years. It is written in a nomenclator code, the most commonly used encryption system at the time. These codes consisted of mini dictionaries with numbers from one to over three thousand, each one of which stood for a different letter, syllable or even word. In this case, the dictionary was only 700 numbers strong, and within three months Wallis cracks this one as well. The rewards are immediate. Aged thirty-two, he is made professor of geometry at Oxford University.

Charles II then comes to the throne in 1660. Being a good mathematician, Wallis works out the odds of surviving as an anti-royalist sympathizer and, realizing they are not good, changes sides and agrees to work for the King. The King is nowhere near as good a mathematician, but he works out that the chances of finding another cryptanalyst like Wallis are not good either and so he decides the smart thing is to forgive him for his past transgressions. Wallis becomes chief code-breaker and—still being a devout man of God— is also appointed chaplain to the King. He then continues breaking ciphers into his old age, serving Charles II's successors William and Mary as well. His decrypts are hugely important, and he provides a conveyor belt of invaluable intelligence, but then learns one of the iron laws of cryptography through the ages: the fees paid to code-breakers—even those with superstar status—are only ever a tiny proportion of the commercial value of the intelligence they reveal, a fact that irritates Wallis through much of his later years. Despite receiving gifts such as a gold chain from the King of Prussia and a medal from the Elector of Brandenburg, he constantly moans and complains about his pay, pointing out in one case that "The deciphering of some of those letters [...] was of much greater advantage [...] than all I am likely to receive on that account."

Wallis dominates English cryptography in the seventeenth century. Exactly a hundred years after his birth, in 1716, another code-breaker who is also a man of God takes over British cryptography. Twenty-two-year-old Edward Willes becomes minister at Oriel College, Oxford. He then embarks on an extraordinary career, in which he performs the alchemical trick of turning his skills into great wealth and promotion within the Church. His first scalp is Sweden. He decrypts 300 pages of their plans to foment revolution in Britain. His reward is to be appointed the Rector of Barton, his first step on the ladder of Church promotion. It will not be his last. He then testifies against the Bishop of Rochester, who is caught plotting against George I, the German-born, non-English-speaking King of England. He is promoted to be Canon of Westminster and chief decipherer to British intelligence. Worshipping at both the Temple of God and the Temple of Mammon, he sets up a family business with his sons—it is essentially a factory production line in which cipher text goes in one end and plain text come out of the other, with language being no obstacle. Cipher texts in Spanish, French, Russian, Italian, German, Polish, Portuguese, Dutch, Danish, Swedish, Greek and Turkish all go into the "machine" at one end and come out in English at the other.

They average one message a day, sometimes storing them up until they have enough cipher text to attack, though not all are acted on.

In 1761, a crucial intercept between the Spanish ambassadors in England and France reveals that they are planning to join the Seven Years War on the French side and attack England. Pitt the Elder goes to the Cabinet and argues for a pre-emptive strike, seizing their treasure ships, which are on the way back from the Americas. His plan is rejected and the Spanish join much of the rest of Europe against England and Prussia. The only problem for the English is that they do not have a sudden injection of Spanish gold to help finance the war effort. Pitt resigns. One British Navy admiral, who by that time had retired in splendor to a stately home in Staffordshire, will have sympathized completely. Admiral George Anson had robbed a Spanish treasure ship in 1743 and then used his share of the booty to build a magnificent stately home, complete with models of Ancient Greek temples, including the Shepherd's Monument, which contains one of the great unsolved codes in this book.

***

Today, codes and ciphers do not just decide the outcome of wars. They are crucial to everyone on the planet, informing huge chunks of our everyday lives. They underpin all international commerce and—when broken—can still be the triggers that cause catastrophic shifts in the restless tectonic plates that divide nations.

Their influence starts with the mundane. Everything we buy in a major store or supermarket carries a Universal Product Code (UPC) or bar code, usually a ten-digit signifier, which allows the scanner to identify and price the product. This codified information is then used by all supermarkets and retail chains to analyze sales patterns and store deliveries.

This book carries a specific code—an ISBN number. The International Standard Book Number system is a code that gives every book published a unique identification that cannot be confused with another. It is an international encryption system, like Morse code, and is both clever and simple to use. The first numbers indicate the country of publication, the second the publisher, and the third is the specific edition of the publication. But this number conceals its own secret. It is called a "modulus 11 with weights 10–2." In plain English, this means that each number in turn is multiplied by 10, 9, 8, 7, 6, 5, 4, 3, 2 and 1, and then added up. The last number in the series is a check number. If the number ten is required, then the Roman numeral X is used instead. When all the numbers are added plus the check number, it must be divisible by eleven with nothing left over. A book with the ISBN 1-84119-947-8 would therefore break down as follows:

ISBN	1	8	4	1	1	9	9	4	7	8	
Weighting	x10	x9	x8	x7	x6	x5	x4	x3	x2	x1	
Total	10	72	32	7	6	45	36	12	14	8	**242**

242 is divisible by 11 to make 22.

In the past, nations moved their wealth about internationally in treasure ships, which were vulnerable to attack by pirates and other nations. Today, nearly eight thousand banks and financial institutions in more than two hundred countries send each other over eleven million messages every day, protected not by heavily armed warships but by very sophisticated computer-generated encryption systems. In value, it is estimated to be equivalent to half the world's gross domestic product, a fast-moving river of virtual wealth unparalleled in history. E-commerce, much of it protected by varying levels of encryption, is growing exponentially, creating a borderless world, the global village predicted by Marshall McLuhan back in the 1960s, an idea that was scoffed at when he was alive, but is now the world we all inhabit.

Without thinking about it, we all use codes all the time. We routinely password-protect our computer files, laptops and mobile phones. Home and business alarm systems require a discrete code to switch them on and turn them off. Anyone who regularly uses an online trading site, like Amazon or eBay, will—for convenience's sake—have their own trading account, accessed by a specific password. The transactions we make, which are run by PayPal, VeriSign or any other Internet-business transaction company, are all encrypted.

When we draw money from a hole in the wall, we key in a number code to confirm that we are the legitimate user of the card. Increasingly, credit cards are used point-of-sale. Though the technology is different around the world, there are two underlying principles at work here: there is something you have—the card—and something that (in theory) only you know—your four-digit code. When you key in your code number, the machine checks that this matches the number stored in the system, and if it does, the transaction will proceed. From this point on, many of the key internal transactions within the financial institutions will be protected by varying levels of encryption. This provides a level of protection, but as always, the technology of fraud is inventive. Criminals use a skimmer, a card-reader that extracts all your information. These are either fitted on to the front of a cash machine or used surreptitiously by a criminal employee when they take your card away to complete the transaction. Increasingly, retailers are using a portable machine so that you key in your own pin number. Nevertheless, in the United States, more than $500 million a year are stolen through fraudulent transactions.

Many Internet users send private documents using SSL (Secure Sockets Layer). This clever protocol was developed by Netscape and uses two keys: a public key known to everyone, and a private or secret key known only to the recipient of the message. The agreed convention is that you type in https:// followed by the domain name, which tells your Web browser (Netscape, Explorer, Mozilla, etc.) to open up a secure communications channel with the website you wish to communicate with. Your browser then connects and there is an initial exchange of non-confidential information, such as which cryptographic methods are going to be used. The server will send back a copy of its certificate (which is given by a certificate authority, a recognized organization that can vouch that everyone is who they say they are). Your browser confirms this and then creates a secret key, which will be used only once during this secure session, encrypts it using the server's public key and then sends it to the server. The server then sends a message back to the client, which it has encrypted with the secret key created by the client. This is like a handshake to confirm the deal has been completed and now all communications between the two computers will be encrypted using the new shared secret key. You can see that this has been done as there will usually be a little icon of a locked padlock in your status bar.

All these codes are there to protect the integrity of our everyday commercial and financial lives—and we are all only too well aware of what happens if the security of any of our credit cards is broken.

Historically, codes and commerce have long been deeply interlocked. With the emergence of increasingly complex capitalist transactions during the Renaissance, merchants and traders protected their businesses with ever more intricate systems of encoding, only too aware that financial ruin would inevitably follow if these were broken.

But long before codes became the clandestine currency of capitalism, they had a rich military tradition, often being more important than weapons, generals, soldiers, strategy and tactics in deciding the outcome of conflict.

William Hall, Tommy Flowers, Jerzy Rozycki, Henryk Zygalski, Marian Rejewski, William Friedman, Frank Rowlett, H. A. Newman, the Reverend William Montgomery and Nigel de Grey are hardly known, even to modern historians. They rarely make it as a footnote in many mainstream histories, yet collectively and individually, they wielded a far greater influence on the twentieth century than many well-known politicians. As cryptographers, they form the riptide running under the great events of history. They are often the fulcrum on which key historical events are based. For the last two and a half thousand years, battles have been turned, wars have been won and lost and kingdoms have been gained and surrendered on ciphers and codes that have been broken—often without the sender's knowledge.

Any army whose secret communications are intercepted and decoded by the other side is immediately at a huge disadvantage. Few armies whose communications have been broken have gone on to be victorious. The converse is also true: successful armies have tended to be the ones that kept their plans and communications secret.

The story of how the Nazi war machine was undermined in the West by the code-breakers of Bletchley Park who broke the Enigma code is well known. Less well known is the fact that there was a spy—code name "Werther"—high up in Hitler's inner circle who betrayed every crucial move the Germans made in the East. In all, Werther sent an estimated two thousand heavily encrypted cables to Stalin.[7] Though the Germans knew they had a spy in their midst, they never managed to identify him or decrypt any of his cables. Had they done so, they could have identified Stalin's spy and realized how their military operations were fatally compromised.

If Werther was a single person, and there is good evidence that he was, then the prime suspect is Hitler's deputy, Martin Bormann, which makes him the most important spy of the twentieth century as it was he—more than any other person—who delivered defeat for Hitler on the Eastern Front and effectively destroyed his dream of a Reich to last a thousand years.

When the might of the German Army arrive in Kursk with 900,000 men, 2,700 tanks and 10,000 artillery pieces, they are—amazingly—outnumbered. Fully briefed beforehand by Werther, the Russians dig 3,000 miles of trenches and lay 400,000 mines. In all, 40 percent of the Red Army is waiting: more than 1.3 million men, 3,444 tanks and 19,000 artillery pieces. As the Russians also have the German battle plan, the outcome is inevitable. The German Army marches into a huge killing field. Hitler's war in the East is over in just a few days in July 1943.

Had the situation been reversed—had Hitler's communications in the Atlantic remained unbroken and had he deciphered the Werther cables—the outcome of World War II would have been very different. The German U-boats would have sunk the bulk of the American merchant fleet, starving Britain to the negotiating table. Without access to the intimate details of the German battle plans, Stalin's divisions would have struggled. Even with this intelligence, the Russians still suffered massive losses at Kursk.

As a group, therefore, cryptographers and cryptanalysts, the makers and breakers of codes, have had a disproportionate though often invisible sway on history.

But as each generation of code-makers has advanced, so the code-breakers have become more sophisticated. It's a constant war. Initially, code systems were constructed manually, written down and then hand-delivered. In the Renaissance, the first mechanical machines appeared and these became increasingly popular in the nineteenth century. In the twentieth century, many of these machines, like the German Enigma machine, became electro-mechanical. Now, the vast majority of encrypted messages are electronic and the systems are generated by computer software. Until recently, the code-breakers were winning the war, even though they had lost some battles along the way. But now, the balance is tipped in favor of the code-writers. Overall, however, the code-breakers have still won. Over the last two thousand years, successive generations of encryption systems have been broken: what was impregnable a century ago is now often easy meat for a contemporary cryptanalyst, with or without a computer. The result is that more codes and ciphers have been cracked than have survived intact—until recently, when the arrival of the microchip allowed much greater levels of encryption. Though even here, modern encryption systems are often only as secure as the operator who uses them.

Historically, many codes have used a key—often an easily remembered word or phrase—or a set of keys, as in a code book. Julius Caesar suggested a simple cipher in which the plain text was encoded by being moved on by three letters, so that A was written as D, B was written as E and so on. Of course, you needed to know that the key was "+3" to decipher it, though anyone reasonably literate may well have spotted it. When a key is stolen or lost, the code or cipher can easily be unlocked and the secrets inside revealed. Key management is the crucial issue, and many codes and ciphers are broken because of operator incompetence, laziness or poor security when handling keys.

Until the twentieth century, all code systems were symmetric: the sender and the receiver shared the same key. In Ancient Greece, where a messenger was shaved, the information written on his head and he was then sent on his way as soon as his hair had grown, the key was quite literally this person.

A more modern solution is called asymmetrical encryption, in which sender and receiver use different keys. Imagine a chest with a hasp and a padlock. I write my message, put it in the chest, lock it and send it to you. You cannot open it, because I am the only one with the key. You attach your own padlock and send it back to me. I remove my padlock and send it back to you. You can then open it with your key. It is a relatively secure transaction, but time-consuming.

A simpler version is that I send you a lock in advance, one that snaps shut and can then only be opened by a key, which I have conveniently kept. When you want to send me a message, you put it in the chest, close the lock and send it. I—and only I—can then open it, as I am the only one with the key.

In 1976, there was one of those quantum leaps in cryptography, as significant as any previous development. In the early 1970s, three British cryptographers—James Ellis, Clifford Cocks and Malcolm Williamson—came up with a brilliant idea: public-key cryptography, in which there is a public key and a private key. I send you a message, which I encrypt using your public key, and you decrypt it using your private key. The public key and the private key are mathematically linked, but the calculation to try to derive the private key is so complex that it is not feasible to even try. Providing my key is secure when I send the message (and it should be as only I know it), then the system is theoretically foolproof. The three men who invented this system worked for GCHQ, the British government's then supersecret listening post, which taps into the world's communications, then translates and decodes them where necessary. This was such a huge breakthrough that they kept it secret until 1997. However, once a brilliant idea is in the ether, it is hard to control.

In 1976, two Americans—Whitfield Diffie and Martin Hellman—publicly floated this idea, which became known as the Diffie-Hellman key exchange. Three Americans working at MIT (Massachusetts Institute of Technology)—Ronald Rivest, Adi Shamir and Leonard Adleman—then did further work and posited the idea of public-key encryption, which they called RSA, after their initials.

As the computer age took hold, electronic communication grew exponentially. Not surprisingly, corporations, governments and individuals wanted privacy, and encryption systems became ever more complex and secure. By 1990, the U.S. government panicked and, the following year, introduced an innocuous-sounding piece of legislation called Senate Bill 266, a catch-all anti-crime bill with a killer clause. In the future, it would be law that every cryptography manufacturer had to include a trap door, allowing the government to read all encrypted communications easily. They didn't try to introduce a law ordering everyone to use postcards rather than letters, but they might as well have.

However, while the Bush Sr. government was trying to force this highly controversial measure through a reluctant Congress, the genie leaped from the bottle, never to return. Phil Zimmermann, a computer programmer from Boulder, Colorado, took the core ideas of RSA and produced a popular version, called PGP (Pretty Good Privacy). He then did something very smart: he had it posted on an Internet bulletin board. Though the Web was still in its infancy, this was enough. In the time it takes to send an electronic message round the world, the bill was history. Two years later, the U.S. government fought back and customs officers visited Phil Zimmermann. He was then subjected to the full might of the Federal government (the FBI and Grand Jury) as they put him through a three-year criminal investigation, based on the allegation that he had illegally exported a weapon, arguing that such powerful cryptography was just as dangerous to the security of the United States as weaponry. In the end, the charges were dropped. PGP is now widely used everywhere, especially by human rights groups operating in dangerous countries. Today, Phil Zimmermann is one of the heroes of the Internet age. The latest version of PGP is available from his homepage, www.phil zimmermann.com.

Though the cryptography of PGP is virtually unbreakable, it is not invulnerable to attack. While you can secure your communications, you also need to protect your private keys, which means protecting the integrity of your computer. It is relatively easy to install a Trojan virus, or key-logging software, on a remote computer, which will scoop up your private keys, allowing the attacker to pry open encrypted mail and anything else on your PC. Think of your computer as a castle with high walls, moat and guards but with an entrance through the drainpipe at the back.

Governments argue that they have to be able to read private mail and encrypted traffic because otherwise terrorist groups and major criminal organizations can use high-level cryptography to protect their communications. Though this can be the case, al-Qaeda often uses personal messengers as the safest means of communication. Bernardo Provenzano, the "Boss of Bosses" of the Sicilian Mafia, who was arrested in April 2006 near the village of Corleone (made famous in *The Godfather* movies), never used codes, laptops, computers, Internet cafés or phones. Instead, all his orders were handwritten and given to his lieutenants on scraps of paper. It worked: he was on the run for forty years and was not caught until he was seventy-three years old. The only picture the anti-Mafia police had was taken when he was twenty-five.

In Britain, under Tony Blair, the Labour government, which was elected on a ticket of civil liberties, passed a brutally draconian law in 2000. The Regulation of Investigatory Powers Act, Section 49, gives the State the right to force anyone who uses PGP to give up their keys. These powers are given to every police force (including all the military police forces and Customs and Excise). The reasons are very broad: national security, the prevention or detection of crime, the interests of the economic well-being of the UK or if it is deemed "necessary for the purpose of securing the effective exercise or proper performance by any public authority of any statutory power or statutory duty." Quite what this means is anyone's guess as you need a legal code book to decrypt it, but it looks suspiciously like a catch-all phrase. Many human rights lawyers believe that—if challenged—it is almost certainly a major breach of the European Convention on Human Rights.[8] The defenses are limited: either you give up the key within the time specified or as soon as possible after that. A conviction means a prison sentence of up to two years.[9]

As Phil Zimmermann argued in an interview:

> We need encryption. The common person needs encryption to function effectively in the information age. So it's time for cryptography to step out of the shadows of spies and military stuff and step out into the sunshine and be embraced by the rest of us.
>
> If our government ever goes bad, as sometimes happens, bad people can be elected, and if democracy is allowed to function normally, these people can be taken out of power by the next election. But if a future government inherits a technology infrastructure that's optimized for surveillance, where they can watch the movements of their political opposition, they can see every bit of travel they could do, every financial transaction, every communication, every bit of email, every phone call: everything could be filtered and scanned and automatically recognized by voice-recognition technology and transcribed. As we extrapolate our technologies into the future, if the incumbency has that political advantage over their opposition, then if a bad government ever comes to power, it may be the last government we ever elect.

***

This book is the story of those great codes and ciphers that got away, a big-handed celebration of the devious code-writers who created those skull-cracking problems—some now hundreds of years old—whose secrets have remained elusive. These were not set by government cryptographers or spies but by a cross-section of humanity—artists, writers, composers and even a serial killer. The shortest is just ten letters long, the longest is over two hundred pages. All have resisted the onslaught of the world's best code-breakers, some of whom are armed with the world's most powerful computers and the most advanced software for breaking encrypted messages.

And now, it is your turn. I have assembled all the evidence as best I can for each story and tried to provide some basic lessons on the key forms of encryption that were around at the time each code was created. These are integrated into the text, rather than being written as lessons in cryptography; the aim is for you to understand through example, not just theory.

CHAPTER I

Kryptos: "There's Another, Deeper Mystery"

"It ain't easy, but it's solvable."

—Jim Sanborn, creator of *Kryptos*

Kryptos, Langley, Virginia, 1990

Since it was first installed, in 1990, many of the world's greatest
code-breakers have walked between the red granite, quartz, copperplate, lodestone and petrified wood, touching, prodding and stroking
the metallic and stone surfaces with their hands, even poking their
fingertips through the many carefully carved holes, each one of
which carries a carved letter. What draws their attention is how
these sculptures change as the light plays strangely on the different
angles, shifting subtly throughout the day as the sun moves. The
change is even more dramatic with the seasons, bleak and harsh in
the winter, but fiery in the summer as the bright Virginia sunlight
fights for a response from the different surfaces, some matte, others
highly polished.

What gives this code its special piquancy is its name and exotic
location. It's called *Kryptos*, the root word for "cryptography," from
the Greek word meaning "hidden." The key cipher is engraved on a
large copperplate screen, just part of a specially commissioned
sequence of sculptures in the courtyards of the headquarters of the
Central Intelligence Agency (CIA) in Langley, Virginia, "wordlessly
taunting everyone to try to read its hidden message," to use the poet-

ic phrase of one of the many CIA analysts who are challenged by it every day.

Though the major interception and decryption work for the Americans is done at the NSA (National Security Agency) at Fort Meade, the CIA has always had its own huge cryptography division—and these students of the incomprehensible have access to the world's most powerful decryption software, those lines of computer code with devastating impact. They have routinely taken apart Russian and Chinese codes, as well as the encryption systems of anyone else who interferes with American interests abroad, but this cipher, right on their own doorstep—in fact opposite their cafeteria—has defeated them. All but one have retired from the challenge, defeated by its wide-ranging symbolism and subtle complexity. Thanks to the Internet, for over a decade now, thousands more code-breakers worldwide (amateur and professional) have also worked on these ciphers, both individually and collectively. Although three-quarters of this cipher has been broken, there are still ninety-seven or ninety-eight letters of intractable text, triumphant and unbroken. Even here there is a mystery within a mystery. The symbol at issue is a question mark, which could be exactly what it seems: a question mark that comes at the end of the previous phrase, which reads, "Can you see anything." This would be the most likely explanation. However, in this cipher, a question mark is also used as the marker between one phrase and the next.

According to the man who set it, this collection of heavily encoded sculptures is "a layered puzzle and we may find that it has layers within layers," so even when the top layers are pulled away and finally yield up their secret, they only open the door to yet another, deeper mystery, one requiring lateral thought, not just deductive reasoning—a conclusion beyond the reach of the banks of supercomputers that are only a short walk away. And if that is not a big enough draw for obsessives everywhere, there are two oblique references to it on the hardback cover of Dan Brown's (definitely not plagiarized) blockbuster *The Da Vinci Code*.[1]

Kryptos took two years to build and is the brainchild of a local American artist called Jim Sanborn, who is based in Washington,

D.C. The total cost was $250,000. It was commissioned when the agency added a new headquarters building in the late 1980s, which was unveiled in November 1990. The overall theme was the information-gathering role of the CIA.[2] However, when the agency commissioned the work, they also added some other key riders: art at the CIA should reflect the positive aspects of life, it should inspire feelings of "well-being and hope," it should be "forceful in style and manner," and it should be worldly yet identifiably American in its concept and in the materials used. The agency was concerned that when the plain text was deciphered, it might be something critical, embarrassing or unsavory. To calm their easily combustible paranoia, Sanborn gave a copy of the plain text, in an envelope with a wax seal, to William Webster, the director of the CIA at the time. Webster presumably felt reassured that the CIA's reputation, which had already been tarnished over the previous twenty years by revelations of bizarre mind-control experiments at home[3] and crazed assassination plots abroad,[4] would not suffer any further damage.

An archaeologist by training, Sanborn was taught encryption techniques by Ed Scheidt, who at the time was a CIA veteran of twenty-six years and the chairman of one of their cryptographic centers,[5] a man nicknamed the "Deep Throat of Codes" by his colleagues. For the project managers of the world's largest intelligence service, choosing Sanborn only required a short leap of the imagination. His previous sculptures involved working with the invisible forces of nature—lodestone, the earth's magnetic field, tornadoes, whirlpools, wind and water. As Sanborn says, "It was all involved in the secrets of nature before the agency chose my work to deal with the secrecy of man." From the perspective of the project managers, the CIA was in a similar business: trying to control invisible global forces, the undercurrents of a complex geopolitical world, and then bend them to their will (or rather the often incoherently expressed desires of their paymasters in the White House). Their notions resonated with Sanborn, for whom this was "a conceptual leap in that I could work equally well with the invisible forces of mankind."

In the finest traditions of intelligence services everywhere, there was a bizarre incident during the construction of *Kryptos* that splits the conspiracy theorists from those who believe everyone makes mistakes.

The story goes, Sanborn arrives for work one day and carefully slides his way through the different layers of security, only to find that the piles of granite he is working on have disappeared. The conspiracy theorists believe it is the CIA's overly paranoid internal security service taking the stone away for analysis—an explanation that is possible, as all the materials coming on site at this time (during the building of the new headquarters) are examined for listening bugs and other surveillance equipment.

Nations intercepting one another's communications has been standard practice since the first ambassadors started presenting their credentials in mid-fifteenth-century Europe. Getting a bug into the new CIA headquarters would have been at the top of the agenda for the huge KGB contingent operating under diplomatic cover out of the Soviet Embassy in Washington, D.C. According to a Soviet spy who was working there at the time, two-thirds of the staff were really spies.[6] The Americans had previously found a tunnel crammed with eavesdropping devices under their embassy in Moscow in 1978, and—only three years before *Kryptos* was commissioned—they had abandoned the idea of moving into a new building in the Soviet Union in 1985 after discovering that the KGB had laced it with bugging equipment. The traffic was not all one-way: while Jim Sanborn was busy at work above ground at the CIA headquarters in Langley, CIA engineers were busy digging a tunnel under the Soviet Embassy building just a few miles away.

Whether the CIA ever found anything in the stone is highly unlikely, as this would assume a high level of competence by the agency's internal security division. At this time, they had a major spy in their midst—Aldrich Ames—who was repeatedly missed despite leaving a string of big clues, like driving a new Jaguar to work that took an impossibly big chunk out of his annual salary.

The simple-human-error theorists believe that the missing granite was removed by contractors who simply cleared the site thinking it is just a pile of rubble. The CIA's own on-the-record version is "no comment," and they never explain why it was removed, but they do give Sanborn the money to replace it. There is a more intriguing possibility here—an outrageous pun in the finest traditions of cryptography—which might be a tangential clue to the final solution of the unsolved section of this puzzle, but more on that at the end of this chapter.

***

It was the arrival of Dan Brown, like much else in this area, that propelled the code from being of interest to a relatively few insiders to becoming a major international puzzle. When *The Da Vinci Code* was first published, the book cover was a crucial part of the marketing. The jacket is a brilliant piece of design as it contains all sorts of clues and allusions to other mysteries, including two references to *Kryptos*, even though neither have anything to do with the subject of the book.[7]

The first clue can be seen by holding the back cover of the hardback edition up to a mirror. Very near the Crais quote are the faint geographical coordinates (light-red on dark-red background) "37° 57' 6.5" N 77° 8' 44" W." These almost match the coordinates in the deciphered text of part two of *Kryptos*, which are "38° 57' 6.5" N 77° 8' 44" W." Dan Brown was asked why there was a discrepancy (the cover says "37," while *Kryptos* says "38") and he claimed that this was intentional, though he has declined to say why or what this meant. A typo is the most obvious explanation, though neither Dan Brown nor his publishers would admit that. The second clue is the faint and tiny phrase "only WW knows" on the back cover. This is another reference to *Kryptos*, "WW" being William Webster, the CIA chief at the time the sculpture was created.

Dan Brown may have a much more intimate involvement in *Kryptos*. When Sanborn was first commissioned to make the sculpture, he worked with an unnamed but "prominent fiction writer," though later on he claims that he dropped the idea, saying, "It was one idea I considered in the beginning. I decided not to do it: why let someone else in on the secret?" In the fevered speculation that surrounds every nuance of *Kryptos*, the question is inevitably asked, was Dan Brown this writer?

Dan Brown has maintained his interest in *Kryptos* even after the publication of his blockbuster: his webpage carried a quiz relating to *Kryptos*. Hundreds of thousands took part, and *Kryptos* was given top billing worldwide.

The *Kryptos* sculptures cannot be visited, as the CIA does not allow outsiders to wander in its grounds. There are no tourist tours, and the few outsiders who have seen the sculptures have been heavily escorted. Anyone wanting to get a real-life flavor of *Kryptos* can go and see a variation on it called *Antipodes*, which is outside the Hirshhorn Museum in Washington, D.C., next to the Smithsonian, on Capitol Hill. This version of *Kryptos* has had other previous names, including *Kryptos*, *Kryptos Untitled Piece*, *Secret Past* and *Covert Balance*. It is just over 2.4 meters tall and is a symbolic representation of the Cold War. On one side, the sculpture text is in Russian, and on the other, it is English, separated by a log of petrified wood. The Russian text is very similar to that on another of Sanborn's sculptures, called *The Cyrillic Projector*, which was deciphered recently and reads in part:

> The highest skill of the Secret Service is the ability to develop a source, which you will handle and control completely so that the source supplies, as a rule, the most reliable information. A controllable source is a source that is considered bought or made otherwise dependent by some means. Traditionally, the goal of the Secret Service professional is to ensnare any potential-value source of information with a psychological net, and pull tight this net at the appropriate time. There are not too many possibilities for this, but those secret agents who develop controllable sources of information will get promotions and the respect of colleagues. However, the methods and behavioral techniques that are needed to attain this goal [...][8]

According to Sanborn, the CIA side relates to their covert activities. The English script at the Hirshhorn Museum is similar to *Kryptos* at CIA headquarters but in a different order, beginning with the final part, which has still not been deciphered, and then followed by the rest of the cipher text. There is one other wrinkle: in the part of the sculpture that deciphers as "only WW knows," the "WW" has been replaced by two dots.

There is something very intriguing about *Kryptos*. Given the shape of the sculpture, there is a fascinating trick of the light, and letters on the far side of the curve are reflected on to the nearest surface. *Kryptos* is straight out of the intelligence world, that parallel universe where little is as it seems and where there are plenty of clues but often far fewer answers. It is a wilderness of mirrors where every detail means something, even if it is only a false trail. However, although as far as most would-be crackers are concerned the original only exists in cyberspace, there are plenty of high-quality photographs available on the Web.[9]

Ironically, the technology that U.S. intelligence developed to spy on the Soviet Union during the Cold War and make the world safe for capitalism is now commercially available, and one of the sites accessible from cameras in space is the CIA headquarters in Langley.[10] The CIA's own website carries quite a lot of detail, though some of it is incorrect or misleading, and this may or may not be deliberate. Are there clues that can be gleaned from their mistakes, or are they just the product of genuine human error?

Kryptos is in two, possibly three related parts, and each section consists of several related pieces.

The first sequence of sculptures is at the main entrance to the New Headquarters Building (known as the NHB—all spies love acronyms), which was opened in 1991. As the intelligence officers walk into work at the NHB, they pass between red-granite and copperplate pieces flanking either side of the path. Stretching about 50 yards, they are about 13 feet wide and just short of a yard high. These stones look like pages jutting up from the earth with copperplate between them. According to Sanborn, this is the first of three elements of his work. He describes it as:

> a large "natural" stone outcropping running parallel to the façade, through which the main walkway passes. This outcropping is composed of 30-centimeter-thick slabs of granite. Between two of these layers is a "seam," in geological terms, of green copperplate. The top of this plate is exposed in several places and perforated with international Morse code. The simplest of all codes. This text can be deciphered easily by those familiar with Morse.

There is nothing clandestine about Morse. The symbols (dots and dashes) are more of a telegraphic alphabet, easily recognizable and decipherable. Morse code was invented in the 1830s by Samuel Morse from Massachusetts, a man who has a special significance for Sanborn as one of Morse's previous inventions was a machine to cut three-dimensional structures in marble or stone. As Sanborn says, the dots and dashes on *Kryptos* can be deciphered easily, though even here there is a twist.

The Morse-code sections contain the words "SOS," "lucid memory," "T is your position," "shadow forces," "virtually invisible," "digetal interpretatu" and "RQ" (or maybe "YR," depending on which way up it is viewed). None of this, though, is entirely simple or clear.

The Morse-code sequences are not just simple messages but a series of palindromic repeats, except that while the dots and dashes read the same in both directions, the words they form are different. To read the words in their reverse direction means using another layer of cipher in which some letters have to be substituted. When this is done, it is possible to construct a small matrix with which to produce a final meaning. The matrix is Q=Y, N=A, D=U, V=B, F=L, G=W and C=AA.[11] To complicate matters further, some of the messages are chopped: some disappear as they go under or come out of a granite slab. To solve these means that there must be some speculation. So the phrase "T is your position" is missing a few letters and is most likely to read, "What is your position?"—a classic message delivered thousands of times by every intelligence service and military unit in every country and throughout history. "Digetal interpretatu" is more difficult. The spelling of both words, "digetal" and "interpretatu," is neither conventional American nor English spelling, but it is reasonable to assume that it means "digital interpretation," again a phrase that speaks to the overall theme of the sculptures.

However, just to confuse matters, Jim Sanborn has teased the international army of would-be code-breakers by implying that the misspelling of "digetal" is deliberate, though he has not given any further clues about why or what this might mean. There are also many dots (which in Morse code stand for the letter E) that appear to be almost random, as if they are padding to fill out the space, though this would be odd as Sanborn rarely does anything without meaning, making this already enigmatic sculpture even more baffling. One thought is that the Morse code has been put through some sort of scrambling filter, although in the absence of a key or even a clue, it will never be more than a collection of random dots and dashes. Ever elliptical, Sanborn added that what the letters say is not that important: "It's more the orientation of those letters that's useful there." On other occasions, he has also said it is the "positioning" that is important, something we will look at later on in this chapter.

The second and third sections of the sculpture sequence are in the courtyard and lawn between the NHB and the Original Headquarters Building (inevitably known as the OHB).[12] Sanborn laid out the sculptures and a duck pond in a green semicircular park area so they can be seen from the cafeteria, which has a wall of windows down one side looking out onto the lawn. There are also free-standing tables for the spies to sit and enjoy their lunch in the summer. According to Sanborn's own description, "The lawn in the courtyard offers a peaceful contempletive [sic] hidden space with the sound and image of water. This was designed as a place to escape from, or ponder, difficult decisions." He then added, somewhat tautologically, that "The encoded texts will remain undeciphered to those unable to crack the code."

This set of sculptures, which includes the key *Kryptos* piece that carries the main enciphered messages, consists of a calm, reflective pool of water between two layered slabs of granite and tall grasses. Sanborn wrote at the time that "Its placement in a geologic context reinforces the text's 'hiddenness' as if it were a fossil or an image frozen in time." Directly opposite is the centerpiece of *Kryptos*, a wavy S-shaped copper screen standing about 2 yards high, engraved with about eighteen hundred encrypted characters. It stands next to the trunk of a petrified tree. In front of it, and enjoying the same shape as the right-hand half of the wavy screen, is a second circular pond, guarded by two large pieces of rock; one red slate, the other white granite. The water in this pool bubbles and "symbolizes information being disseminated with the destination being unknown."[13] According to Sanborn, he chose this particular spot because there had once been a tree there. When it was ripped out of the ground, it left a hole, about 8 feet in diameter, which he used for the pool.

According to the CIA, this sculpture is like a shorthand and visual history of cryptography:

> The left side of the copper screen, the first two sections, is a table for deciphering and enciphering code, a method developed by sixteenth-century French cryptographer Blaise de Vigenère. The Vigenère method substitutes letters throughout the message by shifting from one alphabet order to another with each letter of the key. Part of the right side of the sculpture uses the table from the left side, and another portion uses the cryptographic method of transposing letters or changing their position in a message according to whatever method the writer devised.

When Ed Scheidt taught Sanborn basic encryption techniques, he confined himself to historic systems—those that were already in the public domain—rather than use the virtually unbreakable encryption systems that were being widely used by the world's more advanced intelligence services by 1990. As a man who had learned his craft as a cryptographer on traditional systems, he wanted the code to be solvable by the traditional methods from the golden age of code-breaking: nothing more than pencils, a large amount of paper and sheer undiluted brainpower. Hence the Vigenère encryption system.

The overall sequence of the sculptures was designed to increase in complexity as the viewer walks from the entrance to the courtyard. The original intention was that these pieces should parallel something in the courtyard, but when Sanborn was shown the satellite photographs of the CIA buildings and grounds, he confessed that he was surprised that this effect—whatever it was—had not been achieved.

***

For would-be *Kryptos* code-breakers, Sanborn's choice of materials is packed with meaning. As with many of his sculptures, Sanborn used some of his favorite stones—polished red granite, quartz and lodestone—as well as copperplate and petrified wood. Inevitably, every detail has been eagerly analyzed and re-analyzed for clues. According to the CIA, "In the case of the two-part sculpture, information is symbolized in the chemical and physical effects that produced the materials and in other more literal ways." This sentence itself is written in some sort of code. As Mr. Spock would say, "It is English, Captain, but not as we know it."

Sanborn himself was clearer, giving away some indicators of his thought processes when he first started work. In an open letter to curious CIA employees, he wrote:

> My choice of materials, like code, conveys meaning. At the entrance a lodestone (a rock naturally magnetized by lighting [sic]) refers to ancient navigational compasses. The petrified tree recalls the trees that once stood on this site and that were the source of materials on which written language has been recorded. The copper, perforated by text, represents this "paper." I also use another symbol: water. In a small pool on the plaza, partly surrounded by the copperplate, water will be turbulent and provocative, constantly agitated into standing waves. In the other pool, located among trees in the courtyard and between two massive outcroppings, water will be calm, reflective, contemplative. Other materials around the site—large stones, ornamental grasses, and small trees— are designed to make the natural features surrounding the agency more visually interesting and thought-provoking.[14]

Though this sounds good on the surface, those eager to try and break this code have delved deeper—and with good justification. After all, Sanborn himself has admitted that he too is in the business of dissembling, for a series of very good reasons.

When he first built the sculpture, his agreement was that he would give the plain text to the then CIA chief William Webster, but Sanborn later said, "I wasn't completely truthful with the man and I am sure he realizes that. I mean, that's part of tradecraft, isn't it? Deception is everywhere [...] I definitely didn't give him the last section, which has never been deciphered." Webster is not the only one to be fooled. Sanborn's cryptography tutor, Ed Scheidt, was possibly similarly double-crossed. In the best tradition of espionage and cryptology, he thought he knew what the message was supposed to be but then said of his pupil Jim Sanborn, "Since he's the one who had the chisel in his hands, there could be some changes," though, of course, he too could be deliberately dissembling as well. In this world, you never know. Misdirection is a standard operating procedure. Even the judge in *The Da Vinci Code* alleged plagiarism trial put some misdirection in his cipher, to try and throw would-be seekers of the truth off the scent. Just how accomplished a dissembler Jim Sanborn is can be measured from this exchange in an interview with *Wired News* in 2005:

> **WN:** You don't remember the solution to your own sculpture?
>
> **Sanborn:** No. I've got it hidden someplace, but I'm not going to read it. I have done everything I can to forget [it]. Because I don't want to slip and give somebody information about it. I mean, you read the piece of paper, you burn it, and you forget it. That's the only way information is kept secret. [Otherwise] it's very difficult not to give clues. In the early days, anything I said was a clue. Now things are getting more and more refined the more people [are looking into] this. They are looking for shreds, tiny little slivers of information. So I have to be very careful not to go any further.
>
> **WN:** So if you don't know the answer, how will you know if anyone has solved it?
>
> **Sanborn:** I have the solution hidden someplace. So if somebody cracks it, I can cross-check it.
>
> **WN:** What if something happens to you?
>
> **Sanborn:** The secret will probably pass away.
>
> **WN:** You haven't left it in your will?
>
> **Sanborn:** Well, actually I have. I think it's important that whoever says that they cracked it will in fact find out whether they actually did. So from that standpoint, there does have to be some sort of historic record of what it says.[15]

Faced with such brilliant obfuscation, all that the would-be codebreaker can do is take a holistic approach and assume that everything relating to *Kryptos* might be a clue. For example, take the petrified wood.[16] According to the CIA, it symbolizes the trees that once stood on the site. Trees are cut down to make wood and paper, one of the primary sources on which written language has been recorded and therefore a crucial material in the history of cryptography. But all this seems a bit facile, given Sanborn's love of deeper symbolism and hidden meanings. And in this case, the wood has a special significance, as Sanborn has said that he wrote much of the cipher on the journey to find and collect the piece of petrified wood he ended up using.

Much petrified wood comes from Arizona and Africa. For some, it has other meanings as well as the obvious symbolism of wood equals paper equals writing. It can also symbolize transformation and is seen as a material that induces great levels of introspection, allowing people to see themselves and the world around them with greater clarity. In a similar vein, others believe that petrified wood is good at helping people surmount obstacles, solve intractable problems and ease the way to achieving any task that is jammed with barriers to success and is proving to be excessively difficult to achieve. If petrified wood has these powers, then it is invaluable for solving intractable codes. In the overall scheme of things, it is highly unlikely that Sanborn was not aware of these symbolic meanings when he chose this particular material.

⋏ ⋏ ⋏

The main code is in four parts,[17] of which three have so far been cracked, but the final ninety-seven or ninety-eight characters remain unbroken. The first person to break these three parts was David Stein, a CIA analyst who used only his brain, pencil and paper. He worked on it for many hours, without any joy, until February 21, 1998, when he had his major breakthrough:

> How well I remember sitting at my desk that day, with the bright sunlight beaming through the window and the birds chirping unusually loudly outside. Suddenly, I felt a burst of divine inspiration—the insights I had gained about the *Kryptos* code from hundreds of hours of work came together and combined with all I had learned about cryptography. Everything seemed so clear that I didn't have the slightest doubt about how to proceed, and I was confident that my plan would work.

He was ecstatic; this was every cryptographer's dream, an epiphany as powerful as the moment Howard Carter opened the tomb of Tutankhamun.

> And suddenly it happened—I was hit by that sweetly ecstatic, rare experience that I have heard described as a "moment of clarity." All the

doubts and speculations about the thousands of possible alternate paths simply melted away, and I clearly saw the one correct course laid out in front of me. Taking a fresh sheet of paper, I slowly and deliberately wrote out a new column of letters, followed by another and then another.

It had taken him 400 hours spread over seven years.

A year later, Jim Gillogly, a computer scientist from California, solved the same three parts, but using computer-based decryption software.

For David Stein, cracking the *Kryptos* was the equivalent of running a marathon or climbing a mountain. The challenge was as much a spiritual journey, where the satisfaction came from knowing that he had unwrapped this most intractable of codes using skullwork and nothing else. A wonderfully modest man, he wrote:

> Professional cryptographers almost certainly could have broken these codes much faster, and would have used superior methods. But I doubt that they would have derived as much satisfaction as I have. I didn't use any computers to decrypt the *Kryptos* codes—just pencil and paper, some common sense and a lot of perseverance. Using a computer would have cheated me out of the feeling of accomplishment that I obtained, because I've found that often in life the journey itself can be more gratifying than arriving at the final destination. When confronted with a puzzle or problem, we sometimes can lose sight of the fact that we have issued a challenge to ourselves, not to our tools. And before we automatically reach for our computers, we sometimes need to remember that we already possess the most essential and powerful problem-solving tool within our own minds.[18]

The cipher text reads:

EMUFPHZLRFAXYUSDJKZLDKRNSHGNFIVJ
YQTQUXQBQVYUVLLTREVJYQTMKYRDMFD
VFPJUDEEHZWETZYVGWHKKQETGFQJNCE
GGWHKK?DQMCPFQZDQMMIAGPFXHQRLG
TIMVMZJANQLVKQEDAGDVFRPJUNGEUNA
QZGZLECGYUXUEENJTBJLBQCRTBJDFHRR
YIZETKZEMVDUFKSJHKFWHKUWQLSZFTI
HHDDDUVH?DWKBFUFPWNTDFIYCUQZERE

EVLDKFEZMOQQJLTTUGSYQPFEUNLAVIDX
FLGGTEZ?FKZBSFDQVGOGIPUFXHHDRKF
FHQNTGPUAECNUVPDJMQCLQUMUNEDFQ
ELZZVRRGKFFVOEEXBDMVPNFQXEZLGRE
DNQFMPNZGLFLPMRJQYALMGNUVPDXVKP
DQUMEBEDMHDAFMJGZNUPLGEWJLLAETG

ENDYAHROHNLSRHEOCPTEOIBIDYSHNAIA
CHTNREYULDSLLSLLNOHSNOSMRWXMNE
TPRNGATIHNRARPESLNNELEBLPIIACAE
WMTWNDITEENRAHCTENEUDRETNHAEOE
TFOLSEDTIWENHAEIOYTEYQHEENCTAYCR
EIFTBRSPAMHHEWENATAMATEGYEERLB
TEEFOASFIOTUETUAEOTOARMAEERTNRTI
BSEDDNIAAHTTMSTEWPIEROAGRIEWFEB
AECTDDHILCEIHSITEGOEAOSDDRYDLORIT
RKLMLEHAGTDHARDPNEOHMGFMFEUHE
ECDMRIPFEIMEHNLSSTTRTVDOIIW?OBKR
UOXOGHULBSOLIFBBWFLRVQQPRNGKSSO
TWTQSJQSSEKZZWATJKLUDIAWINFBNYP
VTTMZFPKWGDKZXTJCDIGKUHUAUEKCAR

While the companion text reads as follows:

ABCDEFGHIJKLMNOPQRSTUVWXYZABCD
AKRYPTOSABCDEFGHIJLMNQUVWXZKRYP
BRYPTOSABCDEFGHIJLMNQUVWXZKRYPT
CYPTOSABCDEFGHIJLMNQUVWXZKRYPTO
DPTOSABCDEFGHIJLMNQUVWXZKRYPTOS
ETOSABCDEFGHIJLMNQUVWXZKRYPTOSA
FOSABCDEFGHIJLMNQUVWXZKRYPTOSAB
GSABCDEFGHIJLMNQUVWXZKRYPTOSABC
HABCDEFGHIJLMNQUVWXZKRYPTOSABCD
IBCDEFGHIJLMNQUVWXZKRYPTOSABCDE
JCDEFGHIJLMNQUVWXZKRYPTOSABCDEF
KDEFGHIJLMNQUVWXZKRYPTOSABCDEFG
LEFGHIJLMNQUVWXZKRYPTOSABCDEFGH
MFGHIJLMNQUVWXZKRYPTOSABCDEFGHI

```
NGHIJLMNQUVWXZKRYPTOSABCDEFGHIJL
OHIJLMNQUVWXZKRYPTOSABCDEFGHIJL
PIJLMNQUVWXZKRYPTOSABCDEFGHIJLM
QJLMNQUVWXZKRYPTOSABCDEFGHIJLMN
RLMNQUVWXZKRYPTOSABCDEFGHIJLMNQ
SMNQUVWXZKRYPTOSABCDEFGHIJLMNQU
TNQUVWXZKRYPTOSABCDEFGHIJLMNQUV
UQUVWXZKRYPTOSABCDEFGHIJLMNQUVW
VUVWXZKRYPTOSABCDEFGHIJLMNQUVWX
WVWXZKRYPTOSABCDEFGHIJLMNQUVWXZ
XWXZKRYPTOSABCDEFGHIJLMNQUVWXZK
YXZKRYPTOSABCDEFGHIJLMNQUVWXZKR
ZZKRYPTOSABCDEFGHIJLMNQUVWXZKRY
ABCDEFGHIJKLMNOPQRSTUVWXYZABCD
```

The first thing David Stein did was work out what sort of encryption system was being used here. It was pretty clear that at least part of it used a Vigenère tableau. In this system, you lay out the alphabet twenty-six times, offsetting the start by one letter each time.

```
   A B C D E F G H I J K L M N O P Q R S T U V W X Y Z
A  A B C D E F G H I J K L M N O P Q R S T U V W X Y Z
B  B C D E F G H I J K L M N O P Q R S T U V W X Y Z A
C  C D E F G H I J K L M N O P Q R S T U V W X Y Z A B
D  D E F G H I J K L M N O P Q R S T U V W X Y Z A B C
E  E F G H I J K L M N O P Q R S T U V W X Y Z A B C D
F  F G H I J K L M N O P Q R S T U V W X Y Z A B C D E
G  G H I J K L M N O P Q R S T U V W X Y Z A B C D E F
H  H I J K L M N O P Q R S T U V W X Y Z A B C D E F G
I  I J K L M N O P Q R S T U V W X Y Z A B C D E F G H
J  J K L M N O P Q R S T U V W X Y Z A B C D E F G H I
K  K L M N O P Q R S T U V W X Y Z A B C D E F G H I J
L  L M N O P Q R S T U V W X Y Z A B C D E F G H I J K
M  M N O P Q R S T U V W X Y Z A B C D E F G H I J K L
N  N O P Q R S T U V W X Y Z A B C D E F G H I J K L M
O  O P Q R S T U V W X Y Z A B C D E F G H I J K L M N
P  P Q R S T U V W X Y Z A B C D E F G H I J K L M N O
```

```
Q Q R S T U V W X  Y Z A  B C D E  F  G H I  J K L M N  O P
R R S T U V W X Y  Z A B C D E F  G H I J K L M N O P Q
S S T U V W X Y Z A  B C D E F G H  I  J K L M N O P Q R
T T U V W X Y Z A  B C D E F G H  I  J K L M N O P Q R S
U U V W X Y Z A B  C D E F G H I  J  K L M N O P Q R S T
V V W X Y Z A B C  D E F G H I  J  K  L M N O P Q R S T U
W W X Y Z A B C D  E F G H I  J  K  L M N O P Q R S T U V
X X Y Z A B C D E  F G H I  J  K L  M N O P Q R S T U V W
Y Y Z A B C D E F  G H I J K L M N O P Q R S T U V W X
Z Z A B C D E F G H I J K L M N O P Q R S T U V W X Y
```

Rows go up and down, and columns go across. You then choose a keyword, which can be as many letters as you wish, but as this is his triumph, let us make the keyword "DAVIDSTEIN," and the phrase we wish to encrypt is "KRYPTOS." We then take the letter K and encrypt it with the letter from the D alphabet by looking across row D and finding the equivalent letter under K, which will be N. You then take the next letter to be encrypted, which is R, and you encrypt that from the A alphabet, which in this case will be R. The next letter is Y and that will be encrypted from the V alphabet, which gives us T and so on. When the keyword, "DAVIDSTEIN," has been exhausted, it is repeated. There are many advantages to this. The keyword is easy to remember and easy to change, though encryption and decryption tend to be slow. As a system, it was long thought to be impregnable—the French called it *"le chiffre indéchiffrable"*—until the nineteenth century, when first the great British mathematician Charles Babbage and, then, Major Kasiski, then a Polish infantry officer, came up with methods of attacking it. Both methods are, however, dependent on having a reasonable amount of cipher text to attack. Sanborn and his coach, Ed Scheidt, anticipated this and changed the keyword after a relatively short number of lines.

The keyword for the first section of *Kryptos* was the sort of word only known to crossword enthusiasts, it was PALIMPSEST. Palimpsest is a paper or parchment, but it is more than that. Crucially, its early-eighteenth-century meaning included the notion that it is not just a parchment but more like a slate, a surface that can be written on, wiped and then written on again. In the nineteenth century, the meaning was extended to describe a parchment on which the original text had been rubbed out and then written over. Later in the nineteenth century, the meaning had advanced further to describe a monumental brass that has been turned and re-engraved on the reverse.

All these various meanings hint at the main piece of sculpture, which looks like an unfurled parchment, an ancient metallic scroll where the letters are cut through the sheet so it is possible to look through them to what is beyond, on the other side. The keyword for the second section was ABSCISSA, a term from geometry.

Also incorporating the code word KRYPTOS into the Vigenère tableau and then using PALIMPSEST gives a much shorter cipher text to attack. What David Stein eventually deduced looked like this:

```
   K R Y P T O S A B C D E F G H I J L M N Q U V W X Z
 1 P T O S A B C D E F G H I J L M N Q U V W X Z K R Y
 2 A B C D E F G H I J L M N Q U V W X Z K R Y P T O S
 3 L M N Q U V W X Z K R Y P T O S A B C D E F G H I J
 4 I J L M N Q U V W X Z K R Y P T O S A B C D E F G H
 5 M N Q U V W X Z K R Y P T O S A B C D E F G H I J L
 6 P T O S A B C D E F G H I J L M N Q U V W X Z K R Y
 7 S A B C D E F G H I J L M N Q U V W X Z K R Y P T O
 8 E F G H I J L M N Q U V W X Z K R Y P T O S A B C D
 9 S A B C D E F G H I J L M N Q U V W X Z K R Y P T O
10 T O S A B C D E F G H I J L M N Q U V W X Z K R Y P
```

The first section of the cipher text reads, "EMUFPHZLRFAXYUSDJKZLDKRNSHGNFIVJ."

To decrypt it, you take the first E from the cipher text and run it against the row against P, the first letter in "PALIMPSEST." The second letter, M, is then run against the A alphabet and so on, repeating after the first ten letters. It decrypts therefore as:

1	2	3	4	5	6	7	8	9	10	1	2	3	4	5	6	7	8	9	10	1	2	3	4	5	6	7	8	9	10	1	2
E	M	U	F	P	H	Z	L	R	F	A	X	Y	U	S	D	J	K	Z	L	D	K	R	N	S	H	G	N	F	I	V	J
B	E	T	W	E	E	N	S	U	B	T	L	E	S	H	A	D	I	N	G	A	N	D	T	H	E	A	B	S	E	N	C

The next section of the cipher text reads,
"YQTQUXQBQVYUVLLTREVJYQTMKYRDMFD."

3	4	5	6	7	8	9	10	1	2	3	4	5	6	7	8	9	10	1	2	3	4	5	6	7	8	9	10	1	2	3
Y	Q	T	Q	U	X	Q	B	Q	V	Y	U	V	L	L	T	R	E	V	J	Y	Q	T	M	K	Y	R	D	M	F	D
E	O	F	L	I	G	H	T	L	I	E	S	T	H	E	N	U	A	N	C	E	O	F	I	Q	L	U	S	I	O	N

In all, this reads, "Between subtle shading and the absence of light lies the nuance of iqlusion." According to Sanborn, the spelling of the word "iqlusion" is deliberate. It is a clever way of fooling crypt-analysts, as they would normally look for a U after the letter Q. The word "iqlusion" does not exist anywhere in the English language other than here. It could be a subtle joke at the CIA's expense. By merging the abbreviation "IQ," meaning "intelligence quotient"—a measure of cleverness—and the word "illusion," does he mean the illusion of intelligence, a charge often leveled against the CIA by its critics? The obvious assumption is this is simply a spelling mistake or an error in transcribing the plain text of "illusion" into the cipher text. It is worth noting that elsewhere Sanborn has shown himself to be at the dyslexic end of spelling ability and this may therefore just be a simple mistake; this too cannot necessarily be concluded, however.

The next section of *Kryptos* uses a variation on the Vigenère tableau called Quagmire III. In this, the cipher alphabet uses the code word of KRYPTOS and the keyword ABSCISSA. The alphabet therefore looks like this:

	K	R	Y	P	T	O	S	A	B	C	D	E	F	G	H	I	J	L	M	N	Q	U	V	W	X	Z
1	A	B	C	D	E	F	G	H	I	J	L	M	N	Q	U	V	W	X	Z	K	R	Y	P	T	O	S
2	B	C	D	E	F	G	H	I	J	L	M	N	Q	U	V	W	X	Z	K	R	Y	P	T	O	S	A
3	S	A	B	C	D	E	F	G	H	I	J	L	M	N	Q	U	V	W	X	Z	K	R	Y	P	T	O
4	C	D	E	F	G	H	I	J	L	M	N	Q	U	V	W	X	Z	K	R	Y	P	T	O	S	A	B
5	I	J	L	M	N	Q	U	V	W	X	Z	K	R	Y	P	T	O	S	A	B	C	D	E	F	G	H
6	S	A	B	C	D	E	F	G	H	I	J	L	M	N	Q	U	V	W	X	Z	K	R	Y	P	T	O
7	S	A	B	C	D	E	F	G	H	I	J	L	M	N	Q	U	V	W	X	Z	K	R	Y	P	T	O
8	A	B	C	D	E	F	G	H	I	J	L	M	N	Q	U	V	W	X	Z	K	R	Y	P	T	O	S

The first section of the cipher text reads,

VFPJUDEEHZWETZYVGWHKKQETGFQJNCE.

1	2	3	4	5	6	7	8	1	2	3	4	5	6	7	8	1	2	3	4	5	6	7	8	1	2	3	4	5	6	7
V	F	P	J	U	D	E	E	H	Z	W	E	T	Z	Y	V	G	W	H	K	K	Q	E	T	G	F	Q	J	N	C	E
I	*T*	*W*	*A*	*S*	*T*	*O*	*T*	*A*	*L*	*L*	*Y*	*I*	*N*	*V*	*I*	*S*	*I*	*B*	*L*	*E*	*H*	*O*	*W*	*S*	*T*	*H*	*A*	*T*	*P*	*O*

The next section reads,

GGWHKK?DQMCPFQZDQMMIAGPFXHQRLG.

8	1	2	3	4	5	6	7	8	1	2	3	4	5	6	7	8	1	2	3	4	5	6	7	8	1	2	3	4
G	G	W	H	K	K	D	Q	M	C	P	F	Q	Z	D	Q	M	M	I	A	G	P	F	X	H	Q	R	L	G
S	*S*	*I*	*B*	*L*	*E*	*T*	*H*	*E*	*Y*	*U*	*S*	*E*	*D*	*T*	*H*	*E*	*E*	*A*	*R*	*T*	*H*	*S*	*M*	*A*	*G*	*N*	*E*	*T*

The next section reads,

TIMVMZJANQLVKQEDAGDVFRPJUNGEUNA.

5	6	7	8	1	2	3	4	5	6	7	8	1	2	3	4	5	6	7	8	1	2	3	4	5	6	7	8	1	2	3
T	I	M	V	M	Z	J	A	N	Q	L	V	K	Q	E	D	A	G	D	V	F	R	P	J	U	N	G	E	U	N	A
I	*C*	*F*	*I*	*E*	*L*	*D*	*X*	*T*	*H*	*E*	*I*	*N*	*F*	*O*	*R*	*M*	*A*	*T*	*I*	*O*	*N*	*W*	*A*	*S*	*G*	*A*	*T*	*H*	*E*	*R*

The next section reads,

QZGZLECGYUXUEENJTBJLBQCRTBJDFHRR.

4	5	6	7	8	1	2	3	4	5	6	7	8	1	2	3	4	5	6	7	8	1	2	3	4	5	6	7	8	1	2	3
Q	Z	G	Z	L	E	C	G	Y	U	X	U	E	E	N	J	T	B	J	L	B	Q	C	R	T	B	J	D	F	H	R	R
E	*D*	*A*	*N*	*D*	*T*	*R*	*A*	*N*	*S*	*M*	*I*	*T*	*T*	*E*	*D*	*U*	*N*	*D*	*E*	*R*	*G*	*R*	*U*	*U*	*N*	*D*	*T*	*O*	*A*	*N*	*U*

YIZETKZEMVDUFKSJHKFWHKUWQLSZFTI.

4	5	6	7	8	1	2	3	4	5	6	7	8	1	2	3	4	5	6	7	8	1	2	3	4	5	6	7	8	1	2
Y	I	Z	E	T	K	Z	E	M	V	D	U	F	K	S	J	H	K	F	W	H	K	U	W	Q	L	S	Z	F	T	I
N	*K*	*N*	*O*	*W*	*N*	*L*	*O*	*C*	*A*	*T*	*I*	*O*	*N*	*X*	*D*	*O*	*E*	*S*	*L*	*A*	*N*	*G*	*L*	*E*	*Y*	*K*	*N*	*O*	*W*	*A*

HHDDDUVH?DWKBFUFPWNTDFIYCUQZERE.

3	4	5	6	7	8	1	2	3	4	5	6	7	8	1	2	3	4	5	6	7	8	1	2	3	4	5	6	7	8
H	H	D	D	D	U	V	H	D	W	K	B	F	U	F	P	W	N	T	D	F	I	Y	C	U	Q	Z	E	R	E
B	*O*	*U*	*T*	*T*	*H*	*I*	*S*	*T*	*H*	*E*	*Y*	*S*	*H*	*O*	*U*	*L*	*D*	*I*	*T*	*S*	*B*	*U*	*R*	*I*	*E*	*D*	*O*	*U*	*T*

EVLDKFEZMOQQJLTTUGSYQPFEUNLAVIDX.

1	2	3	4	5	6	7	8	1	2	3	4	5	6	7	8	1	2	3	4	5	6	7	8	1	2	3	4	5	6	7	8
E	V	L	D	K	F	E	Z	M	O	Q	Q	J	L	T	T	U	G	S	Y	Q	P	F	E	U	N	L	A	V	I	D	X
T	H	E	R	E	S	O	M	E	W	H	E	R	E	X	W	H	O	K	N	O	W	S	T	H	E	E	X	A	C	T	L

FLGGTEZ?FKZBSFDQVGOGIPUFXHHDRKF.

1	2	3	4	5	6	7	8	1	2	3	4	5	6	7	8	1	2	3	4	5	6	7	8	1	2	3	4	5	6
F	L	G	G	T	E	Z	F	K	Z	B	S	F	D	Q	V	G	O	G	I	P	U	F	X	H	H	D	R	K	F
O	C	A	T	I	O	N	O	N	L	Y	W	W	T	H	I	S	W	A	S	H	I	S	L	A	S	T	M	E	S

FHQNTGPUAECNUVPDJMQCLQUMUNEDFQ.

7	8	1	2	3	4	5	6	7	8	1	2	3	4	5	6	7	8	1	2	3	4	5	6	7	8	1	2	3	4
F	H	Q	N	T	G	P	U	A	E	C	N	U	V	P	D	J	M	Q	C	L	Q	U	M	U	N	E	D	F	Q
S	A	G	E	X	T	H	I	R	T	Y	E	I	G	H	T	D	E	G	R	E	E	S	F	I	F	T	Y	S	E

ELZZVRRGKFFVOEEXBDMVPNFQXEZLGRE.

5	6	7	8	1	2	3	4	5	6	7	8	1	2	3	4	5	6	7	8	1	2	3	4	5	6	7	8	1	2	3
E	L	Z	Z	V	R	R	G	K	F	F	V	O	E	E	X	B	D	M	V	P	N	F	Q	X	E	Z	L	G	R	E
V	E	N	M	I	N	U	T	E	S	S	I	X	P	O	I	N	T	F	I	V	E	S	E	C	O	N	D	S	N	O

DNQFMPNZGLFLPMRJQYALMGNUVPDXVKP.

4	5	6	7	8	1	2	3	4	5	6	7	8	1	2	3	4	5	6	7	8	1	2	3	4	5	6	7	8	1	2
D	N	Q	F	M	P	N	Z	G	L	F	L	P	M	R	J	Q	Y	A	L	M	G	N	U	V	P	D	X	V	K	P
R	T	H	S	E	V	E	N	T	Y	S	E	V	E	N	D	E	G	R	E	E	S	E	I	G	H	T	M	I	N	U

DQUMEBEDMHDAFMJGZNUPLGEWJLLAETG.

3	4	5	6	7	8	1	2	3	4	5	6	7	8	1	2	3	4	5	6	7	8	1	2	3	4	5	6	7	8	1
D	Q	U	M	E	B	E	D	M	H	D	A	F	M	J	G	Z	N	U	P	L	G	E	W	J	L	L	A	E	T	G
T	E	S	F	O	R	T	Y	F	O	U	R	S	E	C	O	N	D	S	W	E	S	T	I	D	B	Y	R	O	W	S

In all, this reads:

It was totally invisible. How's that possible? They used the earth's magnetic field. X the information was gathered and transmitted underground to an unknown location. X does Langley know about this? They should: it's buried out there somewhere. X who knows the exact location? Only WW. This was his last message. X thirty-eight degrees fifty-seven minutes six point five seconds north, seventy-seven degrees eight minutes forty-four seconds west. ID by rows.

Stein was completely stumped by the plain-text spelling of "undergruund," which was clearly wrong. Stein was so disturbed that he made what was for him a rare visit (only about his third) to *Kryptos* to double-check his copy. He put his hand on the sculpture to be absolutely certain. In the very best traditions of good intelligence analysis, he kept an open mind: "I hesitated to call it an error—it could also have been a purposeful effort by the code's authors to make deciphering more difficult or possibly to provide a clue for interpreting a deeper part of the solution." The latter could certainly be correct as cryptographers from the Renaissance onward have advised code-writers to put deliberate spelling mistakes in codes to fool the code-breaker. UU as a digraph does not exist and will therefore form a wonderful piece of grit in any piece of cryptanalysis.

These geographic coordinates in the plain text (which might give us a clue as to exactly what Sanborn meant when he referred to "positioning") indicate a location on the opposite corner of the plaza courtyard area. The aerial photographs do not suggest anything special in this area, other than the usual clumps of scattered free-range lunch tables.[19] However, as part of the sculpture, on one of the slabs on the south side of the walkway near the entrance, a compass has been carved into the marble. The compass is pulled off magnetic north by a piece of lodestone set nearby, a trick Sanborn has used at two other sculptures in the Washington, D.C. area,[20] though on these the compass is pointing in different directions. One report suggests that in *Kryptos* the compass is pulled south-south-west to 220 degrees. Any potential coordinates that are extracted from this part of the decrypted text might have to take this into account.

Although the solution had been public since 1999, suddenly, in April 2006, the creator of *Kryptos*, Jim Sanborn, contacted one of the Kryptos Group moderators and told them that the last part of the decrypt was incorrect. He had forgotten to put a character on the sculpture, probably something that would have resulted in a plain-text X before that section. He explained that he had assumed that with the missing character, the last section would have deciphered into a meaningless jumble of words. Instead, he said that he was shocked to see that against all odds, it had come out as "ID by rows," which was definitely not what he had intended. What prompted him to suddenly say this is anyone's guess. The new last section now deciphers as "x layer two," whatever that means.

When this new solution was presented to Sanborn, he confirmed that it was the correct answer but refused to say anything more. However, it should be remembered that he had confirmed the previous incorrect plain text to be correct. Sanborn's defense is that when he heard David Stein read the phrase "ID by rows," he thought that the CIA analyst was using some cryptographic jargon about a decryption technique, not that he was reading what he took to be the real plain text. Definitely, one of the more flimsy excuses you might hear in your life.

One of the reasons why the Vigenère method of encipherment was never popular with army commanders and intelligence officers is that though it is difficult to break, it is very delicate and not robust enough to withstand operator error. With a traditional code-book system, a soldier can tap in the wrong key and only one plain-text word will be wrong. In a polyalphabetic encryption system like this, every letter has to be exactly right, in the right order and in the right place. A missed letter will throw out the entire sequence, making every letter after it incorrect. In this case, Sanborn was lucky that the mistake occurred toward the end and so only the last nine letters were wrong. Had he made the same mistake at the beginning, the entire cipher text would have been gibberish.

The big question—apart from whether the CIA is going to ask for a rebate—is exactly what this new plain text means. Right at the start, Sanborn said this was a multilayered puzzle, and this confirms it, but does not really move things any further toward a solution.

The third piece of cipher text, 336 letters in all, reads:

ENDYAHROHNLSRHEOCPTEOIBIDYSHNAIA
CHTNREYULDSLLSLLNOHSNOSMRWXMNE

TPRNGATIHNRARPESLNNELEBLPIIACAE
WMTWNDITEENRAHCTENEUDRETNHAEOE
TFOLSEDTIWENHAEIOYTEYQHEENCTAYCR
EIFTBRSPAMHHEWENATAMATEGYEERLB
TEEFOASFIOTUETUAEOTOARMAEERTNRTI
BSEDDNIAAHTTMSTEWPIEROAGRIEWFEB
AECTDDHILCEIHSITEGOEAOSDDRYDLORIT
RKLMLEHAGTDHARDPNEOHMGFMFEUHE
ECDMRIPFEIMEHNLSSTTRTVDOHW

Stein figured out fairly early on that this was not a Vigenère cipher. He guessed, correctly, that it was a transposition cipher, in which all the plain-text letters were there but in a different order, like a huge anagram.

Stein's task was to work out what sort of order they went in. As he noted ruefully, "At first, it seemed like an impossible task, with a tremendously large number of possibilities." However, being a diligent researcher, he studied the subject and discovered that there are standard ways to encrypt a transposition code. In this sort of encryption, a plain-text message such as "The enemy is approaching. We are all fleeing east" could be written in a six-columnar code. If the code number is "653214," then the letters would be written as follows:

```
6  5  3  2  1  4
T  H  E  E  N  E
M  Y  I  S  A  P
P  R  O  A  C  H
I  N  G  W  E  A
R  E  F  L  E  I
N  G  E  A  S  T
```

The code would then be written out, each column in turn, so it would read, "NACEES ESAWLA EIOGFE EPHAIT HYRNEG TMPIRN." If they are then joined up into one long string—"NACEESESAWLAEIOGFEEPHAITHYRNEGTMPIRN"—or split into a group of a different length, say into groups of four, the resulting cipher text looks very different: "NACE ESES AWLA EIOG FEEP HAIT HYRN EGTM PIRN."

To decipher the message, the reverse procedure has to be carried out, but the tricky question is where to start. The first thing Stein did was to try and work out the basic architecture: how many columns, and how many rows. The total number of letters is 336, a very clever number to choose as there are so many possibilities. It could be 18 x 18, 14 x 24, 42 x 8, 21 x 16, 6 x 56, 84 x 4 or 28 x 12. If the final row was not the same as the others, then there was an even bigger number of possibilities. The grid could be 17 x 20 grid, with thirteen letters left in the final row.

Stein used a lot of guesswork and some software called a digraphic-frequency table, which calculates how often, on average, any two alphabetic letters occur next to each other. He was then able to slowly piece together what he thought might be the correct combinations, a bit like solving a whole series of related anagrams. Eventually, he teased out some plain text, which reads:

> Slowly, desparatly slowly, the remains of passage debris that encumbered the lower part of the doorway was removed. With trembling hands I made a tiny breach in the upper left-hand corner. And then, widening the hole a little, I inserted the candle and peered in. The hot air escaping from the chamber caused the flame to flicker, but presently details of the room within emerged from the mist. X can you see anything q?

"Desparatly" is another misspelling, which again may or may not be deliberate. Sanborn has said this part of *Kryptos* was inspired by Howard Carter's account of opening the tomb of Tutankhamun, in 1922. This may well be another bit of misdirection, as it bears little resemblance to Carter's actual diary account and there is nothing to firmly link it to this event. Elsewhere, Sanborn said the subject matter of *Kryptos* is CIA covert operations, and this could just as easily be the account of any number of underground bugging operations conducted by the agency and its predecessor, the OSS, since 1945.

All of which just leaves the fourth and final section of ninety-seven or ninety-eight characters, which reads:

?OBKR
UOXOGHULBSOLIFBBWFLRVQQPRNGKSSO
TWTQSJQSSEKZZWATJKLUDIAWINFBNYP
VTTMZFPKWGDKZXTJCDIGKUHUAUEKCAR

Over the years, Jim Sanborn and his mentor, Ed Scheidt, have given interviews. In the best traditions of cryptography, they have been elusive in their utterances, but there are some clues that can be used to point toward a potential solution, always bearing in mind that this might be a series of carefully constructed false trails.

In one interview, Sanborn said:

> Mr. Scheidt gave me a whole variety of possible systems to use and ways to modify all of those systems. But as a visual artist, I like to rely on systems that include visual [material] as well as digital material that can be deciphered by machines. It's also well known that I did use some matrix codes Ed gave me, and I have also designed visual systems for encoding, which are much harder for cryptographers to crack because they're individualistic.

In all, he has said he used five or six.

It may well be that *Kryptos* is an outrageous pun. The coordinates in the plain text indicate something in the next courtyard, an area sealed off as an emergency exit, where there is a manhole cover. Suppose it is exactly what it says on the label: not a "krypt" but a "crypt," an underground burial chamber?

Jim Sanborn has been asked directly whether the final part of the code led to something buried in the CIA grounds. He declined to answer.

CHAPTER 2

In the Beginning Was the Code, and the Code Was With God, and the Code Was God

"In the beginning was the code."

Menet Khufu, Egypt, circa 1900 BCE

Long before modern complex languages develop, some of the creators of hieroglyphics in Ancient Egypt use very simple encryption techniques to conceal the meaning of what they are writing. The first known proto-cryptographer is called Beket, a man with one name but two jobs. He is the chief treasurer to a powerful nobleman called Khnumhotep II, a hereditary prince, count and governor of the eastern highlands, who lives at Menet Khufu on the Nile. He has an even more important second job as the chief architect in charge of Khnumhotep II's tomb, the next life being more important for Ancient Egyptians than their often tenuous grip on their earthly existence. Beket writes a detailed dedication to his master's life so "that he might perpetuate his life for ever",[1] but toward the end of the inscription, he suddenly starts replacing well-known hieroglyphs with unusual ones. It is not full-blown encryption as it is known today, but he does use a basic principle of code-writing. He substitutes the plain text—in this case well-known hieroglyphs—for some symbols in cipher text—some different hieroglyphs, which could only be understood by someone who could decipher their meaning, ideally using a code book.

This is generally regarded as the first use of code-writing anywhere, and it sets the tone of much that will follow in Egypt. Like fashionistas in subsequent times, the tomb scribes soon take this to extremes and it quickly reaches the point where crucial parts of epitaphs are incomprehensible to all but the best-connected insiders. However, the journey into the eternal afterlife needs a clearly laidout set of signals to the gods, not one they are going to have to decipher, and the practice soon dies out, but the genie of clandestine communication is out of the bottle—and will never return.

There are few things more addictive for any group than the notion that their communications can be limited to fellow members. Cryptography soon gets a grip and the tomb scribes—who are always very adept at spotting a commercial opportunity—begin to develop a couple of encryption techniques that will still be used more than three thousand years later.

The first technique is to conceal an alternate code meaning in otherwise innocent-looking plain text. The Ancient Egyptian hieroglyph for sailing boat is "*khentey*," which also means "who presides at" and is often used to mean the latter, though the ill-informed would think it is just a nice picture of a boat.

A variant on this technique was used by General Sir Charles Napier after he took the town of Sind, in India, in 1843. According to historical rumor, he sends a one-word telegram, "*Peccavi*," meaning "I have sinned" in Latin, a pun much loved by an overgrown public schoolboy with a classical education. The story of this single-word code is apocryphal, but the real pun is even better: *Punch*, a satirical magazine, carries this as the caption for a cartoon of Napier's conquest. It is a double pun as Napier has sinned on every level: he attacks the town on what he knows to be the thinnest of justifications, an early example of the practice of using palpably dodgy intelligence as a pretext for invasion. But that is just the start of his infamy. If the allegations of his contemporaries are correct, he also lubricates his attack with a large slug of corruption to achieve his aims. The same Latin-based pun as code is used a decade later, when James Ramsey, the Marquis of Dalhousie, annexes Oudh, on another paper-thin pretext to cover for British imperial swagger in India. This time, the wags claim that the one-word cryptic pun used is "*Vovi*," Latin for "I vowed." The full joke then becomes:

> "Peccavi"—*I've Sind, wrote Napier so proud;*
> *More briefly Dalhousie wrote,* "Vovi"—*I've Oudh.*

The second practice of code-making established by the Ancient Egyptian scribes is called acrophony, in which the writer uses a symbol or hieroglyph to represent phonetically the initial letter or syllable of the object being described. For example, the Egyptian word for "ox" is "*aleph*," so the hieroglyph for "ox" was then used to stand for the first letter of "*aleph*"—A.

This process is reversed with acronyms, those well-known phrases that make up some of the currency of everyday life. In World War II, a common expression was "SNAFU," standing for "situation normal, all fouled up," though the impolite version has a more Anglo-Saxon alternative for the word "fouled." Today, everyone in retailing knows that a "BOGOF" is a "buy one, get one free"; computer geeks used "WYSIWYG," "what you see is what you get," a term that then crossed over into common terminology. We use hundreds of acronyms in our everyday language as easy shorthand, but at their heart, they are essentially codes in which a letter stands for a word. Text-speak is a spin-off of the same. The acronym "LMAO" is unlikely to cause offense to a casual viewer, unless you know that it is code for "laughing my ass off."

At the heart of any secret or clandestine form of communication are two basic types: codes and ciphers. Ciphers are almost always focused on a single letter that stands for another letter, number or symbol. With a cipher, the cipher text that has been encrypted will be the same length as the plain text, as each letter of cipher converts into a single letter of decrypted writing. Codes are different. Here, a single encrypted letter can stand for another letter, a syllable, a sentence or even a whole instruction. In the case of the assassination of Che Guevara, the codes were simple: "500" identi fied him specifically; "600" meant that the U.S.-trained soldiers who had captured him were to execute him though not shoot him in the face, so that the government could perpetuate the lie that he had been killed in combat; and "700" meant they were to preserve his life.[2] The orders to the platoon holding him were "500 600," following which he was murdered.

When it came to cryptography, as with many other areas, Egypt was way ahead of everyone, but it would soon pop up in other civilizations. From early history, communication goes hand in hand with the imperative for groups to keep their messages secure from outsiders. Though Genghis Khan did not bother with encryption, preferring speed and brute force, most ambitious military commanders before and since have built it into their planning, either keeping their own communications secret or breaking into their enemies' to give them critical leverage in the ensuing conflict. Inevitably, we only have snapshots into ancient civilizations and much is still opaque, but there is evidence of early cryptography everywhere.

The Ancient Chinese used simple substitution codes in which both sender and receiver would know the real message behind what otherwise looked like an innocent communication. So if both know that a message saying, "Send more camellias" (the plant from which tea-drinking is believed to have begun) really means, "Send more troops," the communication is relatively secure, though anyone who intercepted that during a war ought to be suspicious. More recently, al-Qaeda used the Abdallah Brothers Trading Company as cover in their international emails, but even the dozier elements in Western intelligence spotted that one. For greater security, the Ancient Chinese preferred the technological solution of writing their messages on tiny pieces of silk and covering them in wax before the messenger secreted it about their person, usually choosing the same routes to secretion used by drug mules today bringing cocaine from South America or heroin from Turkey. This is now called steganography and is the science of writing hidden messages so that only the sender and the intended recipient know of its existence. More usually, messages are hidden in a microdot or a single pixel of a computer-generated picture.

All ancient empires had one far greater level of protection: very few people could read and write, so interception was not such an issue, unless it was a similarly well-educated rival at court, in which case the poisoned goblet of wine or the stiletto at close range could easily follow any plotter who was caught making an injudicious move.

Any military commander or intelligence-service chief has to work on the assumption (or at least the hope) that their communications are safe. When they have been compromised and this is not realized, disaster often follows. The first country recorded as having understood this is India, whose ambassadors were advised in 320 BCE to use cryptanalysis to gather intelligence "by deciphering paintings or secret writings," which presumably means that other emerging nation states were using several different forms of cryptography and were certainly sophisticated enough to hide secret messages in pictures—an early form of steganography, perhaps.

Trade follows the flag regardless of era or location, and encryption is always wrapped up in the folds. From the early days of international trade, codes and ciphers were also used to protect commerce; then as now, copyright protection being a key imperative underpinning prosperity. The first known example of a code being used to protect commerce comes from a potter on the Tigris river in 1500 BCE who used primitive encryption to conceal the formula he used for making glaze, though he might have been far better simply not writing it down at all. At the time, patent infringement was even harder to protect against than it is now. In no time at all, many other potters had also realized how to make similar glazes, and with the knowledge out in the public domain, few then bothered to hide their secrets.

The other area of the emerging cryptography was religion, where initiates wanted their route to heaven to be a private path, not to be shared by the unworthy. Between 600 and 500 BCE, the Hebrew scholars who were producing the Book of Jeremiah used a substitution code—what would now be fairly simple, primary-school stuff— by reversing a cipher and a plain-text alphabet so that the first letter of one was the last letter of the other.

A B C D E F G H I J K L M N O P Q R S T U V W X Y Z
Z Y X W V U T S R Q P O N M L K J I H G F E D C B A

Julius Caesar then took this a stage further, creating simple substitution ciphers (which are now named Caesar ciphers) by shifting on the cipher-text alphabet by an agreed number of spaces. So if the number was three, then the plain-text A would be represented by cipher-text D, B would be represented by E, C by F and so on.[3]

A B C D E F G H I J K L M N O P Q R S T U V W X Y Z
X Y Z A B C D E F G H I J K L M N O P Q R S T U V W

Julius Caesar also used simple transliteration ciphers, swapping Latin into Greek. In an age when few were literate and fewer still were bilingual, this was adequate protection for most government communications, though obviously not enough to stop him getting killed.[4]

The Spartans in Ancient Greece had a clever method of secret writing known as a skytale,[5] which used two identically shaped pieces of wood with several flat sides like a pencil. A piece of leather was wrapped round the staff and then the message was written along one face, unwrapped and given to a messenger, who would take it to the recipient. The recipient would wrap the leather round an identically shaped piece of wood. As a means of encryption it is very weak as all the letters of the original plain text are there and are all likely to be displaced by the same number. The word "enemy" might well look like "EDHSJNSJDKEASLKMOKDY" but could easily be broken as the plain-text letters always have four letters between them: "E DHSJ N SJDK E ASLK M POKD Y."

Cryptography was also used by another group for whom secrecy was essential for survival—illicit lovers. The world's most infamous sex manual, *The Kama Sutra*, the definitive encyclopedia of sexual positions in print, still dominates the gymnastic end of the erotica market after fifteen hundred years. Written sometime between 320 and 540 CE, it was first translated into English in 1883 by the epic British explorer and writer Sir Richard Burton, a man who spoke at least twenty-nine languages, discovered the source of the Nile and who neatly split Victorian society into those who were scandalized by his antics and those who admired his intellectual brilliance, his prolific output and his extraordinary courage. In the book, he lists skills that all women should learn. There—between the art of teaching parrots and starlings to speak, applying perfumed ointments to the body, dressing and braiding hair with unguents and perfumes, and making flower carriages—is the art of understanding writing in cipher. This is set in the context of what is clearly by now an advanced science as it includes "writing of words in a peculiar way and speaking by changing the forms of words." He even gives some clues as to the types of cryptography being used at this time, as he writes that "Some speak by changing the beginning and end of words, others by adding unnecessary letters between every syllable of a word, and so on." Transliteration is also used, as he says that the skilled lover should have "knowledge of language and of the vernacular dialects." The key purpose seems to be to allow lovers to send each other messages, especially those involved in illicit relationships, though many of the codes suggested would only fool the sleepiest of cheated wives and husbands, or those who preferred not to know.

Many of the systems proposed are simple substitution codes. "*Muladeviya*" consists of simple substitution, one letter for another, often in a very-easy-to-break code, such as A=B, B=C, C=D. In another system, called "*kautilyam*," vowels are swapped with consonants and some consonants could convert into the same vowel. So KH=A, G=A, GH=I, N=I, CH=U, J=U, DH=E, N=AI, TH=O, D=AU, Y=I, V=U and so on. Another system, which again smacks of schoolboy codes, is to add a syllable to the beginning of each word to create a sentence that sounds like nonsense but decrypts in seconds—e.g. "Beleave beyour behusband beand berun beaway bewith beme beto bethe beland beof bemilk beand bedates." The technical name for this at the time was "*gudhayojya*."

As well as clandestine lovers, the other group who needed to use encryption to cover their tracks were early military commanders. As empires grew, they were increasingly required to manage conquests over ever-greater distances. This should have provoked a huge increase in the use of cryptography, but the evidence for this is scrappy. However, according to the Ancient Greek writer Herodotus (the "Father of History" to some, the "Father of Lies" to others), the fate of the Greek Empire hung on the smart use of a single piece of steganography.

His story goes that Demaratus, the former King of Sparta, Greece, is in exile in Persia when he discovers that his host, Xerxes, is planning to invade his homeland. Though he has no love for the Greeks who are occupying what he still sees as his rightful throne, he does not want his homeland overrun by his (and their) life-long enemies, the Persians. He desperately wants to get a message back home, but knows that any messenger he sends will be searched by guards along the way and so any plain-text warning will immediately be seen. He comes up with a cunning plan and writes what he knows of the intended invasion on wooden tablets and then covers them with wax. This is enough to confuse the border patrols and almost enough to confuse the Greeks at the other end, who stare at it until Gorgo, the wife of one of the military commanders, suggests they scrape off the wax. Whether this is historically accurate or not, the fact is that the Greeks then do two very smart things.

They work out a clever battle plan to defeat the Persian Navy, which has much bigger ships and is three times the size of their own. They build a fleet of smaller, faster vessels, and when the Persians arrive, they ambush them in the narrow straits between Salamis and Attica. Being much nimbler, they are able to ram and sink the Persian ships, preserving the integrity of Greek civilization.

A huge pivotal moment of history turns on a piece of basic steganography and the smart use of military intelligence.

* * *

Codes and ciphers do not really begin to take a serious grip until the Middle Ages. Leading the way and a giant of the craft is a thirteenth-century Franciscan friar, multilinguist and all-round English mega-genius, Roger Bacon, who proposed all sorts of clever encryption systems, which when used together will still make fairly secure encryption today. His expertise in this area and the techniques he suggests make him (in the eyes of many) the hot favorite to be the creator of the Voynich Manuscript (see Chapter 3). Bacon also defined a basic principle of cryptography: the right of everyone to secure communication.

> The man is insane who writes a secret in any other way than one which will conceal it from the vulgar and make it intelligible only with difficulty even to scientific men and earnest students. On this point the entire body of scientific men have been agreed from the outset, and by many methods have concealed from the vulgar all secrets of science.[6]

Though his position is remarkably elitist for a member of a Christian order whose purpose was to sow light where there was darkness, the principle that a smart person may wish to conceal his communication is established. He further clarified this in another book (*Friar Bacon, His Discovery of the Miracles of Art, of Nature and Magick*), in which he argued that "He's then not discreet, who writes and Secrets, unlesse he conceal it from the vulgar, and make the more intelligent pay some labour and sweat before they understand it."

A century later, Geoffrey Chaucer, the first major English writer before Shakespeare, wrote six passages in cipher. He used symbols for letters and helpfully also provided a key and instructions so that the very few who were literate at this time could transpose the codified symbols into plain text.

But while Chaucer was tinkering about with a very basic substitution cipher, something much more profound was happening in mainland Europe, where two popes were competing for the miter and the right to command the direct line to God

In the red corner is the incumbent, Bartolomeo Prignano of Naples, Pope Urban VI. Also in the red corner is Robert of Geneva, better known as Clement VII to some, or the Executioner of Cesena to others, after ordering the slaughter of its 4,000 inhabitants. As soon as he is elected as the spiritual heir to Peter the Apostle and the infallible voice of God, Urban VI begins to behave like a lunatic: he is prone to violent mood swings, overbearing arrogance and spectacular tantrums. After five months, the cardinals have had enough and promptly elect another pope, Robert of Geneva. The Vatican, however—as ever, utterly predictable in its knee-jerk reactions—promptly brands Clement VII as the Antipope and, worse still, the Antichrist. One Church, indivisible under God, splits into two. Clement VII is supported as God's representative on earth by Scotland, France, Portugal (though they waver and renounce him a couple of times), Savoy, some German states, Denmark and Norway. The incumbent is supported by some of the home crowd in the Vatican. He immediately elects twenty-six new cardinals and raises funds for a war in the name of God against God's other earthly representative.

The Antipope and his fellow sinners are condemned to eternal damnation but are not ready to open negotiations with St. Peter just yet. In these circumstances, survival and personal security, rather than a feeling of basking in God's holy light, are at the top of everyone's personal agenda and the worldly wise look to their backs. Vatican spies are everywhere and all communications between the allies have to go via messenger, especially as some of the Antipope's allies, including Niccolo of Naples, the Duke of Monteverdi and the Bishop of Venice, live in the shadow of the papal forces.

The Vatican has the stronger, more unified forces, but to the armies of the Antipope comes a gift—a highly creative and imaginative code-creator, Gabrieli Di Lavinde, who creates a system that will form the basis of much cryptography for the next five hundred years. He develops a set of keys, the first known in Western civilization, which form the basis of what will be known as nomenclator codes—discrete dictionaries so that the forces of the Antipope can communicate securely with their allies against the Church of Rome. Once in place, this form of cipher grows quickly and nomenclator dictionaries end up being unwieldy, with thousands of entries, both code and cipher rolled into one, and with numbers standing for single letters as well as syllables, words and even whole phrases.

The Great Schism is fought out over who should have the direct line to God—a Swiss psychopath or an Italian madman. This now provides rich historical entertainment, especially for non-Catholics, but it had a much more significant and purely secular effect on the life of nations.

It was the starting gun for the race between the code-setters and breakers—a centuries-long historical battle that now began for real. The stakes were huge. As with many other great historic shifts, necessity drove invention. The speed with which major chunks of Europe tipped over from being relatively primitive medieval states into dynamic international capitalist economies was staggering. Huge fortunes were made everywhere in the powerhouse nations of Europe by a newly dominant bourgeoisie, a swaggering merchant class that took huge risks knowing the rewards were literally beyond their childhood dreams. Power and wealth were stimulated by new ideas. If trade was the flesh of the international body politic, information was the lifeblood, and being the most precious resource, it needed protection. The cryptographers —both as writers and breakers of code and ciphers—became superstars, highly paid, key members of the secret state, often with reputations stretching way beyond their national borders.

The twin notions that trade equals wealth and war leads to poverty began to sink in, and nations established permanent presences in each other's countries. And as soon as kingdoms and empires started lying to each other in the name of trade, diplomacy and imperial strut, encryption became a weapon as essential as the factories that were beginning to mass-produce armor and change the face of warfare. Italy led the way in the fifteenth century, and marching hand in hand with the diplomats were the cryptographers, though they often walked along the dark side of the street.

Ambassadors, diplomats and embassies were seen as essential, but—then as now—they were also viewed as legitimate targets for espionage. Every country began to target each other's diplomatic communications, "borrowing" and reading them whenever they could before sending them on. Knowing what others actually thought rather than the platitudes mouthed by a silken-tongued diplomat was top of every intelligence-service agenda. Everyone knew this, and encryption had to get better and very quickly, as no government had any qualms about stealing each other's secret communications and then trying to break them—a pattern of behavior that has not changed since.

The huge impetus, both for diplomatic relations and cryptography, came from the Italian city states—Venice, Florence, Milan and the Vatican in Rome—all hotbeds of dynamic Renaissance creativity, where a person was not judged by whether they did one thing well but by how many things they did brilliantly. There was no sense of specialism and it was perfectly natural for an artist to paint, write, sculpt and—in some cases—be a great cryptographer as well.

Step forward and take a bow, one of the true Renaissance giants—Leone Battista Alberti, born in Florence in 1404 and died in 1472. He was a brilliant mathematician, musician, architect, poet, linguist, philosopher, writer, general Renaissance polymath and, above all, a ground-breaking genius whose shadow can still be seen in modern cryptography.

He wrote one of the definitive how-to books on painting, defining the scientific rules by which a three-dimensional object can be represented on a two-dimensional medium, the first major study of perspective. He wrote fluently in Italian and Latin on subjects as diverse as architecture, sculpture, traction, the law and the family, and even defined the mathematical rules for calculating heights. He wrote comedy, erotica and non-fiction in verse and prose. He was also one of the better musicians of his age.

As an architect, he was brilliant and designed palaces and churches, the Church of San Francesco being widely regarded as one of the best in Italy. Like Leonardo Da Vinci, he was also very commercial and knew that these were dangerous times and there was a huge demand for any artist who could turn his creativity to military invention. His work on how to reinforce towns in the age of sieges and gunpowder set the tone and dominated town planning for centuries.

But he also knew how to have fun. According to his autobiography, he was a supreme gymnast who could jump over a man's head from a standing start. For amusement, he tamed wild horses and climbed mountains.

But above all, Alberti was a brilliant cryptographer. He was responsible for three major breakthroughs that have defined much that has followed. He invented the polyalphabetic cipher, the first encryption machine, the Cipher Disk, making him the "Father of Western Cryptography,"[7] and wrote the first clear exposition of cryptanalysis.

What is extraordinary is that he only comes to the cryptography business late in life, when he is already in his early sixties. He is approached by the Pope's secretary, Leonardo Dato, whose job includes codes and ciphers, to see if he will turn his fabulous brain to the subject. By this time, most of the Vatican's enemies routinely encrypt their communications. The problem for the Vatican is that they do not have any in-house capability and have to farm the work out—a huge security risk. Dato asks Alberti to write him a guidebook—the result is the oldest surviving textbook on cryptography. In it, Alberti lays out the principles of letter-frequency analysis as a start to unlocking enciphered communications. But he also knows the Vatican needs higher levels of protection for its own communications and he advises Dato how he can make the Vatican's secret messages much harder for their enemies to break. All it requires is just a few changes to their own practices. In future, all plain text is run into single strings. He replaces all double consonants with single ones, and just to further confuse the enemy, he recommends a technique first suggested by Roger Bacon, a couple of centuries before—the liberal use of nulls—letters meaning nothing.

A clever and practical cryptographer, Alberti then comes up with a brilliant invention, a code machine "worthy of kings," which consists of two circular copperplates that spin on the same axis, each of which has twenty-four cells. On the outside, he writes twenty letters in red capitals—the full alphabet, though without the letters H, J, K, U, W and Y, some of which do not exist in Latin, and some of which aren't needed. It was a smart move to remove U, as this letter is a cipher-breaker's dream because it often follows Q. The extra cells are assigned the numbers one to four. The inner wheel consists of the Latin alphabet, written in black and lower case, the last slot being taken by the word "*et*," meaning "and." To operate it, the sender simply sets the wheel and then reads off the cipher text. As it stands, Alberti's invention just looks like a mechanical version of a simple substitution code, which can easily be broken, but for his stroke of genius. After writing three or four words, the user changes the settings. Provided the recipient knows what the formula is, he or she can easily decrypt the message. The polyalphabet was created. Code-writing would never be the same again.

However, Alberti had a huge brain and he came up with yet another devastating wrinkle: enciphered code. He put numbers in the outside ring, some of which correspond to words or complete phrases. In other words, another layer of protection was added, as the plain text was enciphered before being processed by the machine and then re-encoded.

Alberti was well ahead of his time, but this was an era of hot rivalry between the Italian city states and there were huge rewards for anyone who could advance the dark arts.

Venice learned the trick of turning commercial information into wealth long before most, creating a huge trading empire from a tiny base. Brilliantly managed, with a ruthless and effective secret police and huge networks of foreign intelligence spies, the city established itself as an epicenter of intrigue and conspiracy, grasping the huge leverage potential of codes and ciphers. The first great man at the wheel was Giovanni Soro, appointed cipher secretary in 1506. He broke foreign encryptions with relative ease. So good was he that his city masters soon realized the foreign-exchange potential and began to rent out his services to other friendly states, who started routing their intercepts through Venice, with Soro running a small workshop, where cipher text was delivered and plain text returned. His masters were pleased, as not only did they make a profit on his skills, they also got first sight of the intelligence take of their allies. Business boomed, apprentices were selected and trained, competitions were held to attract the best and the brightest, with rewards for anyone who could come up with a smart new way of encryption or a clever technique in steganography.

The dominant form of codes was called the nomenclator; "*nomen*" being Latin for "name," and "*calator*" meaning an "attendant" or "servant." Presumably, the name was the plain text and the servant was the cipher text, dutifully in attendance. Nomenclators were a dictionary of numbers, a cross between code and cipher, in which each number stood for a letter, a syllable, a whole word or even a name or phrase. The weakness of these code systems was that the plain-text equivalents were often in alphabetical order, so if the code number for "the" was 115, it was safe to assume that every number less than 115 stood for a letter or syllable before "the" in the alphabet. They quickly became more sophisticated, having hundreds and, in some cases, thousands of entries, as well as homophones— several cipher letters that stood for the same plain-text letter. A common letter like E, for example, could have six (or more) numbers or symbols attached to it, which would reduce the ease of attack using letter-frequency analysis.

But knowing how easily they could break the ciphers of others made the Venetians realize just how vigilant they had to be with their own traffic. Nomenclator codes were changed regularly. They provided some level of protection, but if a code book was ever stolen, copied or sold to the opposition, then all communications immediately became totally transparent. The ciphermeisters of Venice had reason to be worried. Breathing down their necks were the other city states.

This was the Renaissance, when every intellectual activity was celebrated and creativity was the most highly regarded of all commodities. Rome was already well established, but Florence quickly came on stream, building their own local production center around the gifted cryptographer Pyrrho Musefili, the Conte Della Sasseta. In the middle of the sixteenth century, he set up the sort of factory that was being emulated everywhere, with cipher text going in at one end and plain text coming out of the other. His reputation quickly became international: even Edward VI, the King of England, sent him a French intercept that his own code-breakers could not crack.

Inevitably, the Dukes of Sforza in Milan, the great talent-spotters of history, got in on the business. Ruthless aristocrats whose relatives tended to die at convenient times during the relentless tectonic shifts in the family power, they famously took on Leonardo Da Vinci as painter, engineer and designer of killing machines. Less well known, but hugely significant, was the recruitment of Cicco Simonetta as in-house cryptographer. In 1474, he wrote a detailed handbook on how to break monosyllabic ciphers and, like the other superstar cryptographers, quickly attracted an international following. Machiavelli was a fan, as was the competition from the other Italian states, who showed him serious respect, using greater layers of encipherment when communicating with the diplomats in Milan than anywhere else.

By 1600, Shakespeare, Jonson and Marlowe were transforming British theater. Theirs was a rapidly changed world, where traditional values were being ripped apart. All over Europe these were brutally competitive times. No one's neck was safe, no matter how well born. In fact, the more expensive the ruff round the neck, the more uneasy the wearer. Roger Bacon's advice "The man is insane who writes a secret in any other way than one which will conceal it from the vulgar" was over three hundred years old by this time, and only the very foolish ignored it. But even though the advice was good, the technology software was not there. The best code-breakers were rampant, and anyone with weak encryption might as well have sent their top-secret messages by postcard.

By this time, England's most talented spymaster, Sir Francis Walsingham, had constructed a huge web of spies all over Europe. Measured by the number of intelligence officers he had abroad and the positions they occupied, this was one of the greatest spy networks ever. Securing the raw intelligence was one thing, deciphering it another, and Walsingham was obsessed with being at the competitive edge of cryptography. He was able to give an intercepted letter to one of his spies telling him to deal with the decrypt speedily as "The cipher is so easy that it requires no great trouble." If he had heard this, it would have come as a horrifying shock to the King of Portugal and his London-based ambassador, who assumed that their gossip (the diplomat was whining to his boss that Queen Elizabeth pretended to be ill rather than see him) was private to them. Though this intelligence gave the English wonderful opportunities to tease the weak ego of the pompous Portuguese ambassador, it was low-grade stuff compared with the daily intelligence take that the English spies were scooping up all across Europe.

Walsingham, a ferocious hater of the Vatican and all its works—temporal and spiritual—had his unblinking gaze on a much bigger prize: the most important Roman Catholic of them all, Mary Queen of Scots. Walsingham knew from all his intelligence reports that Mary was lonely, isolated and a natural plotter. He knew that she knew that she was running out of time, and that inevitably she would overplay her hand, sooner rather than later. Though she was obsessed with ciphers, codes and secret messages and highly skilled in all the arts of clandestine communication, she was no match for the sorcerer's apprentice. Walsingham's young protégé was a short, slight, pock-marked, thirty-year-old customs official with poor eyesight. Thomas Phelippes, England's first great code-breaker, was fluent in English, Latin, French and Italian, with a good smattering of Spanish thrown in. Their alliance was to lay down a marker in British history so profound that the ripples are still felt in the twenty-first century. They secured the Protestant ascendancy in English public life, which then spread throughout the British Empire.

England has usually been turbulent, but the sixteenth century was especially so, the single biggest hinge in its history. In the space of little more than a couple of generations, England went from being a medieval, backward-looking nation dominated by the clerics in Rome to being Protestant, dynamic and capitalist. A new, fabulously wealthy bourgeoisie emerged, a merchant class whose power and energy ripped away the old social order. Here was social and class war of every kind: the established order against the upstart middle class, old money against new, the city against the country, and, most important of all, Protestant against Catholic. In the 1530s, Henry VIII had smashed the power of the Vatican in Britain, surgically removing what was then the world's most powerful religious institution from the English body politic, a blow from which it has never recovered.

But faith is a powerful imperative and the Catholics regrouped, in great secrecy. Their great hope, the icon round which they could rally and unite, was Mary Queen of Scots. Passionate, beautiful and multilingual, she was—at least in the eyes of Catholics everywhere and the French especially—the legitimate heir to the English crown, a claim that must have worried the incumbent, Elizabeth I, every day. The English Queen dithered, reluctant to execute her rival for the throne, for sound political and personal reasons: she did not want to create a martyr, and besides which, Mary was her cousin. But lurking in the shadows was one who had already short-circuited the part of his brain that linked morality to action, ends to means. If he had ever been asked the old philosophical question about whether the ends justified the means, he would not have been able to answer, as he simply would not have understood the question. Walsingham had no moral qualms and set the gold standard for every British spymaster who followed. He wanted Mary's head separated from her shoulders and he got it—all thanks to some deciphered letters, and a huge slice of cunning.

Mary lived the strange half-life of a cosseted prisoner, but a prisoner nonetheless, in castles across England. She was the bait in Walsingham's trap. Any plot needed her consent, but that meant that the plotters had to communicate with her.

In 1586, her page, Anthony Babington, starts to warm up a three-stage conspiracy. The first stage is to assassinate Elizabeth, which (so the theory goes) will prompt a populist but ultimately Catholic uprising that will underpin the popular surge, putting Mary on the English throne, at which point she will sign treaties with the Catholic monarchs of Europe. As a plan, it is ridiculous. There are few precedents in which the scenario of assassination/popular uprising/new monarch has ever actually delivered in the way the plotters hope. Popular uprisings (Paris 1789, Russia 1917) tend to remove the established order, not replace one parasitical royal figurehead with another. More important, by this time the Protestants are already far too strong and they have a match-winning player: Walsingham is so very much smarter than anyone on the Catholic side.

The year is 1586 and Mary is held under house arrest on the country estate of Chartley Hall, Staffordshire. Her keeper, Sir Amyas Paulet, reports back on all those who make contact with her. Sir Anthony Babington, Mary's page, is easy meat for the worldly genius of Walsingham, who spots him immediately. Though he professes to be Protestant, Walsingham knows him as a vainglorious young man who is also a closet Catholic. Though only twenty-four, he is a prime suspect: his security records show he is close to at least two of the more fundamentalist Catholic priests, men who are high up on Walsingham's watch list. Babington had also spent six months in France, the home of Mary's supporters—perfect conditions to turn him into a Catholic sleeper, an agent to be activated at some future date.

But Walsingham knows all about creating spies and especially double agents. As Mary settles into Chartley Hall, his security services pick up a young Catholic priest at Dover, Gilbert Gifford,[8] and persuade him—presumably with the threat of horrific torture and a slow and desperate death—to spy for the Crown. But Gifford is much more than just a spy; he is also an agent provocateur, and from this point on, Walsingham is running the plot. Apart from the inner core of the conspirators, every other key player is on Walsingham's payroll. The tail is wagging the dog and the dog will die.

In Rome, the Vatican has effectively signed a *fatwa* against Elizabeth I.[9] The parallels with modern-day religious assassins are remarkable. The young Catholic hotheads are seduced by the papal bull, which sanctions the murder of Elizabeth. Just like the Islamic suicide bombers and the Christian fundamentalists who blow up abortion clinics, they believe they are truly blessed and walk in God's holy light, his wonders to perform. In fact, they are deluded pawns being manipulated by Sir Francis Walsingham. What appears to be a secure communication channel is established: messages are concealed in small boxes in beer barrels, courtesy of a local brewer, who of course is on Walsingham's Protestant payroll. Mary is convinced that this is genuine and in no time she is writing to the French ambassador, who is also so impressed by this new channel of communication that he sends her all the letters he has been accumulating for the previous two years—a cryptological treasure trove, as Thomas Phelippes, Walsingham's expert code-breaker, now has a substantial volume of text to attack. He soon discovers that although she changes her nomenclator code, it is not as robust as many others he has been breaking regularly. He quickly works his way through the backlog, and though she is often sending two letters a day, he is deciphering them almost in real time. Little is known of Phelippes, but it's reasonable to assume that, given he was reading every word that Mary wrote in code, he must have been amused by some of the plain text as it emerged in front of his eyes. Among other things, Mary gives the French ambassador advice on steganography, secret writing and message concealment, which must also have brought a wry smile to Walsingham's face. The advice is not brilliant:

> The plan of writing in alum is very common, and may easily be suspected and discovered, and therefore do not make use of it except in case of necessity. And if you should use it, write between the lines of such new books, writing them always on the fourth, eighth, twelfth and sixteenth leaf.

But then she gives the game away, telling the ambassador to put green ribbons on all books that are marked in this way. Her other suggestions are only marginally better: writing on "white taffeta, lawn, or suchlike delicate cloth," adding an extra half-yard to carry the message. She also suggests hiding messages in the cork lining of shoes, but the English have already been wise to that for years.

Walsingham knows that he needs something more solid—something visceral, incontrovertible, which will strike at Elizabeth's soul and hasten Mary's short journey to the executioner's block. Over the summer, she writes an encrypted message to David Beaton, the Archbishop of Glasgow, asking him what he knows about the King of Spain's plans for "revenging himself against this Queen." It is a good hook into her, but not enough. Walsingham is a master of the long, patient game. He does not move against the plotters. Instead, he establishes one of the great standard operating procedures of intelligence services: he lets the action run its course, monitoring and guiding it at every stage, waiting for his moment to strike. As there are no arrests and no action against the plotters, they assume they are safe and that their communications are secure. Feeling bold, Babington writes to Mary about the plans "for the dispatch of the usurper." The plot is there for Walsingham and his code-breaker to see. He describes "six noble gentlemen, all my private friends, who for the zeal they bear to the Catholic cause and your Majesty's service will undertake the tragical execution." Though the law had been tightened to extend the definition of treason, Walsingham needs Mary to respond. Assuming that her letters are safe, she sends a long and detailed reply, throwing herself into the plot, even questioning the logistics for the provision of foreign troops to invade England, restore Catholicism and move the capital of England from London to Rome. It is high treason on every count. But Walsingham still wants more: he knows he has already won, but he also knows there is more he can squeeze from the play. Once he has Mary's letter, Walsingham gets Phelippes to add an addendum, forged in her handwriting and using her cipher key, asking for "the names and qualities of the six gentlemen which are to accomplish the designment."

Mary's motto was "In my end is my beginning." She was right but not in the way she thought. Her end was the end of any Roman Catholic claim to the British throne and the beginning of the Protestant ascendancy that has maintained itself ever since.

This crucial moment in history had been achieved by a man whose name does not often make the history books, Thomas Phelippes, whose skill provided the leverage so that the far more powerful forces of the State could prevail.

When they searched her belongings, they found "about sixty Indexes or Tables of private Cyphers and Characters"—silent testimony to her long-standing interest in all matters cryptological. But for all her excitement about the intricacies of codes and ciphers and her self-regarding knowledge of steganography, she had failed to apply basic common sense and had severely underestimated her opponent. Walsingham was an obsessive. The chances of her actually having her messages delivered intact were low, and—at this time— the code-breakers were in the ascendant. She was not as smart as she thought she was, but then she was desperate. She was a competent cryptographer, but her opponent, Thomas Phelippes, was a genius.

* * *

Codes and ciphers were not, however, just the everyday weapons of governments, merchants, diplomats, clerics and spies (and often these last four groups seemed to be focused in one and the same person). From the early days of Ancient Egyptian cryptography, there has been another tradition, a parallel clandestine world where codes, ciphers, secret signs, symbols and mysterious forms of covert languages are the currency of everyday communication: the world of the occult in all its kaleidoscopic glory.

For over two thousand years, religious groups (both in the mainstream and the more esoteric), plus every type of sect and cult have routinely encrypted their secrets to maintain the integrity of their world and keep it closed to unwelcome, prying eyes. Those in the know, the insiders, the initiates who can decipher the code, feel special, bound together in the warm glow of shared secrets. Those who cannot decipher the code are—by definition—outsiders and therefore lesser beings, compared with the anointed, who are blessed by their access to ancient wisdom and the secrets of the universe.

Priests, sorcerers, necromancers, anyone who dabbled in the dark arts of divination, magic, alchemy, medieval cosmology, astrology, as well as those who cast spells, delivered curses or plugged themselves into the divine energies, all had one thing in common: their marketing and presentational materials—especially in the Middle Ages and the Renaissance—were often elaborate, mystical confections, dressed up with complex codes and weird symbols. The codes often purported to conceal the great secrets of the age: the philosopher's stone, which would turn base metal into gold, the secret of eternal life and that perennial favorite, still popular today— how to make someone else fall in love with you. In an age when religious superstition was often a substitute for thinking, such material easily impressed the feeble-minded and the gullible, whether educated or not, and the net effect was the magical trick in which the money in their purse was rapidly transferred to the person possessing the code. Much of this sort of material has now found a new home and a new lease of life on the Internet. It comes with a long and glorious history, starting with the Ancient Greeks.

Plutarch, an internationally celebrated priest and intellectual, presides over the Temple of Apollo at Delphi later in the century after the death of Christ. His story has all the key ingredients of a Hollywood blockbuster: at the heart of the plot is an esoteric manuscript that no one can read until the chosen one, the hero with the magic key, comes and unlocks it. Plutarch reported that:

> There were some very old oracles which were kept by the priests in private writings and they were not to be meddled with, neither was it lawful to read them, till one in aftertimes should come, descended from Apollo, and, on giving some known token to the keepers, should take the books in which the oracles were.

Of course, there is a catch. Ancient myth has format as clearly defined as a modern Hollywood film, and in the penultimate act, the hero has to prove that he is truly the anointed one. Whereas in much history the code-breaker is airbrushed away, at least in this story he gets top billing, and the moral is a very twenty-first-century one— choosing your leaders from the best and the brightest is better than having a leader inflicted on you by virtue of who their parents are.

> Things being thus ordered beforehand, Silenus, it was intended, should come and ask for the oracles, as being the child of Apollo, and those priests who were privy to the design were to profess to search narrowly into all particulars, and to question him concerning his birth; and, finally, were to be convinced, and, as to Apollo's son, to deliver up to him the writings. Then he, in the presence of many witnesses, should read, amongst other prophecies, that which was the object of the whole contrivance, relating to the office of the kings, that it would be better and more desirable to the Spartans to choose their kings out of the best citizens.[10]

It was in the Renaissance that codes and ciphers were first hardwired into the occult. This was a time when what was heretical and what was orthodox was not clear, shifting sands in which the unwary could easily perish. On the one hand was the all-powerful Vatican, backward-looking and fearful. Ranged against the Church were the thinkers, poets, artists and painters for whom this was the golden age to be alive. Their world was an exciting kaleidoscope of new ideas, fresh ways of thinking, seeing and expressing yourself in ways that were genuinely revolutionary. These ideas had to be expressed within the framework of an all-powerful Christian God, but the tension between the old and the new was palpable. Painters with a message were very careful exactly how they expressed themselves, ambiguity being at least a workable defense against the Christian fundamentalists who still controlled the levers of power everywhere, but who were often terrified of what they saw as a dangerous new world, where the old certainties were under threat. In this world—and in the periods that followed—the wise (and especially those who wished to survive) learned the value of being fluent in the codes of everyday life.

A code is just a method of concealing a second covert meaning, which (it is hoped) is only known to the sender and the recipient, usually unlocked by a key that is discrete to both parties. Many great Renaissance painters did exactly this, hiding meanings and messages in their paintings, though they often failed to leave behind the key, creating an industry so that writers and academic art historians could then squabble about the exact meaning for centuries afterward. It is this rich pageant of carefully coded meanings that sustains Dan Brown's *The Da Vinci Code*. Is the androgynous figure on the right of Christ a man or a woman? By being deliberately ambiguous, was Da Vinci sending a coded message to everyone who viewed this most enigmatic of paintings about a dinner already carrying the burden of two thousand years of conspiracy theory? It's what makes codes such a rich area for fiction writers.

As well as mainstream art, full of traditional Christian iconography (the Virgin Mary, Christ on the Cross, John the Baptist), there was a parallel popular artistic tradition, an earlier version of Russian *samizdat* literature, where a few copies were made and distributed clandestinely. These were often hand-produced, full of mysterious symbols, hints that the writer had some divine connection. The Voynich Manuscript, which consists of more than two hundred pages of a discrete text in a language not seen anywhere else, is the quintessential example (see Chapter 3), but there were many more. As knowledge spread, the desire to control its dissemination grew ever stronger—and what better way to control circulation than write in a language or code that few could understand?

Inevitably, there was crossover: the occultists and the cryptographers were in the same business. As if by magic, the code-breakers could produce plain text and meaning where there had been none apparent, the traditional rabbit out of the hat much loved by magicians. The occultists and those who practiced divination did the same—extracting meaning from things that were not what they seemed to be, whether it was magic stones cast on to the ground, the flight of birds or the movement of the planets.

There is a further underpinning of the cryptography-mysticism link, a quasi-religious set of beliefs that runs both through the occult and cryptography: the Kabbalah, which has been around for at least a couple of thousand years and has recently surfaced into tabloid reality through the celebrity endorsement of Madonna and others. It has strong Jewish links but crosses over into other faiths. At its essence, the Kabbalah is an ancient teaching system, an all-encompassing theory of the universe. It is billed as a secret teaching studied by only a select few in each generation, which from a marketing perspective makes it mainstream occult. Today, it is sold as a total package, a one-stop shop for all those seeking meaning in their lives, providing solutions, unraveling puzzles and deciphering codes, which taken together unlock the keys to the mysteries of human existence.

Kabbalah beliefs were very influential in the Renaissance. Giovanni Pico, one of the leading Renaissance philosophers and a noted humanist thinker, was a great advocate and spread the word. His big idea, which still resonates today, was that each person is a microcosm of the universe. Each of us can find God in our own hearts and we can all be who we want to be. Every one of us, no matter how exalted or how humble, is divine. But at the heart of the Kabbalah is an apparent scientific methodology, a sophisticated system in which mathematics can unlock the meaning of words, a cryptographer's treasure trove.

Under this system, each letter in Hebrew is given a numerical value. The system, called *Gematria*, then calculates those values and compares words with others that have similar values. The argument is that language does not develop organically over time but is somehow fixed. Language is God's speech, and so as part of the divine master plan, each letter carries with it both its surface meaning and a concealed creative power. Once this is accepted, then it is the comparison of these two hidden meanings that is vital to further understanding. When the numerical values match, they reveal the secret connection between their creative potential. These mathematical connections are not random, so when there is a numerical match, then letters, words and even sentences can deliver new and perceptive insights into the complex interrelationships between words and ideas.

The mathematic systems in the Kabbalah are time-consuming and depend on a series of related values: an absolute value, an ordinal value, a reduced value and finally an integral reduced value. Taken together, these complex algorithms have offered code-writers and -breakers a rich feeding ground from the Renaissance onward, but any competent statistician can easily show how this is more about chance than anything else. However, the fact remains that the occult world of sects and cults routinely uses codes, ciphers, symbols and secret writings, many of which have been heavily influenced by Kabbalistic teachings. Any analysis of secret writings, especially in the Renaissance and immediately afterward, must always consider this as a possible influence. In addition, many Renaissance cryptographers were also interested in the occult, forging a link that has never been broken.

The first printed book on cryptography, *Steganographia*, was written by the brilliant scholar, mathematician, devout Christian, self-promoter and mystic Johannes Trithemius, in about 1500. The Vatican loathed it and immediately suppressed it, but the book's contents were so seductive it immediately enjoyed widespread circulation in manuscript and was copied and then passed on with the excitement that only a suppressed book can generate. The Protestants eventually published it in 1606, and the Vatican responded by putting it on the *"Index Librorum Prohibitorum,"* the list of prohibited books, where—for the next few hundred years—Trithemius rubbed shoulders with other intellectual miscreants like Descartes, Kant, Berkeley, Copernicus, Voltaire, Milton, Hobbes, Hume, Rousseau, Zola, John Stuart Mill, Sartre and Jonathan Swift—not a bad club of which to be a member, especially when compared with the crashing bores who did not make the grade.

Johannes Trithemius proposed some simple rules to conceal messages: vowels and consonants were substituted for each other, and like many other contemporary cryptographers, he used nulls—blanks that have no purpose other than to confuse any would-be cipher-breaker. One system he proposed was to write a plain text in Latin in which was concealed a cipher text that could be lifted by extracting every other letter of every other word—a feat that only the really gifted could achieve.

Perhaps his greatest claim was to be able to send encrypted messages over huge distances overnight—long before the existence of the telegraph. Under his scheme, you write your message in rose-oil ink, draw a picture of an angel or some other planetary spirit next to it, along with a picture of the recipient. You then put it in a box, bury it and say an incantation, something snappy like *"In nomine patris et filii et spiritus sancti"* and the angels will then carry the message through pre-electronic cyberspace and it will arrive. Trithemius then also identifies seven angels, giving each a sign. Tireless employees in the service of God, they work a strict rota, each being on duty one hour out of every seven, twenty-four hours a day, seven days a week. Their order is: ☉Michael, ♀Anael, ☿Raphael, ☽Gabriel, ♄Cassiel, ♃Sachael and ♂Samael. This shift pattern is then repeated throughout the week, and they are the celestial message-bearers.

How many have practiced this in the hundreds of years since is not recorded, neither is the number of successful messages sent and received, but the belief in an ethereal message system prevails even today. The latest polls suggest that at least seven out of ten Americans believe in angels, the postal messengers of the spiritual world who know no fatigue.

Trithemius also compiled endless tables, which many assumed were Kabbalistic-inspired for calculating the numerical values of angels. However, an alternative meaning was recently prised out.[11]

Trithemius used a shortened alphabet, missing the letters J, K, U and Y but using TH, SCH and TZ as well as UU or VV for W. Letters were substituted for numbers to which the number twenty-five was added. So his name would be "26, 27, 28, 26, 30, 31, 32, 28, 32, 33," and this is how he constricted the cipher:

	T	R	I	T	H	E	M	I	U	S
	1	2	3	1	4	5	6	3	7	8
Plus 25	25	25	25	25	25	25	25	25	25	25
	26	27	28	26	30	31	32	28	32	33

From this, it is possible to decrypt the text as T=26, I=28. This was in an age when this sort of simple calculation was not routine, besides which Trithemius had (in the great tradition of cryptography) put everyone off the scent. Anyone who looked at the book only saw the occult, not the code, and he did nothing to disabuse people, allowing them to see what they wanted to see. Chinese whispers and gossip then functioned as a brilliant PR machine. But when the numbers were deciphered, they did not reveal the secrets of the universe, but a playful wit. One piece of plain text reads, "Don't take this monk. He likes to drink good wine and is strange." Another reads, "The bearer of this letter is a rogue and a thief," while yet another was the opening of Psalm 21:

> The king shall joy in thy strength, O LORD;
> and in thy salvation how greatly shall he rejoice!
> Thou hast given him his heart's desire,
> and hast not withholden the request of his lips.

which at least was some sort of homage to his employers.

Though Trithemius transgressed into forbidden areas as far as the Church was concerned—and certainly teased generations of cryptographers with his columns of numbers—he is responsible for one of the great breakthroughs of cryptography, the square table, which looks like this:

```
A B C D E F G H I  J K L M N O P Q R S T U V W X Y Z
B C D E F G H I J K L M N O P Q R S T U V W X Y Z A
C D E F G H I J K L M N O P Q R S T U V W X Y Z A B
D E F G H I J K L M N O P Q R S T U V W X Y Z A B C
E F G H I J K L M N O P Q R S T U V W X Y Z A B C D
F G H I J K L M N O P Q R S T U V W X Y Z A B C D E
G H I J K L M N O P Q R S T U V W X Y Z A B C D E F
H I J K L M N O P Q R S T U V W X Y Z A B C D E F G
I J K L M N O P Q R S T U V W X Y Z A B C D E F G H
J K L M N O P Q R S T U V W X Y Z A B C D E F G H I
K L M N O P Q R S T U V W X Y Z A B C D E F G H I J
L M N O P Q R S T U V W X Y Z A B C D E F G H I J K
M N O P Q R S T U V W X Y Z A B C D E F G H I J K L
N O P Q R S T U V W X Y Z A B C D E F G H I J K L M
O P Q R S T U V W X Y Z A B C D E F G H I J K L M N
P Q R S T U V W X Y Z A B C D E F G H I J K L M N O
R S T U V W X Y Z A B C D E F G H I J K L M N O P Q
S T U V W X Y Z A B C D E F G H I J K L M N O P Q R
T U V W X Y Z A B C D E F G H I J K L M N O P Q R S
U V W X Y Z A B C D E F G H I J K L M N O P Q R S T
V W X Y Z A B C D E F G H I J K L M N O P Q R S T U
W X Y Z A B C D E F G H I J K L M N O P Q R S T U V
X Y Z A B C D E F G H I J K L M N O P Q R S T U V W
Y Z A B C D E F G H I J K L M N O P Q R S T U V W X
Z A B C D E F G H I J K L M N O P Q R S T U V W X Y
```

To encrypt the phrase "*manui dat cognito vires*," meaning "knowledge gives strength to the arm," you would take the first letter (M) from the first line, the second (A) from the second, the third (N) from the third.

```
A B C D E F G H I J K L M N O P Q R S T U V W X Y Z
B C D E F G H I J K L M N O P Q R S T U V W X Y Z A
C D E F G H I J K L M N O P Q R S T U V W X Y Z A B
D E F G H I J K L M N O P Q R S T U V W X Y Z A B C
E F G H I J K L M N O P Q R S T U V W X Y Z A B C D
```

The first five letters of the cipher text would therefore read, "MBPXM"—easily enough to defeat the standard decryption of the age, especially the repetition of the letter M in the cipher text.[12]

Giovanni Batista Belaso then added another brilliant layer of encryption. Once the idea of the square was in the public domain, it was very easy to break because of its total predictability. He introduced the idea of the keyword. If the keyword was "BATISTA," then the encryption of *manui dat cognito vires* would be completely different. The key would be laid on top of the plain text:

B A T I S T A B A T I S T A B A T I S T A
M A N U I D A T C O G N I T O V I R E S

To encrypt the first letter, you would use the B alphabet. The second letter would be encrypted using the A alphabet, the third letter would use the T alphabet and so on. The first five letters would then be encrypted using "BATIS" as the key to which alphabet to use:

A B C D E F G H I J K L M N O P Q R S T U V W X Y Z
B C D E F G H I J K L M N O P Q R S T U V W X Y Z A
C D E F G H I J K L M N O P Q R S T U V W X Y Z A B
D E F G H I J K L M N O P Q R S T U V W X Y Z A B C
E F G H I J K L M N O P Q R S T U V W X Y Z A B C D
F G H I J K L M N O P Q R S T U V W X Y Z A B C D E
G H I J K L M N O P Q R S T U V W X Y Z A B C D E F
H I J K L M N O P Q R S T U V W X Y Z A B C D E F G
I J K L M N O P Q R S T U V W X Y Z A B C D E F G H
J K L M N O P Q R S T U V W X Y Z A B C D E F G H I
K L M N O P Q R S T U V W X Y Z A B C D E F G H I J
L M N O P Q R S T U V W X Y Z A B C D E F G H I J K
M N O P Q R S T U V W X Y Z A B C D E F G H I J K L
N O P Q R S T U V W X Y Z A B C D E F G H I J K L M
O P Q R S T U V W X Y Z A B C D E F G H I J K L M N
P Q R S T U V W X Y Z A B C D E F G H I J K L M N O
Q R S T U V W X Y Z A B C D E F G H I J K L M N O P
R S T U V W X Y Z A B C D E F G H I J K L M N O P Q
S T U V W X Y Z A B C D E F G H I J K L M N O P Q R

```
T U V W X Y Z A B C D E F G H I J K L M N O P Q R S
U V W X Y Z A B C D E F G H I J K L M N O P Q R S T
V W X Y Z A B C D E F G H I J K L M N O P Q R S T U
W X Y Z A B C D E F G H I J K L M N O P Q R S T U V
X Y Z A B C D E F G H I J K L M N O P Q R S T U V W
Y Z A B C D E F G H I J K L M N O P Q R S T U V W X
Z A B C D E F G H I J K L M N O P Q R S T U V W X Y
```

The cipher text would therefore read, "NAGCA." It was a fabulous breakthrough. Diplomats abroad just needed to remember their keyword, which could be changed every time a new messenger was sent through. Diplomats were not limited to a short key like "BATISTA." It could be something much longer, like "IN NOMINE PATRIS ET FILII ET SPIRITUS SANCTI" and, of course, they were not limited to a single key. For the anxious spymaster back at base, there was an even bigger advantage. Every diplomat could be given a different keyword. If the system was compromised anywhere, then it would be confined to that one person and only for the time the key was active.

By this time, ciphers consisted of two basic types: transposition, which changed the order of the letters, and substitution, in which the plain-text letter is exchanged for a symbol or a letter from another alphabet. This was a time of intellectual giants, in cryptography as everywhere else.

Giambattista Della Porta was a child genius, a fabulously wealthy, archetypal Renaissance man, being both an empirical scientist and a playwright. Like many others, he turned his fluid brain to cryptography and suggested using both transposition and substitution, but then also gave a huge clue for code-breakers everywhere. It was a massive slice of common sense, but he was the first to suggest it: look for the probable words. If it is a diplomatic briefing going to the diplomat dealing with trade matters, then it will be the language of commerce that is being used. Similarly, if it is military traffic, the language will be of weapons, troops and tactics.

By the middle of the sixteenth century, cryptography was well advanced, both for the writers and breakers of ciphers. Emerging nation states—and the spymasters who served them—needed creative thinkers and they emerged everywhere, developing new systems for both writing and breaking codes.

The truly smart prevailed everywhere, whether they were codewriters or -breakers, but then a single piece of extended cipher text appeared that was so complex it defeated every contemporary cryptanalyst—as well as everyone who has attacked it since ...

CHAPTER 3

The Voynich Manuscript: Let Your Indulgence Set Me Free

"Such Sphinxes as these obey no one but their master."

—Johannes Marcus Marci

MS 408, Beinecke Rare Book and Manuscript Library, Yale University

In 1961, the twentieth century's most powerful rare-book dealer Hans Peter Kraus (known as H.P.K. to everyone in the book trade) buys a manuscript of which there is only one known copy. Virtually everything about it is a mystery. There is no title on the front page, which is plain and white. It is unsigned, so no one knows for certain who the author is. The names of the illustrators who are responsible for the fabulous color plates inside are not mentioned anywhere in the text, and no one even knows when it was made. In one account, it is nearly four hundred years old. In another, at least twice that age. It is clearly written in some sort of code, but it is not clear what encryption system is being used here, or even whether the symbols are derived from a known language. As these symbols are not known to exist anywhere else, it must be assumed that the writers of the Voynich Manuscript used a code book, but there are no clues as to what language was used for the plain text.

There is no clear candidate for the underlying plain text, because the distribution and patterns of the symbols used do not appear to be an exact match for any known language. All the usual suspects have been suggested, including English, Dutch and Latin—in its classical, medieval and/or abbreviated forms—as well as some other sort of Germanic language. But that's just the start. The full range of suggestions also embraces the more unusual, including Ukrainian, a Creole based on Flemish, Ancient Greek shorthand and encoded Hebrew. Other analysts have searched further afield, pointing out that there are similarities to some of the languages of East and Central Asia, where there is an abundance of candidates. There are those with a Sino-Tibetan root, including Chinese, Tibetan and Burmese, as well the Austro-Asiatic languages, like Vietnamese or Khmer and maybe even Thai. But the most exotic suggestion of all is that the Voynich Manuscript is the only surviving manuscript of the Cathars, one of the many religious sects brutally suppressed by the Catholic Church and believed by some to be the true guardians of the Holy Grail. This manuscript is therefore all that remains of their ancient tongue. But even if the surface language is ever deciphered, it is not known if this will just reveal another layer of code, behind which lurks a meaning that has been concealed for at least four centuries.

Ah, what intoxicating secrets could its pages reveal if they could only be deciphered ...?

***

An obsessive with a fat checkbook, Peter Kraus is a risk-taker, well known for outbidding even the seriously rich at auction, paying prices that at the time are regarded as insane—only to then sell the same book a few years later for many times what he paid for it. In this case, he pays $24,500 and then values it at $160,000, totally confident of a rapid resale and a substantial profit. He has reason to be confident; after all, he is *the* dominant global market-maker in antiquarian books and he knows it—so powerful is he as a collector and trader that when he visits the Vatican Library, they ask him what he would like to see that he has not either seen or handled already. His answer is legendary: "Your duplicates!" he tells a shattered librarian.

But after eight years, he cannot find a buyer for the most bizarre manuscript he will ever handle and so, in 1969, he gives it to the

Yale University Library, where he is a trustee of the Library Associates. Today, it is cataloged as "MS 408" and can only be viewed under strict supervision. In today's money, Kraus paid over $500,000 for the book. Its value is now beyond estimate, but is certainly in the millions of dollars.

It is better known as the Voynich Manuscript, a book that is beautifully crafted, haunting and eerie in its illustrations, ranging from the esoteric to the seriously weird. The text is composed by at least two separate hands, though there may well be more. These two hands are called Currier A and Currier B, after a former director of research at the U.S. Naval Security Group, Captain Prescott Currier, who analyzed Voynich, though he then totally confused matters by going on to identify up to ten more individuals with distinct handwriting characteristics.

The Voynich Manuscript, the world's oldest and longest unsolved public cipher, is small in size, roughly 6 or 7 inches wide by 9 or 10 inches. Unlike a modern book, the pages are not all cut to the same size but are slightly different, giving the manuscript a rough-edged look. Though the text is unintelligible, a conventional Western numbering system is used—1, 2, 3 and so on through to 116. This numbering is instantly recognizable but not consistent with the language used in the body of the work, so there is a suspicion that it was added at another time. Eight leaves are missing Several of the pages are folded so that when they are unfolded, they are the size of two pages, and the largest sheet unfolds to make a single sheet the size of six pages. When these are all added, the manuscript has the equivalent of 246 pages, thirty-three containing text only. If the eight missing leaves were at least two pages each, then the book would have been more than 262 pages.

The book is in excellent condition, given its age, though there is some abrasion round the edges, presumably from where it was handled or moved around.

On every possible test, this book is unique. Breaking the code open and finding the plain text lurking behind these pages of weird symbols and even weirder illustrations is the biggest prize in world cryptography. It is the longest single piece of unsolved code anywhere in the public domain. More cryptographers, some with access to the world's most powerful hardware and software, have attacked it than any other unbroken cipher text, yet it has remained invincible, even resisting the very best efforts of code-breakers, who in their professional lives smashed some of the twentieth century's toughest encryption systems.

The roll call of those who have tried to break this cipher reads like a list of the world's greatest cryptanalysts. Though they all have different views as to when it was written, by whom and what it might mean, there is one thing on which they are all agreed: it is a genuine text and not a hoax. Even those who lean toward the hoax theory lay off their bets and allow that it might well be authentic, even if they cannot be specific about when it was written.

William Friedman, a man generally regarded as the greatest American code-breaker of the twentieth century, set up a study group in the 1940s. At that time, there were very few computers. In the pre-microchip age, computers were driven by hundreds of vacuum tubes and then transistors. The very few that existed ranged from the size of a desk to that of a small truck, but Friedman managed to secure what was then very precious computer downtime to try and break the Voynich Manuscript. Throughout much of his life, he worked closely with his wife, Elizabeth, another brilliant cryptographer, who concluded that "All scholars competent to judge the manuscript [...] were—and still are—agreed that it is definitely not a hoax or the doodlings of a psychotic but is a homogeneous, creative work of a serious scholar who had something serious to convey."

Brigadier Bill Tiltman, one of the key figures at Bletchley Park in World War II, also applied his cryptanalytic brain without success, devoting many hours to studying it before concluding:

> I do not believe the manuscript is completely meaningless, the ravings or doodlings of a lunatic, nor do I believe it is just a hoax—it is too elaborate and consistent for either [...] About the worst thing it can be is a deliberate forgery for gain [...] I regard this as rather improbable.

Erwin Panofsky, one of the great American art historians of the twentieth century, said it was "a perfectly authentic document," even though he had an open mind as to when it was made or why. More recently, a group within the NSA (National Security Agency) adopted Voynich as their hobby over thirty years ago, but despite their high level of skill, they too have failed to even leave a mark on the protective shell that has guarded the Voynich secret all these centuries.

Leading the charge for the hoax theorists against the manuscript is Robert Brumbaugh. A professor of medieval philosophy at Yale University, he argues that it was an elaborate fraud to separate a gullible emperor from his soft-earned fortune, but even he believes it still has meaning and "It could be anything from a standard botany textbook to formulae for the elixir of life deriving from Roger Bacon." More recently, a British academic, Gordon Rugg, showed how it was possible to use "a modified form of a Cardan grille and tables of gibberish syllables to produce quasi-random meaningless gibberish," but he too gives himself an insurance policy against error by arguing that it is very difficult, if not impossible, to ever prove whether random letters and numbers conceal a cipher or not: "I don't think it's possible to prove conclusively that a given document is a hoax containing only meaningless gibberish, as opposed to one with a meaningful code hidden among a large quantity of gibberish, so we'll probably never know for sure."[1]

But regardless of what it is, it remains one of the most important medieval/Renaissance documents, because it combines four distinct areas of thought and appears to try to form them into an overarching theory about the nature and meaning of life. If it ever decrypts as coherent text, it may well provide a huge new understanding of cutting-edge medieval and Renaissance thought. If it is a complete fabrication, it is still vitally important as it will provide an insight both into contemporary encryption and the structure of language systems that were in use at this time.

***

The manuscript is named after Wilfrid Voynich, the American book dealer who first prised this book out of its remote hiding place, where it had lain concealed for two and a half centuries. According to his version of events, he came across a most remarkable collection of preciously illuminated manuscripts. It is a fantastical story, which reads like the start of a Victorian mystery novel:

> For many decades these volumes had lain buried in the chests in which I found them in an ancient castle in southern Europe, where the collection had apparently been stored in consequence of the disturbed political condition of Europe in the early part of the nineteenth century. While examining the manuscripts, with a view to the acquisition of at least a part of the collection, my attention was especially drawn by one volume. It was such an ugly duckling compared with the other manuscripts, with their rich decorations in gold and colors, that my interest was aroused at once. I found that it was written entirely in cipher. Even a necessarily brief examination of the vellum upon which it was written, the calligraphy, the drawings and the pigments suggested to me as the origin the latter part of the thirteenth century. The drawings indicated it to be an encyclopedic work on natural philosophy. The fact that this was a thirteenth-century manuscript in cipher convinced me that it must be a work of exceptional importance, and to my knowledge the existence of a manuscript of such an early date written entirely in cipher was unknown, so I included it among the manuscripts which I purchased from this collection. Two problems presented themselves—the text must be unraveled and the history of the manuscript must be traced. It was not until some time after the manuscript came into my hands that I read the document bearing the date 1665 (or 1666) which was attached to the front cover. This document, which is a letter from Johannes Marcus Marci to Athanasius Kircher making a gift of the manuscript to him, is of great significance.

And that is exactly what his account was—fantastical fiction. The truth was very different, though in some ways, just as intriguing. Wilfrid Voynich lied about the origin of his manuscript, but for very good reasons—he had no choice.

In 1911–12, he did in fact meet the Jesuits of Villa Mondragone, Italy, introduced through one of their number, Father Strickland. They needed money to restore their villa and had decided to sell off some of their huge collection of books—exchanging the transcendent knowledge and wisdom that comes from ancient tomes for ready cash in their pure and unworldly hands. As with most Jesuit transactions, especially those in which money is concerned, the whole operation was distinctly clandestine. Voynich had to promise total secrecy before any deal could go ahead, but in the end he secured about thirty books and manuscripts. In 1912, the Jesuits sold another 300 manuscripts—a third of their collection—to Pope Pius X, who gave them to the Vatican Library. This subsequent sale is crucial in establishing the twentieth-century provenance as the catalog describes the Voynich purchase, proving that this part of his story, at least, is true.

Voynich quickly became totally convinced of two things. The first was that this bizarre and incomprehensible manuscript was one of the most important documents in the history of science. The second was that its author was Roger Bacon, a thirteenth-century English genius and polymath.

Bacon was a devout man of God steeped in the primitive knowledge of the Old Testament, but he was also one of the world's great freethinkers who foresaw many of the key scientific break-throughs that define the way we live now, eight hundred years before they happened. Bacon was a brilliant empirical scientist, an early adopter of "scientia experimentalis," empirical, observation-based science, and spoke several languages fluently. As well as his mother tongue, English, he also spoke both Greek and Latin, had a working knowledge of Hebrew, Aramaic and some Arabic. Educated at Paris and Oxford, he was known as "Doctor Mirabilis," meaning "Wonderful Teacher."

In an age when the Catholic Church held sway and monarchs and emperors quaked under the awesome power of the Vatican, narrow-minded religious bigotry was even more intense than it is now. His overactive, relentlessly inquiring mind took him frequently into areas of belief that meant his own life was in constant jeopardy. But he could not stop himself. Passionate and driven, Bacon studied other religions and philosophy, even delving into Gnosticism and the Kabbalah, but running through his religious and spiritual inquiries is a relentless conveyor belt of scientific experiments.

The breadth of his knowledge is amazing. He was fascinated by geography, medicine, alchemy, mathematics, optics, astronomy, education and even argued for the reform of the calendar. Two centuries before Leonardo Da Vinci, Bacon studied lenses, light, rainbows and mirrors, defining the principles of reflection and refraction. Centuries before Sir Isaac Newton, he pieced together the visible spectrum of light through water. He anticipated hot-air balloons by describing how a balloon of thin copper could be filled with "liquid fire," after which it would float in the air, just like some objects do in water. He described a machine with flapping wings and was the first person in the West to describe how to make gunpowder. He was clearly worried by the awesome responsibility he would carry if the secret formula ever got out, so he partially described it but concealed the crucial details in a short eighteen-letter cipher. So clever is this cipher that it would not be broken for another six hundred years, though sadly for the world, the formula for gunpowder did get out in the meantime.

The Roger Bacon gunpowder reference is in his *De mirabili potestate artis et naturae* (1242), and it yields a wonderful insight into how his mind worked and how he used cryptography. In this first document, he writes about saltpeter as a violent explosive, but he also knew that this was only the case when it was mixed with other substances. He wrote that "From saltpeter and other ingredients we are able to make a fire that shall burn at any distance we please." But he was also concerned to disguise his discovery, writing in Latin, "*Item ponderis totum 30 sed tamen salis petrae luru vopo vir can vtri et sulphuris; et sic facies tonitruum et coruscationem, si scias artificium. Videas tamen utrum loquar aenigmate.*" The phrase in the middle—"*luru vopo vir can vtri*"—is, on the face of it, gibberish. It is not Latin or any other known language. The rest of Bacon's piece translates as "The total weight of the ingredients is thirty, however, of saltpeter ... of sulfur; and with such a mixture you will produce a bright flash and a thundering noise, if you know the trick. You may find (by actual experiment) whether I am writing riddles to you or the plain truth." Actually, he was writing in riddles.

Just after the turn of the twentieth century, in 1904, a lieutenant colonel in the British Army, H. W. L. Hime, cracked Bacon's cipher while writing a book about the history of gunpowder.[2] He very cleverly decrypted it by recognizing that Bacon had used two kinds of cipher at the same time—an anagram and an extensive use of abbreviation, which not only revealed the missing ingredient but also the proportions, without which the formula would not work. According to Hime, the full plain text, which includes the phrase "*luru vopo vir can vtri* reads, "*Salis petrae/ r(ecipe) vii part(es), v no(vellae) corul(i), v /et sulphuris.*" In plain English: "Take seven parts of saltpeter, five of young hazelwood and five of sulfur."

Bacon also described spectacles as well as ships and carriages that could be moved mechanically by propellers. Though he was a friar and a man of God, he used a camera obscura, projecting an image through a pinhole to watch the eclipse of the sun. All this at a time when the Old Testament defined a world that was flat and made by God in seven days.

He despised the "stupid crowd" with what he saw as their infinite foolishness. A Franciscan friar, it was inevitable that he would be imprisoned by the ignorant and prejudiced in the Catholic Church, who were terrified by the awesome power of his intellect and the freshness of his thinking—but this was not before he produced many major scientific works. For many, Roger Bacon's polymathic brilliance stands him alongside Leonardo Da Vinci, though this English man of God is even more mysterious, someone who knew far too much and was more ahead of his time than any other scientist, before or since. When he died, he was known to be compiling the great encyclopedia of all knowledge, both scared and profane, though only fragments have ever been found.

As well as being a very clever cryptographer, there is one other aspect of his thinking that makes him a prime candidate for being the Voynich Manuscript author. He was fascinated with every area covered by the manuscript, arguing that "Without astronomical, geometrical and optical instruments and those of many other sciences, nothing can be accomplished, for through these we acquire knowledge of many celestial objects and from them the causes of the things beneath them,"[3] an eloquent description of many of the plates in the manuscript. For the growing army of Roger Bacon fans everywhere, he even advocated the study of witchcraft, magicians and legerdemain.

Voynich knew that Bacon was also a pragmatist. After the death of his patron, Pope Clement IV, in 1268, he was very vulnerable to attack from the primitive, backward-thinking paranoids in the Catholic Church. As a young man, Bacon had studied in France and loved to travel. He went to stay with his Franciscan brothers in Ancona, Italy, who then jailed him for "suspected novelties" in how and what he taught. Such was their fear of the contagious nature of his thought that he was kept in solitary confinement, not even allowed to speak to his guards for fear that he would pollute their innocent minds. He was denied confession or absolution, his fellow Christians booking him a one-way ticket to purgatory and eternal damnation. All this from an order whose founder wrote without a trace of irony, "No one is to be called an enemy, all are your benefactors, and no one does you harm. You have no enemy except yourselves."

And so one of the greatest minds of all time languished in a solitary cell for over a decade, until he was released when a new leader took over who returned to the loving teachings of St. Francis (after whom the order was named), and Bacon and the others who had shown dangerous freedom of thought were released.

After this horrendous experience at the hands of his fellow Franciscans, what better way of covering his tracks than by writing his greatest work, which concealed all the secrets he had discovered of this world and the next, in an unbreakable cipher?

Voynich and the others who believe that Bacon is the master-mind behind this document think that he entrusted it to one of his favorite pupils and it was then hidden in one of the great monasteries of England by his supporters until Henry VIII smashed the power of Rome during the 1530s, seizing their property and lands. Our mysterious manuscript was just one tiny item in the millions plundered in the name of the King and sold off cheap to the aristocracy. Voynich believes that in the chaos the Duke of Northumberland acquired the manuscript and then gave it to John Dee.

This is largely supposition on his part as there are no catalog entries to track the manuscript at this time. Voynich would no doubt counter this by arguing that when the State, in the form of Henry VIII, sets about the wholesale theft of the property of a fabulously wealthy Church, then the thieves are unlikely to be that concerned about the quality of the records they keep and a small book could easily slip through the net. For Voynich, and the other supporters of the Dee thesis, there is some circumstantial historical evidence, but it is very light. It consists of a letter quoting John Dee's son, Arthur, saying he remembers his father working with Edward Kelley on the obsessive medieval quest to turn base metal into gold. The problem is that it is a childhood memory and the letter was written over a century later.[4] As with many of these alchemical experiments, there were two ingredients—a magic powder and an instruction manual, in this case "containing nothing but hieroglyyphicks, which book his father bestowed much time upon, but I could not hear that he could make it out." The young Arthur was eight years old at the time this would have happened, and it is a perfectly reasonable childhood memory; however, it is a stretch to link this mystery instruction manual with the Voynich Manuscript. At this time, there were dozens of such books written in strange scripts, and Dee was an avid collector of anything to do with alchemy, Kabbalism, mathematics and the wilder shores of fringe science and religion, believing that he had discovered the all-embracing formula allowing the spirit to move effortlessly between the earthly world and celestial paradise. Statistically, the odds are not great that the book the young boy saw was the Voynich Manuscript; besides which, there are no images in it that relate to a metal foundry or anything that might resemble the seductive river of gold that would flow toward anyone who could pull off this miracle.

There is a further argument against Bacon being the author. The Voynich drawings are works of the imagination presented as science. Bacon was a hardcore empirical scientist, and although he imagined amazing feats of engineering, his analysis of the natural world was based on what he could observe and work with. Bacon was a ferocious critic of anything he saw as unclear thinking, especially the sort of fanciful "science" that underpins the illustrations in the Voynich Manuscript, whether it is the fantastical plants, the mythological beasts or what the authors see as the celestial relationship between humankind and the heavens. The supporters of the Bacon thesis will no doubt point out that if this was his final statement on the world, it was coming on the back of over a decade in solitary confinement and his mind may well have been unhinged. Such skepticism predictably had little chance of rooting itself in Voynich's mind, which was blinded by the potential prize: if this manuscript was Bacon's final statement on the empirical world, what extraordinary secrets would it reveal if only it could be deciphered? Had this genius, with a foot in both the spiritual and the religious worlds, discovered the secret elixir of life, the elusive and clandestine meaning of existence? If so, then it would not just be a case of having to rewrite the history of ideas. This would be the most important book ever written, certainly worth devoting the rest of your life to understanding.

Apart from wishing it were so, Voynich had good reason for believing that Bacon was the author. The letter attached to the Voynich Manuscript was written by a Czech doctor, living in Prague, called Johannes Marcus Marci. It was addressed to his friend of decades Athanasius Kircher, telling him of the manuscript, which he subsequently gave to him before his death. In this letter, he described how its previous owner had tried to decipher the deeply encoded language but had failed: "His toil was in vain, for such Sphinxes as these obey no one but their master."

The letter, written in Latin, provides the clue that set Voynich off on his search for Roger Bacon. It reads, "*D. Doctor Raphael Ferdinandi tertij Regis tum Boemiae in lingua boemica instructor dictum librum fuisse Rudolphi Imperatoris, pro quo ipse latori qui librum attulisset 600 ducatos praesentarit, authorem uero ipsum putabat esse Rogerium Bacconem Anglum,*" which when translated reads, "Dr. Raphael, tutor in the Bohemian language to Ferdinand III, then King of Bohemia, told me the said book had belonged to the Emperor Rudolph and that he presented the bearer who brought him the book 600 ducats. He believed the author was Roger Bacon, the Englishman." Though Dr. Raphael Missowski was only guessing at Roger Bacon, his source was, after all, good: Ferdinand III, whom he was tutoring as a young man. There was a second clue to help solidify the Roger Bacon link, and that is the reference to the Emperor Rudolph II, a von Habsburg, Holy Roman emperor, King of Bohemia and King of Hungary, who died in Prague in 1612, when the manuscript's existence is first recorded.

At the time, Rudolph was described as "the greatest art patron in the world," who blew his colossal fortune turning Prague into the intellectual and cultural capital of Europe. Eccentric, prone to depression and withdrawal, he was also willfully extravagant, practicing the traditional alchemy of the super-rich, turning money into art. His taste leaned toward the fantastical, the bizarre and the extraordinary. According to popular rumor, he collected dwarves and his army included a regiment of giants. He was fascinated by chemistry, astronomy and astrology, and inevitably, his court attracted artists, alchemists, thinkers and fraudsters, including a spirit medium called Edward Kelley. Kelley was a devious, clever conman who had the wit to team himself up with John Dee, who was well connected at court, as he was astrologer to Queen Elizabeth I, as well as her mathematics tutor. John Dee looks like just the right sort of man to be the spiritual heir to Roger Bacon. He was one of the great mathematicians, herbalists, alchemists, philosophers and mystics of the Elizabethan age, and even wrote weird books dictated to him by angels, inevitably in a strange script. Such was Dee's prominence in Elizabethan England that he is—at least in the eyes of many—the short-odds favorite to be the man whom Shakespeare chose as the model for Prospero in *The Tempest*.

As Voynich dug deeper, there was further circumstantial evidence suggesting John Dee as the man who had sold the manuscript to Rudolph II for 600 ducats, a huge sum in those times. Dee and Kelley together visited Poland and Bohemia, putting on what were basically magic and alchemy shows. They had an audience with Rudolph II, though he did not adopt them into the menagerie of freethinkers who peopled his court. But despite this, the connection was there. Even better, there was circumstantial evidence that when Dee returned from Prague he had just over 600 ducats, which was an extraordinary feat given that he had just travelled across Europe and back, an expensive enterprise.

For Voynich, the John Dee-Rudolph II association was the missing link, giving him a clear line of provenance from the Jesuit library, through the court of Bohemia back to Elizabethan England and through the Protestant connection to the man he regarded as the fount of all modern wisdom, the greatest one of them all, the thirteenth-century oracle and all-round guru, Roger Bacon.

Even better, he soon found himself supported by a philosophy professor from the University of Pennsylvania—William Newbold, a man with all the right credentials. He had a first-class brain, and his range of interests and knowledge reads like a checklist for anyone wanting to pit their wits against the Voynich Manuscript. He was an expert on the occult, mysticism, the Gnostics, medieval philosophy and science, especially the Kabbalah. He was also fascinated by the history of the Great Chalice of Antioch, which some believe to be the actual chalice held by Jesus at the Last Supper. He was fluent in many languages and was a proficient cryptanalyst, working for the U.S. government in the 1920s and breaking many ciphers where the official intelligence organizations had failed. He was personally thanked by Theodore Roosevelt Jr. for his great work.

Newbold made a whole series of exotic claims, all of which hardwire Roger Bacon into the Voynich Manuscript as its author. First of all, he examined Bacon's intellectual status as someone with the depth and breadth to write such a book and concluded that he—above anyone else—had every credential, whereas no others did.

Newbold then took the forensic cryptography route to link the two, pointing out that Bacon was not only familiar with codes, but was something of an early adopter and expert, suggesting he used eight different types of encryption.[5] The basic levels of protection he proposed (shorthand, dropped vowels from the plain text, simple substitution of one plain-text letter for one cipher-text letter) seem innocent now, but he was writing in an age when books were hand-produced and few could read and write. But Bacon also leaned toward the intellectually exotic, suggesting geometric figures with dots and—crucially for those who support him as the author—he also suggested artificial, discrete, made-up alphabets, as well as the liberal use of nonsense words.

As with the hidden formula for gunpowder, Bacon used two of these (anagramming and abbreviation) in his own writing, as well as something much cleverer. Some analysts of his work believe that he also concealed short messages inside much longer ones, a code system that allowed him to conceal plain text in what would otherwise appear to be innocuous Latin. Newbold argued that a variation of this was used by the author of the Voynich Manuscript; the conclusion being therefore that the two documents had the same author— Roger Bacon. A good example would be where Bacon used nonsense words in his own works as well as gibberish to destroy the brain cells of the unwary, who could easily waste many hours on the sentence "Here ends vcrdhsm mcnezdhsar Rlicrh azdsn ad fratrem hlgznunc de ozrht Alk," which Bacon uses to end one of his treatises.

He also argued that there was a second, far more devious encryption system, using long-string anagrams. Newbold also discovered tiny, almost microscopic shorthand symbols attached to the core letters that constitute the Voynich alphabet. He translated these into Roman letters, which then gave him a secondary text of seventeen more letters. This first phase of Newbold's analysis is generally dismissed by most experts now. One argument against him being that what he argued were crucial pen-strokes were actually cracks in the ink, a long-term casualty of the age of the manuscript and its poor storage.

The other route back to Bacon via Dee could be the historical one, but this is not available. Sadly for Voynich, there is no mention anywhere in the court records of Rudolph buying the book from John Dee, though again there are many who believe that Dee did, in fact, sell the book.[6]

Although its history cannot be definitively traced back much before the early seventeenth century, there is little doubt that the manuscript existed in Prague around this time. Marci's letter indicates that Rudolph II bought it for 600 ducats, which dates this purchase sometime between 1572, when he was crowned king, and 1611, when he ceded power, dying the following year. It is clear that Marci is referring to the Voynich Manuscript, as he subsequently refers to the same book in his letters to the Vatican. There is one other clue placing it in Prague at this time—a small signature on folio 1r, in the name of Jacobus de Tepenecz. From a poor family, he starts life as Jacobus Horcicki but becomes an affluent pharmacist, growing wealthy by curing the rich, and is then given the title "de Tepenecz" after he cures the richest of them all, the Emperor Rudolph II, in 1608.

Sometime later, the manuscript is acquired by Georg Baresch. In 1637 and then again two years later, he writes to Athanasius Kircher, a leading Jesuit scholar in Rome who has established a reputation for translating difficult languages after writing a book about the Copts and their tongue. Baresch encloses copies of part of the Voynich Manuscript, which he has very carefully transcribed to see if Kircher can break them. He cannot, but there is no shame in that. Baresch and Kircher are the first to put their names down on the distinguished list of the vanquished who have been defeated by this manuscript.

Finally, Baresch gives the manuscript to Marci, who in turn hands it to Kircher, in 1666, who presumably buries it away in the vast Vatican libraries, where it stays submerged as it not seen again publicly until it surfaces when Voynich visits the Jesuits in 1911.

Given its total opacity, the Voynich Manuscript has inevitably attracted a full range of interpretations. At one end of the spectrum, Voynich and his supporters have argued that the historical evidence (flimsy though it is) welds Bacon and Dee into the manuscript. At the other end of the spectrum, his detractors argue that there are anachronisms in the manuscript, suggesting it is a fake. Much is made of an image of a clock that has both a short and a long hand,[7] the argument being that clocks did not have a short and a long hand at this time. But this is a case of the viewer seeing what he wants to see. Any common-sense viewing would question whether it was in fact a clock, but whatever it is, the two hands are the same length. The other claimed anachronism is Sagittarius wearing a fifteenth-century Florentine archer's hat. But hanging the dating on a piece of fashion history is about as insubstantial as it gets. Besides, this bit of the manuscript may well have been touched up later. Meanwhile, there is one very strong argument in favor of it being pre-Renaissance and that is the quality of the drawing. There are many hands at work here, but the artwork is rather crude. There is none of the swagger or photorealism of even the average Renaissance painter.

The artwork is distinctly medieval in tone and texture, which probably precludes it from being a Renaissance fake but of course does not prevent it being an earlier one.

In the end, though well argued and well researched by the various protagonists in the Voynich Manuscript debate, all of this is supposition. The best that can be said is that this book existed in the early seventeenth century in Prague, was subsequently given to the Catholic Church, who then sold it in 1912. Only carbon dating would resolve roughly when it was made, but that would require the destruction of part of the manuscript.

**

According to the catalog of the Beinecke Library at Yale University, "Almost every page contains botanical and scientific drawings, many full page, of a provincial but lively character, in ink with washes in various shades of green, brown, yellow, blue and red. Based on the subject matter of the drawings, the contents of the manuscript falls into six sections."

Part I is the botanical section, in which there are drawings of 113 unidentified plant species. The flowers, leaves and root systems of each plant are fantastical and—apart from one drawing—none of these plants have been positively identified as having existed, then or now. This failure to achieve a positive identification for any of the plants is not due to a lack of effort by successive generations of botanists who have studied them. There were early claims that one of the plants was an American sunflower[8] and that elsewhere a green pepper can be found,[9] but the drawing of this plant does not look much like such a vegetable, and there are many European plants that carry a closer resemblance to the drawing here. At best, this is another example of the wishful thinking that impedes much of the analysis of Voynich. People (no matter how well educated or qualified) simply see what they want to see, regardless of the evidence, and this is the enduring measure of the author's genius, whoever, he, she or they may be. Though there is not one indisputable positive identification of any plant in Part I, this may not that be that significant, as they are often poorly drawn, lacking the photorealism of other contemporary herbal drawings. Many of the plants may be composites, as if the flowers, stems and roots are taken from different sources.

Many contemporary readers of Voynich would have recognized the format immediately. This was a time when life was much shorter than it is now, and there were many medical perils that could easily remove a person from the planet. As in developing countries now, everyone lived in a world where the pharmacist, with his potions made from roots and plants, had as much influence on the texture of everyday life as a king. In a more immediate and intimate way, they had the power of life or death over their customers, and their reputation was always enhanced if they were able to source the latest exotic plant tinctures that were one of the many byproducts of the explosion of international trade at the beginning of the seventeenth century. Equally important in the pharmacologist's life were the herbals— beautifully illustrated manuals itemizing plants and their curative properties. One part of the format was to link poisonous animals with the plant that carried the cure by placing them next to each other—a visual shorthand in an age when the majority of the population could not read or write. The same pattern can be seen here, where a plant with a huge and disproportionate fruit conceals a snake in its tubular roots. The idea that such a plant with tubular roots may protect against snake bite is not so farfetched, as a plant with tubular roots has recently been shown to be highly effective against cobra venom, giving a high degree of life-saving protection against the complex cocktail of toxins that would otherwise deliver a slow and painful death to their victim.[10]

To add to the fantastical nature of the plants, many have animals and humans woven in as part of the overall presentation. Some of the plants look positively mammalian, with plant roots that are full of flowing movement like dancers. For lovers of the surreal—and there is plenty here for them—one set of roots has half-faces attached to them where you might otherwise expect to see nodules.[11]

All the plant drawings are wrapped by text, which presumably is a description of what they are, where they are grown and what properties they possess.

Part II is the astronomical or astrological section, with drawings of the sun, moon and stars. Here, there are astral diagrams, swirling circles with segments that are either concentric or radiate outward. There is clearly an attempt to define some complex mathematical formula linking the heavens with life on earth. In one, fifteen men and women populate two concentric circles, which sounds fine except that nine of the thirteen women are naked, they are all standing up to their waists in barrels, and floating above them, like helium-filled party balloons, are seven-pointed stars. In the middle, a goat is eating a huge berry, like the one on top of the plant that has the viper in its roots.[12] Another picture in the same series has six-pointed stars radiating outward, like spikes on a wheel, from a central face, which may be the Man in the Moon, who has a down-turned face.[13] In another, they radiate from a rather spectacular flower.[14] In others, the segments are filled with stars and inscriptions. Some have the signs of the zodiac, while others have drawings of many naked women. Some of these naked women are free-standing, others are drawn coming out of open-topped pipes, like fully formed adults coming out of a fallopian tube.

Part III is the biological section and consists of drawings of small-scale naked women with fat bellies and Rubenesque hips. For the most part, they appear to be coming out of some sort of liquid, probably water, or weird linked tubes. According to the Beinecke Library catalog, "These drawings are the most enigmatic in the manuscript and it has been suggested that they symbolically represent the process of human reproduction and the procedure by which the soul becomes united with the body ... "

Part IV, the cosmological section, which is stranger than the pages before, consists of nine medallions "filled with stars and cell-like shapes, with fibrous structures linking the circles. Some medals with petal-like arrangements of rays filled with stars." The cylinder motif is here again, and in one picture, there are the Four Ages of Man round a central sun. The figure which represents old age is bent double, has a cane in one hand and a huge symbolic chain in the other.[15] Again, there is the recurrent motif of interlocking pipes, as if the pages from an ancient plumbing manual or an anatomy handbook had somehow merged with an esoteric guide to the spirit world. Many of the zodiac signs are incorporated in the text, and there are neat little drawings for Pisces, Taurus, Scorpio, Leo, Virgo, Libra and Gemini.

Part V, the pharmaceutical section, is full of exquisite painted depictions for more than a hundred species of herbs, plants and roots. The assumption must be that these have a medicinal purpose as there is detailed text to accompany the drawings, along with depictions of the sort of jars you might expect to see in an apothecary full of healing potions in mysterious but comforting primary colors—red, yellow and blue—as well as green. The text is continuous, presumably detailing the miraculous healing properties of these distillations of nature's finest offerings—the only problem is that none of these plants exist, either then or now. But in a world where trade with the Caribbean, the Far East and Africa was beginning to seriously open up for the rich and well connected, it would have been easy to pass these plants off as real, items in a catalog of truly exotic goods available in lands beyond the setting sun.

Part VI consists of continuous text, decorated with stars in the margins. There are also animals dotted around the pages, including a dragon, strange insects, a deer with horns on its head shaped like a horse yoke, what looks like a lioness, a woman with a crossbow, a woman casting seeds, a bird that looks like a cormorant, a bird nesting and even a hermaphroditic person with a penis and breasts.

This complex mixture of the surreal, the unique and the truly bizarre is all wrapped up in a script that has defied every attempt at decryption. In part, this is because of the absence of a crib or key to unlock the code, though some cryptanalysts over the years believe they have found one and there have been claimed breakthroughs and even partial decrypts.

***

Any attack on the Voynich Manuscript has to start with an assessment of what it is and, just as important, what it is not. To quote Sherlock Holmes, "Once you eliminate the impossible, whatever remains, no matter how improbable, must be the truth."

Taking a clue from the great master of deductive reasoning, it is possible to eliminate those encryption systems that cannot underpin the Voynich Manuscript. It is clearly not a simple substitution cipher, in which a symbol is matched with a letter: there is an acute shortage of one- or two-letter words, very few double letters but many sequential repetitions. The cipher text does not flow like a living language, and the final confirmation of this is the lack of any "parallel context"—when one common word appears, then statistically other words will tend to appear alongside. For example, the word "of" is often followed by the word "the," yet that sort of pattern is not evident here.

Neither can it be a polyalphabetic substitution cipher, in which different letters represent the same letter in the plain text. When this sort of encryption system is used, the frequency of letters tends to be flattened out, but this does not happen here. There is far too much structured repetition: some characters appear frequently, like E in English, while others appear rarely, like Z does in English plain text.

It could, in places, be ideographic, like Egyptian hieroglyphs, where a symbol represents a single word or even a piece of language. This could well apply to parts of the manuscript, especially the images. For example, the bare-chested dumpy women might represent all pregnant women, or even all women. Many of the animals and plants could be ideographic and carry much heavier levels of meaning. But this still leaves the text, most of which looks like a cipher in which each symbol represents a single letter of plain text. Though even here there is the possibility that the authors have mixed cipher and code together. Some of the characters in the manuscript may be symbols representing syllables, words or even phrases. In the absence of a code book or anything to act as a crib, it is impossible to say.

So what remains for the modern Sherlock Holmes? Sadly, there is no single remaining truth here, just many shades of possibility, though some more likely than others. Whoever wrote the Voynich Manuscript obviously wanted to protect their contents from outsiders and the uninitiated—but equally they needed an encryption apparatus that was relatively easy to decipher for those who were deemed worthy of the secret knowledge secured within. The Voynich Manuscript has always attracted the weird and the wonderful, but with over 250,000 characters to be decrypted, some common sense needs to prevail. Any esoteric or highly sophisticated system in which the symbols have to be put through half a dozen filters—each more complex than the last—can therefore be ruled out. Even though it is for the initiates, the authors would still want it to be comprehensible. The reverse engineering involved with a decryption system like the one proposed by William Newbold (and many others) is huge. With each page taking many hours to decipher and there being so many variations and possibilities, there is far too high a risk of mistranslation along the way. Whoever wrote this wanted to share their wisdom and insight with a select group, that is, those with the key—and like all good keys, it has to fit.

***

First off the blocks, with some plain text prised out of the hundreds of lines of bewildering symbols, was Voynich's greatest supporter, Professor William Newbold. The key page for him—and many others who have followed—is the last one, 116v, twenty-three words of clear text, some linked by a plus sign, which many believe holds the key and may even be a crude anagram of the document's putative creator, Roger Bacon. In the margin is one of the ubiquitous pregnant women wearing what looks like a Rastafarian hat, above her is some sort of four-legged animal, and above that is what looks like an abstract of the human body with a representational heart in the middle.

After Voynich himself, Newbold was the second major player in the story to fall under the intoxicating spell of this manuscript, performing a series of truly spectacular mental conjuring tricks. In no time at all, a few lines of cipher text were yielding up exactly what he wanted them to say—and better still, it could all be justified as advanced and highly sophisticated cryptanalysis. It was a brilliant piece of intellectual magic. In front of your very eyes, he soon had dozens of plates spinning, all apparently defying the inevitable pull of gravity.

Initially, he extracted the phrase "*Michi dabas multas portas,*" which he translated to mean, "Thou has given me many gates," a deliciously ambiguous phrase. It can easily be read as a huge but circumstantial pointer to Bacon as the author: after a lifetime embracing comparative religions, it could mean that he had discovered that his Lord had given him many routes to salvation and eternal life. But Newbold had other desires. The obvious had no interest for him, when an elaborate concoction could be spun out of very little. He read "*portas*" to be Latin for "gates," but these were not just any gates. These were the portals to a Kabbalistic wonderland of esoteric mystery.

The first plank of his case was to argue that Bacon used what was to become a classic method of cryptography, a long stream of gibberish, lurking in which was a small section that was the encrypted part. The thinking is that only the seriously determined will wade through all the chaff to get to the crucial part and most will give up along the way. This was used very effectively by the Russians throughout the Cold War, the practice having the extra bonus of wasting a huge amount of British and American intelligence resources.

From here, Newbold went through a tortuous six-stage journey. He started by selecting the key symbols. Each was examined under a magnifying glass, broken up into its constituent parts and then transliterated, matching them with a system of Ancient Greek abbreviations, in sequence. He then doubled all but the first and last characters, then rearranged them in strings so that the last letter in each pair matched the first letter of the next one. In every pair where the second letter was part of what he called a "commuting" set, he then changed the letter according to some formula he had invented. Obviously, if both letters in the pair were from the commutation set, then both were changed. Once he had a string of symbols, he then gave them English alphabet letters from another table he had constructed. But there were still two steps to go. These letters were then given phonetic values, according to some opaque formula, and then all the letters were rearranged into long-string anagrams from which emerged some plain text.

Initially, it was heralded as one of the great breakthroughs of modern cryptography. It suited everyone to go along with it: here were the first steps toward solving an ancient mystery, a huge triumph for a society still reeling from the destructive shock of World War I. It created a new hero, Roger Bacon, a man billed as the "Father of Modern Science" who was also a devout Christian and therefore a contemporary copywriter's dream. Even the Catholic Church went along—after all, he was one of their own, even if they did then have to apologize for their grotesque excesses back in the thirteenth century.

Sadly for them all, there was only one problem: Newbold's work was total nonsense. All the academics and camp followers who had leaped onto the bandwagon without thinking were made to look very foolish when common sense entered the equation. Various cryptographers performed what was the adult equivalent of the story of the small boy who pointed out that the king did not in fact have any clothes on.[16] Despite creating the illusion that he had discovered the rules of the iron-clad cryptographic systems underpinning the manuscript, Newbold's system was totally subjective: any set of symbols could be read to say anything. Even if all the steps to get to the final strings of letters could be justified (and they were nothing more than deranged fantasies), the fact remains that long strings of letters can be rearranged to make them read almost whatever you want them to. Friedman had a field day amusing cryptographers everywhere by taking long sentences and turning them into something else completely different, even providing a long-string anagram of his own: "I put no trust in anagrammatic acrostic cyphers, for they are of little real value—a waste—and may prove nothing—*finis*," pointing out that an anagram of this length is virtually impossible to solve. That was back in 1959. Today, a PC could churn out every possible variation and then filter them to weed out those that were total gibberish, selecting those which had a high level of known language. But this was not available in the sixteenth century and any long-string anagram would have needed its own key.

After this, many otherwise serious cryptographers left Voynich alone. Having seen one group savaged, they did not want to be associated with Voynich for fear that they too would be contaminated.

Next up was an American lawyer, Joseph Feely. In the middle of World War II, he went back to first principles, though assuming that

Bacon was the author. Feely's previous book, *Shakespeare's Maze: Deciphering Shakespeare* (filed under "Cryptologic Follies" by Friedman) did not inspire confidence, but when he sat down to Voynich, he adopted an entirely sensible approach, starting by analyzing Bacon's various Latin treatises, counting up what he called the "leaders," the most commonly used letters. This gave him E, I, T, A, N, U and S, which he then matched with the symbol frequency in the Voynich Manuscript. So far so good, but then he ran into a wall: the Latin used in Bacon's text was heavily abbreviated, on his estimate by as much as a third, throwing all his calculations out, as common letters would be the first ones to be deleted. He then tried a different approach and tried to link the text with the images, where the subject matter was clear, starting with folio 78r, a page of text with two large flowers linking two shallow bathing pools full of naked women, seven in one and eight in the other. The flowers are clearly fantastical, but provide a pair of matching canopies sheltering the text underneath. Parts of the images are clearly labeled, which at least gives any would-be code-breaker a lever, no matter how small, into the plain text. To Feely's fevered wartime imagination, the flowers became ovaries, the tubes linking them to the naked women underneath were delivering the ova to the waiting gaggle of fecund women below. This was five years before Kinsey first told Americans about the basics of reproductive biology and Feely's misunderstanding is hilarious. Plants contain seeds, ovaries are inside women, and if there was any reproductive mechanism, it was the delivery of seeds (sperm) to women who were already lined up in what looks like a birthing pool underneath.

Though his grip on biology was scant, he used these labels as "clews," as he called them, from which emerged a rough, heavily abbreviated Latin, which then inevitably produced some exotic plain text, including the diary of a scientist who was studying living cells under heavy magnification but who had to disguise his work from a brutal, unyielding Church authority. If true, this would have demanded a heavy rewriting of the history of science. Anton van Leeuwenhoek first used a microscope to describe bacteria, a world of life in a drop of water and the circulation of blood corpuscles in capillaries in 1674, well over half a century after the Voynich Manuscript was written. Once again, the manuscript had cast its magic spell and continued to do so.

The next major attack on the Voynich Manuscript came from a well-respected oncologist, Professor Leonell Strong of Yale University. He tried a twin-pronged attack, using medical science and cryptography. Claiming that he had broken the structure of the encoding system used, "a peculiar double system of arithmetical progressions of a multiple alphabet." From this, he concluded that this was an herbal guide, written by Anthony Askham (often written Ashham), the brother of Roger Askham, the Yorkshire-born scholar who was one of the world's first educationalists, a humanist who argued against schoolmasters' obsession with beating their pupils for every minor mistake. It was not such a strange choice as author. A physician, astrologer and polymath, Anthony Askham shared many of the same obsessions as the Voynich Manuscript author, besides which, he wrote almanacs and an herbal guide.

With Roger Askham firmly fixed as the author, the plain text began to emerge, revealing the Voynich Manuscript to be a graphic guide to what would now be called "women's problems" as well as a pre-*Kama Sutra* guide to the mysteries of the marital bed. In no time at all, he had an herbally based oral contraceptive made from pine-tree bark, honey and something that translated as "oil of spindle," which he then tested in the laboratory. He discovered that this mixture was very effective in slowing down sperm, making them much less mobile, from which he concluded two things: one, the recipe worked, and two, his decipherment was correct. Just how effective, though, can be measured by just one sentence that he prised out of the Voynich Manuscript, a string of medieval English, which reads, "*When skuge of tun'e-bag rip, seo uogon kum sli of se mosure-issue ped stans skubent, stokked kimbo elbow crawknot.*" To many, this is gibberish in its pure form, the phrase "*kimbo elbow crawknot*" resembling something out of the "Jabberwocky" by Lewis Carroll, which begins:

> *Twas brillig, and the slithy toves*
> *Did gyre and gimble in the wabe:*

All mimsy were the borogoves,
And the mome raths outgrabe.

But professors from Yale are made of sterner stuff. According to Strong, this sentence translated as "When the contents of the veins rip (or tear the membranes) the child comes slyly from the mother issuing with the leg-stance skewed and bent while the arms, bent at the elbow, are knotted (above the head) like the legs of a crawfish."

Another Yale professor, Robert Brumbaugh (specialist subject medieval history), then took up the attack, after the manuscript was given to the university library by Hans Kraus in 1969.

Like his predecessors, he looked for the keys on the last page, folio 116v, where he found what he called "a standard thirteenth-century cipher," along with what he saw to be keys in the margins of five other folios (1r, 17r, 49v, 66r and 76r) as well as the second ring on 57v. In the case of 1r, he believed that the paired sequences in the left and right margins indicated a simple monoalphabetic substitution of symbols. The same string that had yielded "*Michi dabas multas portas*" for Newbold now read "*Michi con olada ba*" for Brumbaugh. Not surprisingly, it produced a completely different plain text. After some rearrangement of the letters, he got "Rodgd Bacon." He also deciphered some High German, "*Valsch ubren so nim ga nicht o*," which translates as "The above is false so do not take it."

From this, he reached two conclusions. The first was that the entire document was a fraud, designed to separate the gullible Emperor Rudolph II from his money. The relatively easy decipherment of "Rodgd Bacon" was there to prove authorship and give the manuscript some serious cachet as a great work of science, a bargain at 600 ducats for an emperor who wanted to expand his knowledge and secure his place as Europe's preeminent cultural icon. The second conclusion was that the manuscript is written in an artificial language "based on Latin but not very firmly based there; its spelling is phonetically impressionistic; some passages seem solely repetitive padding." But as with the other attempts to break the Voynich Manuscript, Brumbaugh's solution depended on exotic but opaque decryption systems provided by the code-breaker, which others have found difficult to reproduce. And—just like the others—the plain text ranges from the incomprehensible to the bizarre.

**

For nearly a century now, the Voynich Manuscript has weaved its seductive spell on analysts, proving to be just as devastating against professionals as it is against amateur code-breakers. The result is that there is a wider range of solutions proposed here than there is for any other unsolved cipher, and it is simply not possible to eliminate all but one and so neatly arrive at a Sherlock Holmes-type solution: "One of the most amazingly complex ones I have ever had to solve. A five-pipe problem, Watson!" A better variation on his advice would therefore be to "Eliminate the impossible, discard the improbable and focus on the likely," which at least narrows the search down to two areas.

The first issue is what language is used for the plain text. Statistically, the most likely is Latin. Though the Roman Empire had collapsed centuries before the Voynich Manuscript was written, Latin was still the most widespread language in Europe up to the time of Rudolph II and beyond. It was the main language both of court and academic discourse, with most major thinkers and communicators using it. The odds therefore on it being Latin underneath the bizarre Voynich script are significantly better than they are for any other language. If it is Latin, then the previous exclusions also apply. It is not a simple substitution of one Voynich character for one Latin, neither is it a polyalphabetic code, in which several letters can stand for the same letter in the plain text. The standard mathematical analysis, which precludes this, applies equally well to Latin as it does to most other languages. If such a substitution had been used, the distribution of letters would be much flatter than they are.

This does not leave many options, though at least Holmes would be happy to know that we have eliminated the impossible and at least we have started looking in the right place.

If the plain-text language is Latin (or actually most others), then the writers of the Voynich Manuscript could have constructed a relatively easy code that would nevertheless be very difficult to break using three related techniques. At its core is a discrete group of words and symbols relating to the main subject areas of the manuscript—astrology, botany, biology, astronomy, mathematics, chemistry and pharmacology. This may well be polyalphabetic, with more than one Voynich symbol being used for the same word or concept. Having established the core lexicon of key words, the cipher constructors could then use abbreviations extensively throughout, combined with nulls dropped in at random. Frequently used words, like the names of some of the plants, could also be concealed if they are represented by a single Voynich symbol. A further—and relatively simple level of concealment—could be achieved by using a trick mentioned by Roger Bacon, which is to conceal the plain text in much longer strings of other material. These could be gibberish or plain text that clearly relates to something else. There is a huge clue here that this may well be the case. Consider the task of enciphering over a quarter of a million characters by hand, and then imagine being the code-writer who also has to make up long strings of gibberish to use as material to bracket the actual encrypted material. This is much harder than at first might appear. Writing completely incomprehensible random gibberish is more difficult than it looks, though some might argue that newspaper columnists manage it frequently. For the medieval scribes, having to produce each page without a mistake and also ensuring that the plain text neatly fitted was a mammoth task. Fatigue and boredom would inevitably triumph, and any scribe would end up making short cuts—reusing lines they have already created, making tiny tweaks here and there. This would explain both the inconsistent phrasing and the recurrent pattern in which very similar words are endlessly repeated.

This theory at least fits and explains much of the architecture of the script.[17] It also explains why the Voynich Manuscript has remained unsolved. Using a code manual and a selection of these techniques, the scribes who produced the manuscript could easily have transformed the plain text into a virtually impregnable cipher. The advantage would be that it would be relatively easy to decipher for any initiate who was lucky enough to have the code book, but very difficult for anyone without the key or keys.

The other alternative in the most likely category of solutions is that the Voynich Manuscript is written in an artificial language, probably one developed at the time and maybe even one that was created solely for this one document, making this a variation on the world's ultimate one-time pad. One-time pads were invented in the early twentieth century and are a virtually unbreakable system of cryptography. Typically, sender and receiver have the same set of pads, which contain the key. This is randomly generated, is as long as the plain text and is only used once. Provided the two pads are secure and only used once, it is almost impossible to break.[18]

By the time the manuscript surfaced at the court of Rudolph II, Latin was beginning to lose its resilient power as the international *lingua franca* used by the courts, aristocracies and academics of Europe. There was a vacuum, as national languages were growing stronger and becoming more accepted, but capitalism and growing European trade needed a means of fluent international communication. Transnational commerce was opening up new markets. Merchants and adventurers were travelling greater distances and in far greater numbers than ever before, bringing back with them souvenirs from different cultures, everything from spices to jewelry, as well as new ideas and new ways of thinking. From the Far East came a different way of composing language. Instead of building words from tiny components, like bricks in a house, symbols could be used instead. So instead of writing the word "window," a single symbol could be used to express this concept. It was an intoxicating idea: a universal system of signs that could form the core of a new international language to replace Latin, which was now well past its sell-by date and becoming distinctly frayed round the edges.

Many egomaniacs attempted to construct such languages. After all, what greater expression of the self than to define a language used by millions in different countries across the known world?

The creation of artificial languages quickly became a crowded market. Typical of many such new "languages" was that constructed by William (Gulielmi) Addy in London in 1695. His short book *Stenographia*, billed heroically as "The Art of Short-Writing compleated in a far more Compendious method than any yet extant," appeared in the same year. Here are columns of symbols covering all the usual linguistic needs, plus some that are never going to be used, and which help define the sort of madness that can quickly infect anyone starting to build a language from scratch. There are symbols here for circumcision, uncircumcision and a state of penile deformity that is neither circumcision nor uncircumcision, a concept as baffling as any page of the Voynich Manuscript, chosen randomly. Addy also strays into the truly poetic—having specific single symbols for concepts like "to be as miserable as lovers of the world are miserable" and "as high as the highest heaven."

Move over, Shakespeare, your greatest and most complex thoughts can be reduced to a shorthand flourish.

Though none of these synthetic artificial languages ever made it into the mainstream, they enjoyed substantial, though niche, popularity, especially within cults and other religious groups who either wished or needed to keep their secrets safe.

Meanwhile, Voynich remains as elusive as ever—and the single biggest prize in cryptography.

CHAPTER 4

Shugborough: the Shepherd's Monument

> "Yea, though I walk through the valley of the shadow of death, I will fear no evil: for Thou art with me; Thy rod and Thy staff, they comfort me."
>
> —Psalms 23:4

Shugborough Hall, Staffordshire, England, 1748–58

One of the first to try to crack the puzzle at Shugborough was Josiah Wedgwood, the celebrated eighteenth-century potter and design genius.[1] Blighted by smallpox as a small boy, he devoted his life to research; inventing new and wonderful ceramic glazes before becoming a leading figure in the campaign to abolish the slave trade. His distinctive Jasperware blue-and-white china is now an instantly recognizable global brand.

A brilliant businessman, he was highly creative in every area of his life. Two hundred and fifty years before modern campaigning, he realized the value of fashion in politics. A non-conformist Christian, he joined the committee of the Society for the Abolition of the Slave Trade, designing and producing their seal, a prototype of the modern charity bracelet. "Am I Not a Man and a Brother?" showed a black slave in chains, kneeling, his hands pleading in supplication. This design, a little black-and-white cameo, was used on bracelets, hairpins and teapots, as well as on tokens, which were sold to raise money for the cause. As his fellow campaigner, Thomas Clarkson, wrote, "The taste for wearing them became general and thus fashion, which usually confines itself to worthless things, was seen for once in the honorable office of promoting the cause of justice, humanity and freedom."

The Shugborough code and many of the clues were right on Wedgwood's doorstep, and though he had a brilliant mind and thought about it for more than forty years, he never managed to extract its meaning.

The text is just ten letters long and can be found in the gardens of one of Wedgwood's favorite places, Shugborough Hall in Staffordshire. It is engraved on a stone monument that was commissioned by Thomas Anson, paid for by his brother, George, started by their architect, Thomas Wright, and completed by one of the foremost designers of the age, James "Athenian" Stuart. The Shepherd's Monument was commissioned in 1748 but built and then extended over the next decade or so.

On the top is a carved marble scene depicting shepherds round a tomb on which are carved the words "ET IN ARCADIA EGO." Underneath this is a marble plaque, measuring 51.5 inches across by 18 inches high.[2] Exactly 2.5 inches from the exterior edge at the top is a row of letters, which reads, "O.U.O.S.V.A.V.V," and beneath that, on either end, set 6.5 inches from the top, are the letters D and M. The full inscription reads:

O.U.O.S.V.A.V.V

D   M

Above the inscription is a substantial picture, measuring 57.6 inches across by 72.25 inches high. This is a carved marble relief of a painting by Nicolas Poussin, called *Les Bergers d'Arcadie II*, which was painted over a century earlier, in 1640, but has been subtly altered by the man who carved it, a Flemish artist called Peter Scheemakers.

***

Shugborough Hall is a magnificent neoclassical Georgian stately home, built originally in 1695 on the site of the former manor house at what was known locally as "the Place of the Witch." Here, one of the great English rivers, the Trent, meets one of its subsidiaries, the Sow, with the house nestling where they flow into each other. This is picture-postcard, tourist-trap Britain. There is a sense of English aristocratic history everywhere, from the perfect proportions of the architecture to the neatly sculpted gardens, which include a huge and magnificent yew tree, now covering an acre. Yew trees, which have long been regarded as both a symbol of renewed life and the keepers of the dead, line the river and form an avenue leading away from the house, carrying with them the idea that the dead live on in nature.[3] This notion that life can transcend death by the monuments we leave behind is everywhere in the house and grounds.

Traditionally, Shugborough is the ancestral country seat of the Anson family, whose aristocratic title became Lichfield in 1831.[4] Until he died, in late 2005, the society photographer Patrick Lichfield lived in part of the house, but like many English aristocratic families, the big money has largely come and gone. The entire contents had to be sold in 1842 (in an auction that lasted a fortnight) after the then Earl of Lichfield (described as "extravagant and imprudent") had blown the family fortune on low politics, high living and slow horses. It was ultimately given to the State in 1960 to settle outstanding death duties. The National Trust now owns the house and grounds, and Staffordshire County Council imaginatively runs it as a very attractive working historic estate and tourist attraction.[5] Each year, more than a hundred and thirty thousand people visit Shugborough Hall, many joining the long and illustrious queue of their predecessors who have looked at the Shepherd's Monument from every angle, scratched their heads and then left. This queue has included some of the smartest minds of the last two and a half centuries.

Josiah Wedgwood's grandson Charles Darwin (his daughter, Susannah, was Darwin's mother) also took his turn at trying to locate the elusive meaning concealed within this ten-letter code. Though he is the architect of modern evolutionary theory and a man with one of the most inventive and fluid scientific minds ever known, he too was defeated.

The English novelist Charles Dickens also took a look, and applied his fertile mind to try and crack open the monument's hidden secrets. Like many great Victorian writers, he was obsessed by mysteries, especially ones in which the clues were sparse and elusive. Even though he was a master of complex (and often improbable) plots, he too had to retire from the struggle, defeated by what looks like a simple and easily breakable code.

More recently, in 2004, the code-breakers from Bletchley Park, including some of the brilliant men and women who cracked the German Enigma messages in World War II, began to try and unlock Shugborough's enduring mystery. Over the years, Bletchley Park has received hundreds of proposed solutions, ranging from the crazy (often based on little evidence) through to the highly exotic, some of which are based on esoteric history and complex mathematics. These have come both from amateurs and professionals (including some of the world's most advanced code-breakers from the NSA, CIA and those back offices of British intelligence that are not on anyone's formal budget), but so far no one has come up with an indisputably correct answer.

The solutions so far presented to Bletchley Park are a predictable round-up of the usual suspects and read like a check list for Dan Brown's ongoing research program: the Freemasons, the Knights Templars, the Cathars, the Merovingians, the Rosicrucians, all sorts of Kabbalistic groups, the Priory of Sion, Solomon's Temple and many other occult sects, along with UFOs, the Pyramids, the Dogon tribe (who live in Mali, near Timbuktu) and Nostradamus. Throw Rennes-le-Château into the mix and it makes up a fairly comprehensive list of ancient mysteries and the cults who wander in and out of most of them. Some require a death-defying leap of the imagination, such as the notion that it was inspired by the final Jacobite uprising in 1745, when a ragtag army tried to install Charles Stuart, a Catholic who was born in Italy, with a Polish grandfather and a Prussian mother, on to the English throne, which was then occupied by a German. The self-styled King of Scotland, Bonnie Prince Charlie, got as far as a public house in Derby before returning back to cosseted obscurity. Lady Anson was shaken by it, but it did not really impact the security of their world.

Others have suggested that the monument holds precious clues to the location of the Holy Grail. But this requires an even greater leap of faith: as mentioned earlier, the marble relief on the monument, which was carved by Scheemakers, comes (in part) from a copy of Nicolas Poussin's painting *Les Bergers d'Arcadie II*. Poussin used a background for his painting that looks a bit like a view of Rennes-le-Château, a key location in Dan Brown's *The Da Vinci Code*. However, like many painters, Poussin used backgrounds from other paintings, and he never visited Rennes-le-Château. There is an even bigger hole in this theory: the Priory of Sion, the would-be caretakers of the Holy Grail, who are linked to Rennes-le-Château, is a myth invented in 1956 by a French fantasist, Pierre Plantard, nearly three hundred years after Poussin died, which would make him one of the most prescient human beings of all time.

Another well-publicized solution from an anonymous (but professional) cryptographer has suggested that there is a visible key on the monument, which reads, "1223," though after spending several hours there, I have not been able to see it. He argues that it then decrypts as a ten-letter answer: "Jesus H Defy," the letter H being the most significant as it stands for the Greek letter X or "chi," meaning "Messiah" or the "Anointed One." Quite why the Ansons should choose to hide what would be a clear demonstration of their faith in what was a dominant Christian society is not explained and this solution can be filed under F for fanciful, along with many other similar solutions.

***

Though many of the solutions are sophisticated and exotic, in contrast the Shepherd's Monument looks deceptively uncomplicated. But despite its simple allure, this tiny cipher has remained intact for more than two hundred and fifty years, an extraordinary feat given the battery of tools available to the modern cryptanalyst. Once again, an original cryptographer has defeated the finest minds of successive generations of code-breakers.

It was written at a time when (in general) good records were kept, especially by the British aristocracy, but here, there is a lack of verifiable and therefore trustworthy information. This acute shortage of hard facts means that there are few foundation stones on which to construct any sort of robust critical path toward a solution. Many unsolved codes have kept their secrets, protected by thickets of information. This code has done the opposite: it has protected itself brilliantly through its very lack of armor. It is not even clear if it is a cipher or a code. Does each letter stand for a single other letter, making up a ten-word plain text? Is it a simple acrostic, in which each letter stands for either a word or a set of words, or even a larger amount of enciphered code? The basic problem for any cryptanalyst tackling this code is that there is simply not enough basic material on which to get any sort of handle.

The only facts known for certain are what it says and where it is. Everything else is, to a greater or lesser degree, speculative.

As the great spinner of fictional mysteries Charles Dickens wrote in a different context, "The mystery of the future, and the little clue afforded to it by the voice of the present, seemed expressed in the whole picture."[6] Taking our cue from Dickens, cracking this cipher means searching the surrounding context for clues, no matter how tangential.

**

Code-writers are very specific animals. They are often at the autistic end of the psychological spectrum and tend toward the anally obsessive in their attention to detail. So, in any code, every nuance has to fit. Mistakes are possible and do happen, but they tend to be rare and only occur in very long and complex ciphers where it is easy for boredom to set in and mistakes to happen. There are mistakes in *The Beale Papers* (see Chapter 5), where the code-setter starts miscounting after writing 480 numbers. In the case of the *Kryptos* sculptures at the CIA (see Chapter 1), the creator, Jim Sanborn, simply misses a letter, though by this time he has already cut over sixteen hundred into sheets of metal, a good example of a code-writer who is creatively obsessive but careless in his technical application. But the Shugborough code is too short for mistakes like this. Carved in marble, it is precise in its detail. Those who commissioned it were exceptionally rich and knew exactly what they wanted. If it had not been completed to their precise specifications, they would have given instructions for it to be done again. It is fair to assume therefore that it is exactly what its creators wanted. Though there are only ten letters, they are laid out in a very specific formation and so the layout is rich both with potential meaning and (unfortunately) questions.

The first mystery to try and solve is why there is no period (called a *punctum* in Latin) after the third V, i.e. the final letter on the top line. Some argue that this was just a mistake and was a common error made by stonemasons at the time. But this is palpably incorrect. The layout of the letters is specific and accurate to less than a millimeter or two in virtually every place. If you measure the top line of letters, the distance from the left-hand side of the first O to the left-hand edge of the marble is exactly the same as the distance from the right-hand edge of the last V to the right-hand edge of the marble. In other words, the spacing is exact, and the totality of the letters without the final period fits exactly in the middle of the marble. The missing period is therefore deliberate, and any explanation of the code has to be able to explain this.

The second, and related, mystery is the issue of the D and the M and why they are on a separate line below. D and M often appear on tombstones and other monuments, which are *in memoriam* to a lost one. In this instance, therefore, the most likely explanation is that "D M" stands for "*dis manibus*," meaning "to the spirits of the departed," which is a traditional abbreviation on Roman tombs. Statistically, this is the most likely explanation. Alternatively, it could be the initials for the author of the phrase contained within the eight letters, if that is what it is.

A first step to try to solve this mystery is to resolve what language is used here and, as a subsidiary issue, whether there is more than one language, even though there are only ten letters.

Statistically, there are two likely candidates: English and Latin, with a remote possibility that it might be German, French or even

Italian. However, there is no clear candidate and there are drawbacks to each possibility.

The letter V appears three times in only ten letters, and there is no language in which it enjoys a 30 percent frequency. Traditional letter-frequency analysis would suggest that it is therefore not English, as V is the twenty-first least used letter, appearing about 1 percent of the time, and sentence structures in which two Vs appear next to each other are rare. Latin looks like a better candidate, especially as the V digraph (two-letter pairing) of letters is relatively common and one instantly familiar phrase is "*valeria victrix*," or "valiant and victorious," the title of the Twentieth Roman Legion, which played a crucial role in subduing the English. However, this does not mean that this is the meaning of either DM or VV.

Though Latin looks the hot favorite for the language used here, there are two powerful arguments against it. The Romans used V to stand for both U and V, so why would they use both U and V in the same phrase? This can be explained by putting the cipher into its correct historical context. Though Romans used the letter V to stand for both U and V, the English in the eighteenth century did not always do this and were quite happy to use both V and U. However, this is unlikely to be the case here: the great architect of Shugborough was James "Athenian" Stuart. He was the preeminent influence on contemporary taste, and his long shadow is everywhere in the house and gardens, not only at Shugborough but throughout the upper echelons of Georgian society.

In January 1751, James Stuart and an architect, Nicholas Revett, left Venice for a lengthy trip to Greece to catalog and draw those classical monuments that had survived. His great work *Antiquities of Athens* followed, the first volume of which was published in 1762. As a contemporary cultural icon, Stuart had no peer. His trip and work were sponsored by the cream of the wealthy and well connected. Inevitably, Lord and Lady Anson as well as Thomas Anson gave him money, along with fifty earls, seventeen dukes, numerous lords, marquises and marchionesses, His Grace the Lord Primate of Ireland, His Serene Highness the Prince of Orange, Lord Walpole and the Irish writer Laurence Sterne (author of *Tristram Shandy*). Even one of the greatest Americans of all time, Benjamin Franklin, a scientist, inventor, philosopher, writer and economist, who was living in England and representing the states of Pennsylvania, Georgia, New Jersey and Massachusetts, was not spared the aristocratic begging bowl and he too—along with the Library at Philadelphia—put money in.

The books—in four large-format crimson leather bindings—are exceptional.[7] There are dozens of line drawings of Ancient Greek monuments, plus plans, elevations and detailed descriptions. Their scholarship is immense, and their passion for their subject is palpable. The introduction, written by Stuart, gives one substantial, though not obvious, clue as to the ultimate meaning of the Shepherd's Monument. It ends with a beautifully engraved epitaph, which reads:

DIS MANIBVS

QTVRANNIO MAXIMO

PRAECEPTORIET

AMICOBONORVM

CONSILIORVM

SAGARIS ALCIMIAVGSER

VERNAE ARCARIPROVINC

ARCHAIAE VICAR

MERENTI MEMORIA

The first clue is "DIS MANIBVS," which, as we have seen, means "to the spirits of the departed," and this must remain the most likely meaning for the D and M on the lower line. More important, throughout this dedication, Stuart never uses the letter U at any time, preferring the correct use of the letter V to stand for both letters. As a writer, Stuart is relaxed and fluent in English, Latin, Greek, French and Italian. He is also meticulous and precise. Not for him (or any of his followers) the misuse of U and V.[8] And there is no way he would have allowed such misuse by his clients or anyone working for them.

There is a further problem with Latin as the language of this code and that is the context. None of the Shugborough monuments is Roman. They are predominantly Greek and mostly inspired or copied from Ancient Athens. There are no specifically Roman pieces, and apart from the Latin phrase *"Et in Arcadia ego"* (copied from a French painting), there is little anywhere to suggest that the Romans were a source of inspiration for anything on the estate. This can be countered by the argument that Latin was the most commonly used language on tombstones at this time, but in *Antiquities of Athens*, Stuart uses Greek where it is the correct language to employ.

The other—but remote—possibilities are that the language used here is either German or French. The man occupying the throne at this time, George II, was born in Schloss Herrenhausen, Hanover, and was to all intents German, but there is nothing to suggest a Teutonic connection anywhere in the house or grounds. Again, letter-frequency analysis would not suggest German, as V is a relatively uncommon letter, being twentieth in order of usage, and the V digraph is unusual. French is a possibility. V is much more commonly used here than it is in English or German, and OU is a relatively common pairing in French, though not when followed by U. Both Thomas Anson and his sister-in-law were bilingual, French still being the language of much international diplomatic discourse, but there is little in the estate or house that suggests that France cast any sort of shadow over their everyday lives. Besides which, George Anson had thrashed the French Navy at Cape Finisterre in 1747, and so the family was unlikely to be endeared enough toward them that he would tolerate a code in the French language on their estate. The final possibility is Italian, but there is nothing anywhere to suggest that they would use modern Italian, especially when Latin was available and in common use.

As with everything at Shugborough, for each step toward a solution, there is one (and often more than one) step back. Some speculation is required, and the most likely language in use here is Latin, at least for part of the code. The beginning D and the terminal M are set apart and therefore most likely to be *"dis manibus,"* which means this is a funerary monument, an explanation supported by the subject matter of the carving above.

Above the marble plaque with the ten letters is a substantial picture, carved in marble. Typical of many of the marble carvings that went on top of mantelpieces in Georgian homes, this is a carved relief of a painting by Nicolas Poussin, called *Les Bergers d'Arcadie II*, painted in 1640. The first version of this picture (painted in 1629–30) also carries the phrase *"Et in Arcadia ego"* and is in the Devonshire Collection at Chatsworth House. The history of the Anson family at this time is intimately linked both to this painting and the whole Arcadian ideal. There is a portrait of Lady Anson at Shugborough in which she is holding in her hands a small scroll of a picture with the words *"Et in Arcadia ego"* clearly visible.

In the second version of Poussin's painting of the Arcadian shepherds,[9] three shepherds stand round a large stone tomb on which is carved the phrase *"Et in Arcadia ego,"* which they are pointing out to a well-dressed woman who is standing to their right. The inhabitants of Shugborough at this time (and the other members of their social circle) were steeped in historical antiquity. Under James Stuart's influence, they turned the house and grounds into a microcosm of Athens. The opening picture in Volume One of his book has a huge two-pillared arch in the foreground, on top of a hill, which Stuart believed had been part of Hadrian's Aqueduct. It is remarkably similar to the Triumphal Arch at Shugborough. In the picture, Athens is in the valley below. At Shugborough, it is the main house, which has the same geographical relationship to the arch as Athens does in the picture, which explains why they chose this location for the arch and confirms how they saw Shugborough. They lived their dream. In the picture, in the background is "a mountain in the confines of Arcadia." In their eyes, it was Ancient Athens in an eighteenth-century setting, a modern tribute to a previous golden age.

The inhabitants of the house read the Arcadian classic called *Astrée*, a desperately slow and convoluted five-part romance by Honoré d'Urfé, the Marquis de Valromey.[10] This book was a breakout hit in Georgian England. With its endless plots and intertwining love story, this was an early version of the television soap and served much the same purpose, consuming many relaxing hours of mild diversion. When they looked up from their reading and gazed out of the windows on to the estate grounds, the sight of their animals roaming free must have confirmed their emotional belief that they had created an Arcadian idyll in the middle of the English country-side. For them, the meaning of this painting was clear.

Arcadia was a region of Ancient Greece, a remote, earthly paradise populated by simple, rustic people who tended their cattle and enjoyed a life of rural bliss, singing and playing their pipes. The memorial to the dead person in the tomb, "*Et in Arcadia ego*," means "I am now in Arcadia." This is generally assumed to carry two meanings. The first is that the occupant is now at peace from the troubles of the world. The second meaning is more somber, a reminder that there is nothing so beautiful in life that it cannot be taken away in death. One Georgian visitor, Thomas Pennant, first planted this interpretation, writing in 1782 that "The moral resulting from this seems to be that there are no situations of life so delicious but which at length death must snatch us from." Either way, it is not only a reminder of the transience of life but also a spiritually uplifting message of how we live on after death in the memory of others, the predominant theme of the estate.

The monument is flanked by much cruder stone columns, made up of five carved blocks on each side. Each cylindrical block is carved differently, and together they support the arched roof. On the top of the monument are nine upright circular shields, now rather worn by time and weather.

The monument is surrounded by trees and makes up the focal point at the end of a small glade, a corridor of trees slightly wider than the monument itself. It looks like some sort of funerary monument covering a grave, but this is not the case. The marble picture was removed twenty years ago, as it was becoming unstable and had to be repinned into position. According to the accounts from the time, there was nothing behind it and nothing buried there. The treasure-hunters were disappointed: there was no hidden treasure. The heavens did not open. The lightning did not crack as the final resting place of the Holy Grail was revealed.

***

The marble tableau of the shepherds was carved by one of the major sculptors of the day, the Flemish artist Peter Scheemakers, who also made the statue of Shakespeare in Westminster Abbey. However, he has substantially altered the two original Poussin pictures in the Shugborough Hall version, adding layers of symbolism to further entice and torment. In both Poussin pictures, the tomb is predominantly horizontal and longer than it is high. In the carving, the proportions are reversed and the tomb is taller than it is wide. In the paintings, the tomb is flat-topped and oblong, whereas in the carving, it is essentially rhombus in shape. Above this, Scheemakers has added an ossuary, a funerary casket to carry the bones of the dead, and above that, forming its lid, is a pyramid.

The appearance of the pyramid excites attention. Is it just a visual souvenir of Thomas Anson's visit to Egypt, or is it symbolic of something much deeper? Pyramids provided endless fascination in the eighteenth century, but they were also a symbol used by Freemasons, as is seen on the back of an American dollar bill. Masonic watchers also add in the geometry in the carving to support their view that the whole image is redolent with obvious symbolism. In the paintings, the shepherds hold their crooks in a loose V, and this is then heavily accentuated in the carving, in a very pronounced V, which visually leaps out of the marble. This V is then echoed in the letter Vs that are cut into the marble underneath, which at least raises the question as to whether they are related in some way.

The most common interpretation is that this V is part of standard Masonic symbolism. It is often assumed that given their position in society, the Ansons would inevitably be Freemasons and that this is a huge symbolic clue to their secret beliefs and their affiliations. But this is by no means certain. It is more of an assumption made from a modern viewpoint, which ignores the historical context of the time in which the Ansons were living.

In the mid-eighteenth century, Freemasonry was split between the "Ancients" and the "Moderns" and was not held in particularly high public esteem, so it cannot be said with any certainty that the Ansons would be members of their local lodge. Though their descendants within a generation were Masons, there is no evidence that either Thomas or George were members of the Fraternal Order. Masons traditionally put a small upturned V on their tombs, to symbolize the compass of the Great Architect, but there is no such Masonic symbolism on the family crypt.

To further confuse matters, in the paintings, the shepherds are examining the inscription, but in the carving, it is bizarrely different. One shepherd is looking away from the tomb but has a hand above the lettering with his thumb up. The other shepherd is looking at the phrase. He too has his thumb up, and it is pointing at the letter R in "Arcadia."

But the final intriguer is this: the marble carving is the reverse of both paintings, a mirror image of the original, with the spectating woman on the left rather than the right. This reversal could be explained by a common technique used by artists at the time: the camera obscura, which Peter Scheemakers probably used to trace the basic figures from the original Poussin painting and which would reverse the layout. Though this is the best explanation for the reversal of the image, the changes and additions still have to be explained. And what they all mean is—quite frankly—anyone's guess, though this does not mean that some of the more obviously foolish suggestions cannot be removed.

***

Though members of the Anson-Lichfield family have lived on the site since the Shepherd's Monument was built over two hundred and fifty years ago, the meaning of the code died with its creators, and this has inevitably led to endless speculation by their descendants. Writing in 1987, Countess Margaret of Lichfield recounted:

> One day I was showing some friends round the garden and when we came to the Shepherd monument I told them the story about Alicia the Shepherdess and suddenly I looked at the letters and the penny dropped, and I quoted, "Out of your own sweet vale Alicia vanish vanity twixt Deity and Man, thou Shepherdess the way."[11] I was absolutely astounded and positively shaken that suddenly these words had come to me ... it was all so quick and spontaneous and vivid.

She added:

I think I ought to tell you what gave me the tip-off to my own translation, it was the VV at the end of the top line and "Vanishes Vanity" popped straight into my head, and the rest followed. As you know from the time that Thomas Anson put this monument up everybody from great scholars to ordinary everyday people have been trying to find out what these letters meant, but none had succeeded—and suddenly the words came to me![12]

It is an elegant insight, but this solution only fits in part. The letters D and M surround the letters and fit as "twixt deity [D] and man [M]." They "shepherd" the eight letters in the middle, in the sense of surrounding and guiding them, which is an alternative meaning of "shepherding" instantly recognizable to crossword fanatics.

But though her interpretation helps explain the D and the M, it does not really fit. For a start, the acrostic from the poem reads, "O [Out] O [of] Y [your] O [own] S [sweet] V [vale] A [Alicia] V [vanish] V [vanity]," which shakes out as "OOYOSVAVV," whereas the code actually reads, "OUOSVAVV."

She explains this difference by arguing that the letter U in "OUOSVAVV" stands for "your." Her contention is that "In those days when young men scratched with a diamond on the glass of his loved one's window, he scratched 'I L U' for 'I love you'." But this means stretching the acrostic even further to make it fit. As a shorthand link, U means "you." It does not mean "your." The "I L U" code of love-swept adolescent men in the eighteenth century has changed little in the last two hundred and fifty years and the use of the letter U to mean "you" is instantly recognizable to anyone who has ever sent a text message on a mobile phone or used instant messaging on a computer. "Your" is something very different, is rarely written as U and is more commonly transcribed as "YR" or, more rarely, "UR."

Despite this, the acrostic solution remains deceptively seductive. But common sense suggests that if there was a recognizably matching phrase from classical or even contemporary Georgian literature, then, after two and a half centuries, it would have been identified. No convincing match has appeared, even though many hundreds of classical scholars, both amateur and professional, have been looking.

Related to the acrostic solutions are those code-breakers who claim that it is an anagram. There is no convincing anagram for the existing letters, so the anagram solutions all require creative additions to the basic letters.

Typical is one recent claim that this is an anagram of "devout mason," but it is a reach to make this work. The reasoning goes like this: the two Vs together are really Roman numerals, each meaning five. Added together, they make ten, which is then written as in words. Instead of reading, "D OUOSVAVV M," the letters now read, "D OUOSVA(TEN) M," which can be read as an anagram of "devout mason." But there are a host of problems with this. Apart from the lack of evidence that they were members of their local Masonic lodge, this solution is logically inconsistent. If the second and third Vs are Roman numerals, why not the first as well? If that was the case, then the code would read, "D OUOS(FIVE)A(TEN) M," giving a pool of letters that throw off dozens of anagrams, including a phrase that could easily be George Anson's motto: "a noted use of vim," "vim" meaning "punch," "verve," "dash" and "energy," an apt description of George Anson's leadership style.

***

There are four prime suspects who knew the code's meaning, all major figures in Georgian society, and one of them knew its meaning for sure: Thomas Anson, who commissioned it and who oversaw the rebuilding of the house and gardens. Three others probably knew its secret as well, though this requires various degrees of speculation: Thomas's brother, George, who financed the project, their first architect, the celebrated astronomer, mathematician and garden designer Thomas Wright; and his successor, James "Athenian" Stuart, would all be at the top of any list of the usual suspects. After that, there is also the possibility that Thomas Anson's other immediate relatives were in on the secret: his eldest sister, who would ultimately inherit the estate, his younger sisters, though they have largely been airbrushed from history, and finally, the most important woman at Shugborough at this time, his sister-in-law, Elizabeth, who was married to George, whose money was financing everything.

Thomas Anson was a leading aesthete, politician and cultural opinion-former. George was the leading naval figure of the day and probably the most influential British sailor of all time, while Thomas Wright was one of the most original thinkers of the eighteenth century, whose ideas still inform modern astronomy. James Stuart continued Wright's work and became one of the most powerful neoclassical designers in eighteenth-century England. His influence can still be seen everywhere.

The secret of the code is locked up in these relationships. Any serious attempt to break this puzzle begins and ends with these four men, their history, their beliefs, their vision of themselves in Georgian society and their world picture. The clues (if there are any to be unearthed nearly two hundred and fifty years later) are in what they believed and therefore what could have influenced them.

***

Shugborough Hall was originally bought in 1624 by William Anson, a successful lawyer, but it was his two great-grandsons, Thomas and George, who transformed it from a square three-story block into the splendid neoclassical mansion that stands in 900 acres of woodland today. Both were worldly, alpha males, urbane, cultivated and accomplished and, in their different ways, men of action. If they were alive today, they would be high up on any list of the most powerful in British society.

The elder brother, Thomas, was a member of the Royal Society and a founder member of the Society of Dilettanti in 1734, a society for aristocrats who had been on the Grand Tour round the Mediterranean (Italy, Greece and Egypt) to dip themselves in the enriching and ennobling atmosphere of ancient civilizations. These members of the cultivated elite were early cultural tourists; visiting classical sites, bringing back maps, drawings and plans of ancient monuments. But this was far more than an expensive travel and dining club for heavy-drinking aristocrats. They were hugely influential in setting the cultural tone in which all things classical were the drivers of good taste.

Thomas Anson himself traveled extensively throughout the Middle East, visiting Aleppo in northern Syria, a city with one of the world's great citadels, which can also make a good claim (along with Sana'a and Damascus) to be one of the world's oldest surviving urban settlements. He also visited Alexandria, Rosetta and Cairo, where he was one of the first British visitors to immerse himself in the spectacular richness of Ancient Egyptian civilization.

When he returned to Staffordshire, his head was spinning with antiquities and a desire to build a permanent and commanding monument that would resonate to the rhythms of the ancient world. On a modest budget, he began to enlarge the family house in 1740. But then, thanks to his brother, George, he suddenly got a massive injection of capital—after which the only limit to his ambition was his own imagination.

Born on April 23, 1697, George joined the Navy when he was just fifteen. By the age of twenty-one, he was an officer, and by twenty-seven, he was captain of his own ship. In 1737, he was given command of the *Centurion*, the flagship of a fleet of six. At the time, England and Spain were slugging it out around the globe, pitting their navies against each other in an attempt to establish supremacy on the seas. With naval supremacy came control of global trade. As a young commodore, Anson's orders were to disrupt Spanish imperial and commercial power.

In 1740, he set off with six ships, the first formal attempt to circumnavigate the world by a naval expedition.

By the time he reached Macao, in November 1742, the *Centurion* was the only survivor, the rest of his squadron having been lost along the way or wrecked. Only four of his crew had died through fighting, but thirteen hundred had succumbed to disease, mostly scurvy. Many of the rest were "turned and idiots." He spent the winter in China becoming ever more depressed and fatalistic, writing home to a friend, "I am certainly unfortunate, and a fatality awaits me."

During the winter, Anson's intelligence officers picked up some gossip that would change their lives forever. Once he had checked it out, an audacious plan began to formulate in his head.

On April 29, 1743, he tells his crew that they will not be returning home just yet. Instead, they are going on a treasure hunt—for the Spanish galleon the *Nuestra Señora de Cavadonga*.[13] Flying the red ensign of the British Merchant Navy, he hides by Cape Espíritu Santo, just off the island of Samar in the Philippines. After a month of anxious waiting—and with morale dropping—his lookouts finally spot their target.

It is daybreak, June 20, 1743. The painting of the attack hanging at Shugborough Hall shows the two ships—the mighty Spanish galleon and the British hunter-killer—to be roughly the same size. In reality, the Spanish galleon is about 20 feet shorter. Laden down with cargo from Acapulco, the Spanish captain never really has a chance. With sixty guns, twenty-four of which can fire twenty-four-pound cannon balls that can smash through a ship's side, the British warship is built for speed and fighting. In contrast, the Spanish vessel only has minimal defenses.

The crew hurl cattle and lumber overboard, while the Spanish captain tries to outrun Anson and get to port before the British guns take down his ship. The Spanish are no match for Anson's better-trained crew, and after ninety minutes it is all over. His men then board and seize the *Covadonga's* treasure. The Spanish captain surrenders, giving Anson his ceremonial sword and horse-tail fly-swatter, a symbol of the respect shown by one professional seaman to another. Admiral Anson then treats him and his crew with great humanity and respect, and there is no abuse or mass slaughter, as often happens at this time.

As well as cochineal and various other commodities, their haul consists of 1,313,843 pieces of eight (Spanish dollars) as well as 36,682 ounces of virgin silver. At that time, it is valued at $810,000, worth around $97 million in today's money, though other estimates are much higher. After the inevitable legal wrangling, George Anson ends up with $185,000—a fortune. In today's currency, it is well over $20 million, but an idea of just how far this could stretch comes from the builder's invoice for moldings like the ones on the Triumphal Arch. It was just about $532.

Back home, the capture of a Spanish treasure ship was even better news than a military victory. The newspapers were full of praise,

John Wallis, a brilliant seventeenth-century mathematician, Puritan and amateur code breaker, who works out that his odds of survival are much better if he changes sides and works for King Charles II.
(Mary Evans Picture Library)

Phil Zimmermann, whose software PGP (Pretty Good Privacy) allows us all to communicate with each other away from the prying eyes of nosy governments everywhere. *(© Bryce Duffy/CORBIS SABA)*

Jim Sanborn's sculpture, *Find The Lodestone*, 7200 Wisconsin Avenue, Baltimore, Maryland. Set in an office courtyard it consists of related pieces and, like all his other major works, combines his favorite materials: granite, lodestone, quartz, slate and sandstone. The meaning is encrypted and elliptical.

Jim Sanborn's sculpture, *Invisible Forces*, 2580 Clarendon Boulevard, Arlington, Virginia. In the late afternoon sunshine it changes color continually. The underlying themes are attraction and repulsion.

Almost an exact copy of the CIA Kryptos sculpture outside the Hirshhorn Museum, Washington, D.C. Previously called *Secret Past* and *Covert Balance*, it is just over eight feet tall and is a symbolic representation of the Cold War. On one side the sculpture text is in Russian, while on the other it is English, the texts are separated by a log of petrified wood.

Geoffrey Chaucer, author of *The Canterbury Tales*. One of England's greatest writers and one of the earliest cryptographers, he used symbols for letters. Like many artists who are talented in a particular field, he could not resist the lure of codes. *(Getty Images)*

Leone Battista Alberti, the "Father of Western Cryptography," who only became interested in codes in his sixties and created the polyalphabetic cipher, built the first cryptanalysis. A brilliant mathematician, he was also a musician, architect, poet, linguist, philosopher, writer and gymnast, who could jump over a man's head. For relaxation, he tamed wild horses. *(Mary Evans Picture Library)*

Sir Francis Walsingham, the world's greatest ever spymaster, whose team broke the codes of the plotters who wanted to remove Elizabeth I and secured the Protestant ascendancy in England. *(National Portrait Gallery)*

Mary Queen of Scots, a capable cryptographer, but no match for Thomas Phelippes, England's first great code breaker. She was good, he was a genius. *(Bridgeman Art Library)*

A fully functioning World War II German Enigma machine. The Nazis believed their communications were secure, but many were broken at Bletchley Park. Codenamed ULTRA, the intelligence it offered was invaluable. Without this, Hitler may well have prevailed.

Roger Bacon, a thirteenth-century Franciscan friar, who hid the formula for gunpowder in a code that was not broken until 600 years later. He also defined one of the key principles of every code writer ever since: "The man is insane who writes a secret in any other way than one which will conceal it from the vulgar." *(Getty Images)*

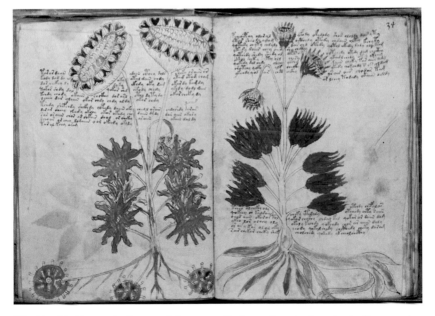

The *Voynich Manuscript* is one of the most alluring and mysterious texts discovered anywhere in the world. The world's greatest cryptographers have tried to reveal its secrets, without success.

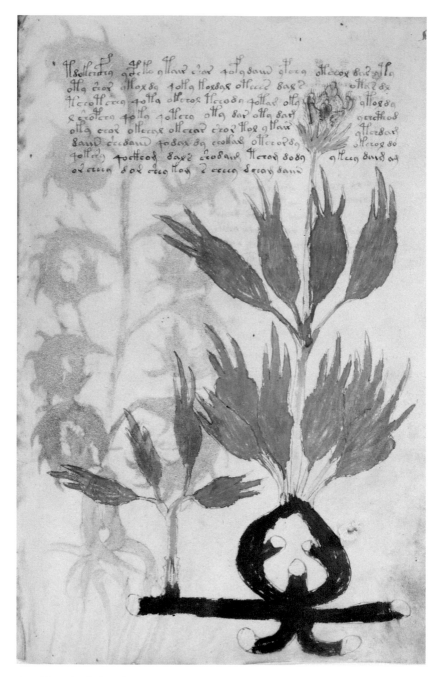

A guide to herbal medicine.

The *Voynich Manuscript*. Women in what look like birthing pools, linking their sexuality to strange plants. Even if the text could ever be deciphered, what messages are hidden in the illustrations?

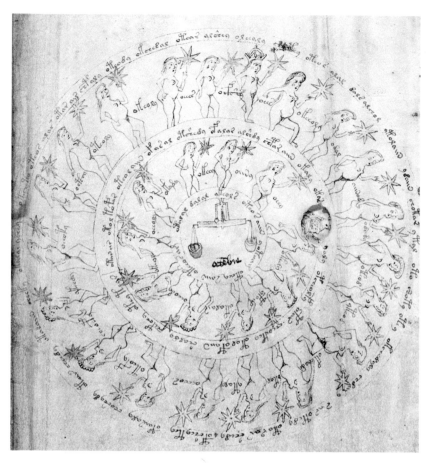

The *Voynich Manuscript*. Fecundity and the celestial dance. Could it be the final outpourings of a brilliant but badly damaged mind, after Bacon had been kept as a prisoner in isolation for more than a decade?

Les Bergers D'Arcadie. A heavily symbolic painting by French artist Nicolas Poussin. What coded messages were taken from here and hidden in the marble statue at Shugborough? *(Bridgeman Art Library)*

The marble relief above the Shugborough code. Coded messages have been added by the sculptor, hinting at a much deeper meaning to the overall code.

The *Shepherd's Monument* at Shugborough.

The Shepherd's Monument code in close up, simple and elegant—but does it conceal a terrible family secret?

A further clue to the hidden meaning behind the Shepherd's Monument: the obsessive need of Thomas Anson to define his family's place in history through the gods of ancient Athens.

The Memorial Arch at Shugborough, modeled on a similar arch in ancient Greece. It confirmed the Ansons in their world view that they were living the Athenian dream, the embodiment of exquisite Georgian taste.

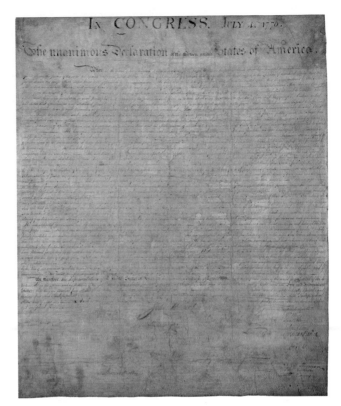

The U.S. Declaration of Independence, one of the world's most famous and influential documents. But few realize that it was used as the key for the code to describe the gold hidden (but still never found) in Buford County, Virginia.

Edgar Allan Poe, one of America's most gifted short story writers, best known for horror and mystery, but also a gifted cryptographer and hoaxer, who may be the hidden hand behind the *Beale Papers*. *(Getty Images)*

Edward Elgar, one of Britain's greatest composers, best known for the *Enigma Variations*, where music and cryptography overlap.

Caroline Alice Elgar, Edward's wife, whose initials were encoded in the *Enigma Variations* and used by him to help make up the coded name of his house, Craiglea.

Arthur Leigh Allen. The short odds favorite to be the Zodiac Killer, who terrorized Southern California, killed between nine and thirty-seven people, sent coded letters to newspapers and inspired the Clint Eastwood movie, *Dirty Harry*.

and the procession of thirty-two wagons from Portsmouth to London on Admiral Anson's return was front-page news. Anson and his men were national heroes. Fame and fortune followed, despite the inevitable row over exactly whose treasure it was and what share each person was entitled to have. The book (written by the ship's chaplain) became an instant bestseller. A story of great heroism and triumph in adversity, it recounted Anson's exploits. As well as seizing the Spanish ship, he had maintained the morale of his officers and crew (no mean feat in these times) and sailed round the world, the first formal naval expedition ever to do so. But who the British media builds up they bring down—even in the eighteenth century. Though Anson's crew only got a small reward each, they quickly reached the status of what would now be regarded as tabloid villains as they drank, whored and fought their way round the bars and inns of London, followed by journalists in search of instantly good copy.

Anson was a master naval tactician, and four years later, he defeated the French fleet off Cape Finisterre, then rising quickly through the ranks: first vice admiral, full admiral the year after, then First Lord of the Admiralty and finally Admiral of the Fleet in 1751, the highest naval rank. Despite his prominence, he remains an enigmatic figure. He left little in the way of private papers, hating both "ceremony and correspondence," and was something of a blank canvas even to those who knew him well. His critics remarked that "He had been round the world, but was never in it," a cowardly jibe from those for whom the corridors and waiting rooms of government were their battlefield and the bravest decision was what color shoes to wear.

The two brothers were both political creatures, masters of the Georgian universe. In 1747, Thomas became the local member of Parliament, while George went into the House of Lords after first instituting a whole series of reforms in the British Navy, many of which have survived through to today, including the establishment of the Royal Marines. He was also smart enough to marry well. Elizabeth Yorke was the highly intelligent and well-read young daughter of his friend and contemporary the Lord Chancellor, a man who was described as one "who had a talent for politics without having the appearance and inclinations of a politician."

The brothers, one a leading cultural and society figure and the other a global player who swaggered over the planet's oceans, needed a magnificent property that defined them and their place in the world. And they got it in Shugborough. No expense was spared as it was transformed into a magnificent mansion, still one of the finest in Britain.

They began to decorate the gardens with stone monuments, some inspired by Stuart's trip to Athens, one by Anson's trip to China, while at least one was heavily influenced by some of their more exotic pagan beliefs.

The third member of the original triumvirate behind the Shepherd's Monument was a self-taught astronomer, mathematician, architect, navigation expert and designer, Thomas Wright. He was not born into high society, but through a combination of hard work and natural intelligence, managed to spend much of his adult life in their company. He surveyed great estates, taught mathematics and the other emerging sciences to young members of the aristocracy who wished to be molded into well-rounded figures fit to take their place in Georgian society. He started work at Shugborough in 1748, and before that had been offered the post of professor of navigation at St. Petersburg but had turned it down.

For the middle class, the rich and the aristocratic, the Georgian world was safe, secure and stable; a time for optimism, a celebration of all things prosperous and, above all, a time to make one's mark for future generations to see. Dissent was brutally crushed both at home and abroad. George II was on the throne for thirty-three years from 1727 to 1760—and though clearly rattled by Bonnie Prince Charlie in 1745, this attempted *coup d'état* turned out to be little more than a damp squib. The Scots were put back in their box with the brutal slaughter at Culloden in 1745 and then further crushed as the Duke of Cumberland and his army of psychopaths practiced savage ethnic cleansing against the Highlanders. Known as "Butcher" Cumberland, he is one of the most hated figures in Scottish history. After the battle, his men roamed the Highlands looking for rebel supporters. Rape was widespread. Women and children were slaughtered. In one case, a group of men found in a barn were locked in and burned to death.

Wearing the kilt, tartan, playing the bagpipes or speaking Gaelic were all banned. Hundreds were executed or deported in a killing spree of ethnic cleansing, making Cumberland an early prototype for Slobodan Milosevic. Overseas, the British military fought and defeated the French wherever they met, taking territory in Canada, the U.S., the Caribbean and Africa. Trade and commerce were booming. The locals (backed by the French) were smashed in India. The East India Company then used its monopoly to systematically loot the subcontinent, creating fabulous wealth back home and providing the cash to finance the building of spectacular estates all over the country. The British Museum was founded to house some of the great collections, fabulous souvenirs of imperialism. For those members of Georgian society who were wealthy and well connected (and they always went hand in hand), it was literally the case that everything in the garden was lovely.

In this world where expansion of every sort—commercial, imperial and intellectual—was the defining imperative of everyday life, a man like Wright could find his place. Not only was he industrious and useful (he could turn his hand to most things), his ideas resonated with the zeitgeist. His various intellectual arguments confirmed his masters in their beliefs. He published, and this reflected well on his patrons. Though none of his books were big sellers, he was highly influential and wrote on antiquities, architecture and astronomy.

In 1734, he argued that there is a "sacred throne" that is the epicenter of the physical world and from which spring the irrefutable laws of nature. He also argued—and this is very useful in informing any thinking about the Shugborough code—that the universe is laid out in magnificent symmetry from this central core. At the heart is heaven, from which all goodness comes, "the more excellent body from whence the whole is governed." The universe, which includes the sun and the stars, surrounds this. But keep traveling onward and there is only the outer darkness of hell, a bleak vastness to which there is no end. By the time he started work at Shugborough, he had extended his ideas to say that the universe consisted of a series of interlocking stars, each with its own supernatural center.

He is best known for his publication *An original theory or new hypothesis of the universe* (1750), which he completed while he was at Shugborough. In it, he explains the appearance of the Milky Way as an optical effect due to our immersion in what he believes to be a flat layer of stars. Being self-taught, he was never truly accepted by the scientific establishment, even though he was widely read and influenced Immanuel Kant, the German philosopher whose own work *General Natural History and Theory of the Heavens* appeared five years later.

Wright also speculated on the idea of life on other planets, though in a theological rather than scientific sense. He became interested in the transmigration of souls, the belief that the human soul would inhabit a series of other worlds after death, becoming more and more perfect.

But while he looked forward to the ever-increasing perfection of the human soul, he (and his clients, the Ansons) also looked back to what they saw as a previous golden age, one that stood as comparison with the one they inhabited. The cradle of exquisite taste was Greece, and Athens was the place. In 1748, the Dilettanti spoke for them all when they declared:

> There is perhaps no part of Europe more deservedly excites the Curiosity and Attention of the lovers of Polite Literature than the province of Attica in particular Athens, its capital City [...] But Athens has been almost completely neglected, and unless exact drawings from them be speedily made, all her beauteous Fabricks, her Temples, her Theatres, her Palaces will drop into oblivion, and Posterity will have to reproach us!

So, with at least one eye on securing their place in the warm admiration of future generations (who they believed would share their views of what constituted good taste), Thomas Anson, his brother and their architects began the task of rebuilding Shugborough as an eighteenth-century classical idyll, a contemporary echo of the glorious days of Ancient Greece.

There are ten monuments in all, though only eight have survived, plus a cave. Some were built by Thomas Wright's successor, James "Athenian" Stuart, who also worked on the Shepherd's

Monument. The house, monuments and grounds reflect both brothers as major travelers. Two are Chinese, and four are Greek. The decorations include a Persian cat, Corsican goats, the honeysuckle and a Gothic Druid. There may have been an overall plan from the start for all the monuments begun by Wright and completed by James Stuart, but there are no surviving papers to indicate this. The search for clues must therefore start with the monuments that were built at the same time as the Shepherd's Monument.

The first monument, completed in 1747, is the Chinese House, modeled on sketches made by Sir Peircy Brett, one of the officers on the *Centurion* who made the round-the-world trip with Anson and who stayed with him in Canton. Set over water, this was one of the first ever Chinese buildings in England, a style that quickly became *the* fashion accessory in the next decade. Soon, anyone who was anyone just had to have a Chinese house, whether they had visited the country or not. Thirty-five years later, in 1782, the writer Thomas Pennant noted that the house at Shugborough was the real deal, "a true pattern of the architecture" of China, "not a mongrel invention of British carpenters."

One of the many Chinese buildings that followed was the Temple of Confucius in Kew Gardens, built a couple of years later for the Prince of Wales, Frederick. The Anson brothers then built a five-stage pagoda in the grounds in 1752, which was swept away by floods in 1785. It too was copied at Kew, a decade after the Ansons built the original.

The key point here is that the brothers and the designers they employed—Thomas Wright and James Stuart—were early adopters, setting the pace and the style for everyone else. Assured and confident, they were leaders not followers. They were meticulous men with a big vision, the shakers not the stirred. Though tangential, this is a clue to the mindset of the Anson brothers at this time—and therefore the decryption of the cipher.

Wright started work on the Shepherd's Monument in 1748, the year after the Chinese House was finished, and it may well have formed part of the wall of the kitchen garden, which provided the house with vegetables. The germ of the idea is described in a book

Thomas Wright published in 1755, *Six Original Designs of Arbours*. In it, he describes how this building:

> must be situated so as to be well back'd with Wood, of the hardy Forest Growth, and the more retired the better, as in a Salon or Lawnet, being chiefly designed for the Enjoyment of Objects near the Eye, yet so as to be relieved with Prospects, more remote, without being too conspicuous of itself.

The swirling on the inner stone pillars may well be an attempt to emulate the free-form patterns of nature.

At the same time as the Ansons were finishing the Chinese House, they were beginning work both on the Shepherd's Monument and the Cat's Statue, which is near the Chinese House and just a short distance from both. Again, this is enigmatic and raises more questions than it answers. It is a square monument, with a huge circular stone vase on the top. Sitting on top of this is a cat, and as always with anything involved with Shugborough, there is more than one theory. The first suggestion is that this is a memorial to Admiral Anson's cat, which had traveled round the world with him. The second is that it was put up by his brother, Thomas, in the memory of the rare breed of Persian cats that he kept and bred for years but which died out through disease. There is a further clue that points to this being a memorial for Thomas. For years, he kept a herd of Corsican round-horn goats, and they guard the four corners of the plinth on which sits the urn, on top of which sits the cat.

Either way, it was conceived, designed and built around the same time as the Shepherd's Monument, which must, at least, raise the possibility that the two were linked in some way at the time. Furthermore, this monument also fits Wright's desires for one which is "well back'd with Wood." The back of the monument is rough and unfinished, suggesting that there was a plan to either incorporate it into something else or surround it with trees and bushes like the Shepherd's Monument.

During this period, Thomas Anson and Thomas Wright were busy. Courtesy of the poor military sense of Spanish naval intelligence and the brilliance of George Anson, they had a small mountain of pieces of eight and began work on yet another monument, in some ways just as enigmatic as the Shepherd's Monument.

The front of Shugborough Hall is perfectly proportioned and neoclassical. The gardens at the back lead down to the river. They are precise, geometric, man imposing his will on nature. But there on the river bank, in full view, is a deliberately constructed ruin, which was originally built from stone taken from the previous house when it was knocked down, as well as some pieces from the former palace of the local bishop. On top of it, Wright put a Gothic pigeon house. Being designed as a ruin, it inevitably declined, and today it looks like a pair of stone chimney stacks after the rest of the house has blown away. Still sitting on a ledge halfway up the taller of the stacks is a Druid.

At best, this is a further clue as to the Ansons' thinking. The stone for the Druid's Monument came from different sources, and so do the influences. Wright (like the Ansons) was an intellectual crow, plucking ideas and influences from everywhere, which he shared with his patrons. Thomas Anson was fascinated by the Druids and their culture, believing that in some way they held ancient secrets and wisdom that could unlock the current mysteries of the universe. The Druids held a number of core beliefs that clearly heavily influenced the Ansons. At the core of their belief system are three linked ideas, all of which relate to the past, that taken together provide the key to unlocking this code. These beliefs are underpinned by the notion that your ancestors are the very essence of how you define yourself and your place in the world. The key words here are blood, tribe and land. Blood is your family lineage and that comes first. But your family is part of the tribe, and that sets the wider context for your bloodline, and then there is the land. The land—especially your land—has a spirit attached to it that defines your place in the cosmos. For the Ansons, the 900 acres of land at Shugborough was not just their home; it was home to their spirit, and it placed them both in this world and the next. And the huge yew tree in the heart of the estate was the central point, being the Druidic link between birth and death, earth and sky, this life and the next.

Having completed the first phase of the Shepherd's Monument, Wright moved on, and a new architect, James Stuart, took over. He was fresh from his sponsored trip to Greece, where he and the architect Nicholas Revett had made detailed plans and drawings of many of the key Athenian monuments. Once established at Shugborough, he began to make replica copies in the grounds, turning the souvenirs of his cultural tourism into three-dimensional artifacts, which defined the Ansons as the cultural masters of the age, with a direct link to the very best of classical antiquity right on their own doorstep. He built the Lanthorn of Demosthenes, a copy of an Ancient Athenian building, which recounts how a brilliant Greek sailor, Dionysus, outwitted a group of pirates. This building links directly back to the Shepherd's Monument. The shields on the top are honeysuckle and inspired by the Choragic Monument of Lysicrates in Athens, which is also called the Lanthorn of Demosthenes or Lantern of Diogenes. The same trim can be seen on Regency cutlery, the roof of the North Carolina State Capitol Building[14] and many other neoclassical buildings. They then built four more monuments, each in the neoclassical tradition, including a Greek-style Doric temple just further along the path from the Shepherd's Monument.

After George died and Thomas inherited his fortune, budget was no problem. Thomas then commissioned Stuart to build the Tower of the Winds, a marble octagonal building, again inspired by an Ancient Athenian building. Each side characterizes a different wind. Spiritually, a building like this is also about harnessing the winds and channeling them—and the human soul—toward the heavens.

But Stuart's most important creation is the Triumphal Arch. When you trudge past the uncomprehending cows across the fields to get to this monument, you are struck with one overwhelming question: what were the powerful thoughts and emotions that drove someone to build such an imposing yet incongruous monument? It's huge. It stands on top of the hill and dominates both the estate and the skyline. In 1774, Wedgwood was commissioned to design a ceramic dinner service for Empress Catherine II of Russia, decorated with scenes depicting the very best of English life. He put the arch on the soup tureen.

Work on the arch started in 1761, but when Admiral Anson died the following year, Thomas changed its purpose and it became a huge shrine to George and Elizabeth Anson, both of whom are named on the monument underneath their funeral ossuaries, which sit on either side at the top. Standing there underneath and looking up at the arch leaves the visitor with only one thought: this is a magnificent testament to Thomas Anson's grief, a heart-stopping, heaven-defying memorial to his brother and sister-in-law. He clearly missed them every day for the rest of his life.

***

By 1762, Thomas was sixty-seven years old. He had lost his brother and sister-in-law. His parents were long dead. Many of his friends and contemporaries were dead or too far away for regular contact. His political life had been and gone, and he largely had his memories to serve as his daily companions. The house and grounds epitomized all he believed and had ever wished for. They were the focus of his life—and the epicenter of his emotional existence was the Shepherd's Monument. As he stood in front of it, what thoughts passed through his head? The travel writer Thomas Pennant, who wrote about the monument in 1782, portrayed "the amiable owner" of Shugborough as a man who had built it as a memento of the certainty of death. He then speculated that perhaps it was "also as a secret memorial of some loss of a tender nature in his early days, for he was wont often to hang over it in affectionate and firm meditation."[15]

Could Pennant have stumbled across the key here? What did Thomas Anson know that troubled him so, particularly as he faced his own mortality alone?

If we rerun key parts of the history of the monument and the interlocking Anson story, it is possible to come to an elegant solution toward helping unravel this cipher, one which has the virtue of actually matching what is known about the family.

The first issue to be resolved is when the code was actually written. The marble panel containing the letters is physically very different from the rest of the monument: the color is much lighter, and the patterning is substantially less intense. It is clearly a different piece of marble that was added to the rest of the monument. The question is, when? Was it attached at the same time as the shepherds' carving above, or at a later date?

Work on the Shepherd's Monument began in 1748 and was completed by 1758, when some verse entitled "Hermit Poem" appeared, written by Anna Seward, a young woman with literary pretensions who lived nearby. It refers to the "famous picture of Nicolas Poussin, Representing Shepherds pointing to the following Inscription on a Monument in Arcadia; *Et In Arcadia Ego*." However, there is nothing in these turgid lines that could even be taken as an oblique reference to the code itself, which must prompt the suspicion that this part of the monument was not present at this time. How could you write a poem about the Shepherd's Monument and not mention its most intriguing feature?

By 1782, when Thomas Pennant wrote about the monument, both brothers were dead: George Anson died in 1762, and his older brother, Thomas, followed him in 1773. Pennant's sources must therefore have been their descendants or others at the hall. Pennant does not mention the code at all, an extraordinary omission, for which there are two possible explanations.

One explanation is that he was an early member of the Worshipful and Fraternal Order of Esteemed Travel Writers (WFOETW), who never actually visit the places they write about so eloquently, a tradition of which Marco Polo was an early trailblazer; the evidence strongly suggesting that he was a skilled plagiarist of other works who never actually reached China or got anywhere even close.[16] A careful reading of Pennant's text supports this interpretation. Although he indulges in some outrageous name-dropping ("My much respected friend, the late Thomas Anson, Esquire, preferred the still paths of private life and was the best qualified for its enjoyment of any man I ever knew"), he may not have actually been to the hall or even met Anson. He chooses his words carefully, never actually placing himself at Shugborough Hall or in the grounds, and the giveaway is that his description of the monument is incorrect. According to him, "The scene is laid in Arcadia. Two lovers, expressed in elegant pastoral figures appear attentive to an ancient shepherd, who reads to them an inscription on a tomb, *Et In Arcadia Ego*." But this description is completely wrong. There are no lovers. Instead, there is a single woman with three shepherds, just as there is in the painting on which it is based, all of which supports the view that he was a recycler of secondhand information and not a visitor.

The most likely explanation is that Pennant cribbed this description from another contemporary account, but this still leaves the mystery of why the code was not mentioned in whatever source he used. One explanation is that this was the eighteenth century and travel was not as easy as it is now, even for the rich. The story of the Shepherd's Monument could easily have been an item of gossip in polite society, where the issue of the cipher was lost as the story bounced around the drawing rooms of Georgian England before Pennant picked it up. The other possibility is that the code was not in place at this time and was added after 1782. It is not mentioned again until the 1950s. If this had been added sometime during this 170-year period after the Ansons lived, then decipherment would be impossible without some item of original paperwork from the Anson family papers. Thankfully, this is not the case—a poem, written on July 7, 1767, contains the lines:

> *Observe you rising hillock's form,*
> *Whose verdant top the spiry cypress crowns*
> *And the dim ilex spreads her dusky arms*
> *To shade th'ARCADIAN Shepherdesses tomb*
> *Of PARIAN stone the pile: of modern hands*
> *The work, but emulous of ancient praise*
> *Let not the Muse inquisitive presume*
> *With rash interpretation to disclose*
> *The mystic ciphers that conceal her name.*

This poem was written six years before Thomas Anson's death, which suggests that the plaque with the code was added between 1758 (when it is not mentioned in the "Hermit Poem") and July 1767 (when it is mentioned here). This poem is clearly talking about the monument: "th'ARCADIAN Shepherdesses tomb" cannot refer to anything else. The final line—"The mystic ciphers that conceal her name"—is clearly a reference to the ten letters on the monument.

The author is anonymous but wrote these lines when Thomas Anson was still alive, and he would have approved them, as he was, by this time, the richest and one of the most powerful men in the area. They remain the best clue to the meaning of this code. We can safely assume that the reference to "her name" is not a lighthearted jape. All the contemporary accounts suggest that Thomas Anson was a fairly serious fellow, and there is nothing in any account of his life that suggests that he would play what would essentially be a prank—especially with something as serious as an epitaph or memorial tablet—which at least helps focus this mystery.

All of which brings us back to the intriguing portrait that Pennant paints of Thomas Anson hanging over the Shepherd's Monument "in affectionate and firm meditation." The anonymous poem refers to a mysterious woman, who was clearly hugely important to Thomas Anson. Pennant's recycled gossip says this was "a secret memorial of some loss of a tender nature in his early days." Are they both talking of the same thing? Was Thomas Anson's grief sparked by the carving or the code beneath, or both?

The last line of this section of the poem refers to a "she." "She" could be the poet's muse, but this reference is so pointed and so obviously written by an insider that the clear implication is that there was a woman in Thomas Anson's life. The big question is who "she" was. Her identity is a mystery, as there are few family papers and Anson left nothing behind that hints at a woman in his life.

There are no definitive records of Thomas Anson ever marrying, though his elder sister, Janette, and his younger brother, George, both did. There must be some suspicion therefore that he was homosexual, though given the social imperatives at the time and his position in society, he would have been under enormous pressure to find a wife. He had land, power and prestige and had he wished it, there would have been no shortage of suitors who would have married him, regardless of his sexuality, if this was the explanation for his bachelorhood. Intriguingly, a "Thomas Ansin" did marry in 1729 in "St. James, London," where Thomas Anson had a house at 15 St. James's Square, just off Pall Mall, making it a likely possibility that this is him. It is a romantic, but highly speculative, thought that the "she" of the poem is the long-lost love of his life, which might help explain why he never married. But there are no other known references to Thomas Anson having a wife, and she certainly never lived with him at Shugborough.

Apart from his putative wife, there are a few possible candidates: his mother, his elder sister, his younger sisters or his sister-in-law, Elizabeth, George's wife.

One of the most credible acrostic solutions comes from World War II cryptanalyst and Bletchley Park veteran Sheila Lawn, who believes that it is an ancient love note, and that the code is Latin.

She says, "I'm a romantic at heart," and believes that it stands for "*Optima uxoris optima sororis viduus amantissimus vovit virtutibus*," which translates as "Best wife, best sister, widower most loving vows virtuously."

"Best wife, best sister" can only refer to George Anson's wife, Elizabeth. Elizabeth died childless in 1760; her husband died two years later. For this to be the correct translation, it would have to have been added during that time, when George Anson, the "widower," was alive to vow virtuously. Sadly, there are no estate records to indicate that it was built at this time. There are several problems with this explanation. First, the only person to whom it could apply is George Anson, but he did not live at Shugborough. His home was Moor Park, in Hertfordshire. If he was the grieving widower, then surely he would have put the memorial up in his own grounds. Second, James Stuart would not have tolerated the use of U rather than the correct V (even though many others did at the time), and finally, Thomas was unlikely to grieve at a monument that his brother had put up for his sister-in-law.

Lurking at the back of Thomas's mind was something much more serious, a dark family secret, a stomach-crunching, hush-hush, "only whisper it behind closed doors to your very nearest relatives" kind of secret, about which no one spoke, but which must have gnawed away at him for much of his adult life and certainly was reinforced on his brother's death. It is this that is the most likely key to help unlock the Shugborough code.

***

By the mid-1750s, there is one imperative driving Thomas Anson: his consuming desire to establish a family dynasty. He has created the dynastic monuments in the perfect location. Shugborough is Athens in miniature, the distillation of good taste and ancient wisdom—and every new tribute to the Greeks only confirms its status—but this is not enough. Though he does not have a title, his brother does, becoming Lord Anson, Baron of Soberton in 1747. Furthermore, George Anson has married well, Lady Elizabeth Yorke being the daughter of the First Earl of Hardwicke.

But then, on June 1, 1760, Thomas Anson's dreams are shattered. Lady Elizabeth Yorke, his sister-in-law, dies, without producing an heir. Two years later, in 1762, George dies too, not having remarried in the mean time. The title dies with him, leaving Thomas behind to carry on the family name, with no wife, no title, no heir and no prospects of being able to rectify this situation in the remaining years of his life. Without immediate descendants to carry on the title, he has to look to his ancestors, but here he runs into the family secret, a source of infinite embarrassment.

On April 6, 1663, his grandmother Elizabeth Anson went to the Heraldic Visitors in Stafford to try to persuade them to give the family its own title and the right to bear its own coat of arms. She argued that her husband, William Anson, was "a gentleman of coat armor"—that is, someone who was entitled to use a heraldic shield. To succeed, she had to show one of two things: either that the shield had been in continual use in the family since the Battle of Agincourt in 1415, when Henry V and a heavily outnumbered English Army had massacred the French in the mud of northern France,[17] or that a coat of arms had been given to an ancestor and she could prove an unbroken bloodline back to that person. Her husband was too ill to make the journey and plead his case, and she was poorly prepared. The Heraldic Visitors turned her down. At the time, William Anson doubtless thought that the arms would be granted without question, as the Ansons were one of the most important families in the area. The Visitors from the College of Arms gave her a second chance, telling her what evidence she needed to provide and giving her a period of respite to get it. But neither she nor her husband ever returned to plead their case.[18]

The grim truth facing Thomas Anson in retirement is that, despite a lifetime of service to King and country, he has nothing to show for it. There is to be no hereditary title, no coat of arms and no public recognition beyond the grave—even though their record has been exemplary.

Thomas has made his mark, nationally and locally. Locally, the Triumphal Arch with the funeral ossuaries of Lord and Lady Anson can be seen for miles. Nationally, he has done more than most to establish good taste and make neoclassicism the style of choice for his peers. George has helped make the world's oceans safe for British ships, reforming the Navy and establishing the Marines, a completely new concept in naval warfare. Thanks to a poorly protected Spanish treasure ship, the family name is known throughout the land.

Though their wealth was immense and they enjoyed exceptional social preeminence, ultimately this all counted for nothing. Georgian England was a rigid and stratified class system where there was only one ticket to entry—a hereditary title. For members of the aristocracy, the title had (and still does have) a mystical, transcendent quality, more powerful than any drug. To paraphrase a famous football manager,[19] some say this is about life and death, but it's more important than that. For the aristocracy, title defines everything. It sets them apart as people and guarantees their place in society and in history. It is the unyielding imperative that drives their lives. For Thomas Anson, to lose the hereditary title was a disaster that brought unimaginable misery: it destroyed all his ambitions to secure the dynastic presence of his family in British history. More immediately, it meant losing the family's position in the strict social hierarchy. His brother, George, already had plenty of enemies. There were many in polite society who were jealous of his achievements and his wealth. After all, they were old money, he was *nouveau riche*. Worse still, Thomas Anson knew that his ancestors had previously asked for a title and been rejected. This meant he could not go back and ask again. There was nothing in the family lineage that could bring the title back—an agonizing embarrassment, without compare.

The responsibility on Thomas Anson is huge; but he has a plan. His brother, George, plays the first card. In his will, George Anson leaves an annuity of £300 a year to be split between his sisters, but the estates and his colossal fortune go to his brother, Thomas. He also leaves an annuity of £500 to his nephew, also called George, who is the son of his sister Janette, who has married a local man called Sambroke Adams.[20] The hopes of the Anson line now lie with him.

By 1762, although Thomas Anson does not have a title, he has something almost as powerful: the enormous wealth he has inherited. He can now play the British aristocratic game and leverage wealth for title. The following year, the young George Adams marries well. Mary is the daughter of the First Baron Vernon, in 1763, otherwise known as Venables-Vernon. Four years later, they have their first son, Thomas, and then a second, George, who will become equerry to Queen Victoria's mother, the Duchess of Kent, further securing the position of the Anson family.

The next stage of the plan is to secure the position of George Adams as an Anson, and Thomas Anson does this through his will, which he originally writes in 1771 and then finalizes at Shugborough Hall in February the following year. A decent man, he leaves money to his servants, his sisters and an annuity of £100 a year to James Stuart, the key architect of Shugborough, but the estates and the bulk of the family fortune go to his nephew, George Adams. There is a very strict condition attached. The estates and wealth go to any "heirs of his body by his present lady," but if there is "failure," then they will go to "any other he may have hereafter according to priority of Birth." By making this stipulation, Thomas makes sure that even if there is no title, the land and the money will stay in the Anson family. When Thomas dies, George Adams duly inherits the estates and immediately changes his name to Anson by royal license in April 1773. His first son, called Thomas, then further secures the family position by marrying Anne Margaret, the daughter of the Earl of Leicester. In 1806, he becomes First Viscount Anson, also called Baron Soberton, after his great uncle. His son, also called Thomas, then becomes the First Earl of Lichfield, the family title of the Ansons, and they acquire the heraldic shield, which had been so desperately desired for generations.

The plan of the brothers, Thomas and George, back in the mid-eighteenth century had succeeded—and it may help explain at least part of the code on the Shepherd's Monument.

One of the enduring mysteries is the missing last period, which makes this code open-ended. Thomas Anson believed in the power of his ancestors, which can be explained by the letters D and M, but given his preoccupations, there must a strong suspicion that he was also establishing the family line and that this code is some sort of recognition of this. The first five letters—"O.U.O.S.V."—are probably some phrase celebrating this, but the key is "A.V.V," the last three letters. At the time this monument was being built, Thomas Anson wanted to establish the family dynasty. The future depended on his nephew, George Adams, soon to be Anson, and his wife, Mary Venables-Vernon, whose initials together are "A.V.V."—Adams, Venables-Vernon—and given that this was the union on which the future fortunes of the Anson family would depend, this would explain why there is no final punctuation.

It was the beginning of the future.

The Beale Papers: Accursed Thirst for Gold! What Dost Thou Not Compel Mortals to Do?[1]

"A greedy person and a pauper are one and the same thing."

—Swiss proverb

Buford, Bedford County, Virginia, 1822

Anyone who can crack this code will—in theory—discover the secret location of a huge hoard of nineteenth-century treasure buried in a stone-lined vault nearly 6 feet below the ground in the shadow of the Blue Ridge Mountains in Virginia. The exact location is somewhere in Bedford County, an area of 764 square miles. To be more precise, it is reachable within a couple of hours' walk from Buford's Tavern, a brick house built in 1822 by Captain Paschal Buford of Locust Level, who—not surprisingly—named the settlement Bufordsville. The town changed its name to Montvale in 1890, and it can be found on U.S. 460, 13 miles west of the city of Bedford.

Here, the lucky treasure-seeker will find jewelry worth $13,000 in the early nineteenth century but many millions now. And as well as the jewelry, there is the gold—2,921 pounds of it—as well as 5,100 pounds of silver. Melted down, these precious metals would fetch just under $30 million today. But that is just the spot value of the metal. The exhibition and media rights are worth many times more. The interlocking ciphers that will reveal the secret location of the treasure have all the lure of untold wealth—as well as the bragging rights and international fame that will come to the man, woman or child who breaks this intractable series of numbers.

But before anyone reads on, they should beware. These ciphers come with a brutal health warning: they are highly addictive. For the best part of the last hundred and fifty years, they have baffled obsessive code-breakers and treasure-hunters, breaking the spirits and emptying the bank accounts of many who have come under their subversive spell. Some of the best American code-breakers of the twentieth century have pitted their fertile brains against them.

First up was Herbert Yardley, who founded the unit that became the American Black Chamber, the forerunner of what is now the world's biggest code-breaking institution, the National Security Agency. Though he cracked Japanese-government codes throughout the 1920s, he was defeated by *The Beale Papers*. Colonel Fabyan, whose laboratories at Riverside served the U.S. Army during World War I, tried his luck, as did the greatest American twentieth-century cryptologist of them all, William Friedman. All retired, defeated, by a series of numbers—1,283 in total.

According to the only historical account, the man who was first touched by these codes was left broken by "pecuniary embarrassments." His successor, who then brought the codes to the world's attention, was similarly destroyed:

> I would say a word to those who may take an interest in them, and give them a little advice, acquired by bitter experience. It is to devote only such time as can be spared from your legitimate business to the task, and if you can spare no time, let the matter alone. Should you disregard my advice, do not hold me responsible that the poverty you have courted is more easily found than accomplishment of your wishes, and I would avoid the sight of another reduced to my condition.

Despite these warnings, successive generations of would-be code-breakers and treasure-hunters have been enticed into the trap of believing that they will be the chosen one who will break this cipher, and after all, the bait is irresistible: one of the three ciphers, the one describing the treasure and its rough whereabouts, has already been broken. How difficult can it be to find the key to unlock the remainder and find its exact location? In the great tabloid tradition of never underselling a story, the first journalist to write about it, in 1885, told his readers, "Buy a book, get a pick and shovel ... dig, grow rich or starve."[2]

If the story sounds familiar to modern moviegoers, it's because many of the elements form the skeleton of the plot of the film *National Treasure*, in which Nicolas Cage plays Benjamin Franklin Gates, a third-generation treasure-hunter who has spent his life looking for a treasure no one believes exists. It is—inevitably, this being Hollywood—the greatest treasure the world has ever known. Originally hidden by America's founding fathers, the clues are everywhere in the icons that form the birth of the United States as a nation, including that perennial of mystery-code-hunters, the arcane symbols on the American dollar bill. Gates finds a map hidden on the back of the Declaration of Independence, also a key document in *The Beale Papers*.

***

The story of the Beale ciphers starts in 1885 with the publication of a small pamphlet by James B. Ward of Lynchburg, Virginia, called *The Beale Papers*, containing Authentic Statements regarding the TREASURE BURIED in 1819 and 1821, near Bufords, in Bedford County, Virginia, and Which Has Never Been Recovered (entered according to Act of Congress, in the year 1885, by J. B. Ward, in the Office of the Librarian of Congress, in Washington. Virginian Book and Job Print 1885).[3]

The book is now very rare. I visited the Library of Congress in Washington full of eager anticipation that I would get to see this little gem from the world of unsolved codes, but they did not have a copy and did not appear to have ever had one, even though—according to the front cover—it was lodged there back in the nineteenth century. The only copy was in the New York State Library in Albany.[4]

But even this turns out to be not a copy of the original but the text typed by a secretary twenty years ago, copying it from a mimeograph that is now lost. Though she was very diligent, typing a page a day and checking for mistakes, there are still errors—for example, where some of the numbers in the cipher text do not exactly match the numbers in the deciphered text. However, these are clear typos, and the numbers of the second cipher are clearly far more accurate than the various versions of *The Beale Papers* that are available on the Internet. The text is different too, but this is the version of *The Beale Papers* that I have tended to use as it has the best provenance. The Internet version of the ciphers is to be found in the Appendix on page 242.

Whichever version of *The Beale Papers* you read, inside is a tale worthy of Edgar Allan Poe. The author is anonymous, but he recounts the tale of a man who has to give up a precious secret worth millions because he is financially desperate and needs to devote his time to his family. His motive is saintly: he "only hopes that the prize may fall to some poor but honest man, who will use his discovery not solely for the promotion of his own enjoyment, but for the welfare of others."

The first character to be introduced at length in *The Beale Papers* is an innkeeper, Robert Morriss, who is the first custodian of the secret. According to the pamphlet, Morriss is born in 1778, in Maryland, but goes to Loudoun County, Virginia, where, in 1803, he marries Miss Sarah Mitchell, a saint in human form: "As a wife she was without reproach, as a generous and sympathizing woman she was without an equal; the poor will long remember her charities, and lament the friend they have lost." He quickly becomes rich as a tobacco merchant, constructing the first brick building in the town. This is a time of frontier capitalism, raw, intoxicating and unyielding. A smart trader can make a lifetime's fortune in weeks, and the foolish can lose it in days. Morriss gambles heavily in the tobacco market, but the price collapses and he gets cleaned out. Despite his folly, he is supported by his ever-loving goddess of a wife who "exhibited the loveliest traits of her character. Seemingly unmindful of her condition, with a smiling face and cheering words, she so encouraged her husband that he became almost reconciled to his fate." Morriss picks himself up and, in the great tradition of American entrepreneurs, uses his first failure to define himself. Described as "an old Virginia gentleman" of "unblemished character," he takes the lease on the town hotel, the Washington. His business prospers and he becomes well known and liked, taking his place among the other respectable local figures and his devoted personal friends, Jackson, Clay, Coles, Witcher and Chief Justice Marshall.

But Robert Morriss is a man with a hefty secret, one that burns away at him throughout much of his adult life and eventually proves too weighty for one man to carry. In 1862, aged eighty-four, he cannot hold out any longer and he seeks out a trusted friend on whom he can unburden his secret. Morriss chooses the anonymous story-teller for several reasons: he is a friend, he trusts him, and knowing that he is young and smart, Morriss believes he has the time and intelligence to solve the puzzle. Despite being well into his eighties, Morriss cuts a hard though incomprehensible deal: if and when the storyteller breaks the cipher and finds the treasure, half is to go to Morriss's relatives and friends and the source of the Beale papers story gets to keep half. The "remainder" (though how you get a remainder after 100 percent has been appropriated is not explained) then has to be held back for twenty years in case any claimants come forward, after which it reverts to our anonymous hero.

The narrative begins with a low-key event, which takes place some forty-two years earlier.

In January 1820, a man called Beale comes to stay at Morriss's hotel along with two friends. Beale says he wishes to stay for the winter, though his friends leave after a few days to go back to their homes in nearby Richmond. Beale is striking, a character cut straight from the pages of a cheap adventure thriller. As Morriss recalls:

> In person, he was about six feet in height, with jet-black eyes and hair of the same color, worn longer than was the style at that time. His form was symmetrical, and gave evidence of unusual strength and activity; but his distinguishing feature was a dark and swarthy complexion, as if much exposure to the sun and weather had thoroughly tanned and

discolored him; this, however, did not detract from his appearance, and I thought him the handsomest man I had ever seen. Altogether, he was a model of manly beauty, favored by the ladies and envied by men.

Beale is very much his own man and will not tolerate anyone who might offend him by being supercilious or presuming. But Beale, this archetypal nineteenth-century adventure hero, is also a man of mystery. No one knows his past, how he made his money or what he does for a living. The only things they know for certain are not to cross him (probably to keep an eye on their wives and sweethearts when he is around) and that he comes originally from somewhere else in Virginia. He stays for the winter until his friends return, and then—just as mysteriously—he disappears, before returning again in January 1822, "if possible, darker and swarthier than ever", the assumption is that he has been down south, the Virginia winters being bleak and brutal.

In the spring of that year, Beale leaves the hotel, but when he does so, he leaves behind a locked iron box full of "articles of value," which he asks Morriss to store in a safe place. In the great tradition of all Gothic mysteries, that is the last Morriss ever sees of him.

Writing years later, the pamphlet writer assumes that Beale has been "slain by Indians, or killed by the savage animals of the Rocky Mountains, or whether exposure, and perhaps privation, did its work can never be told." He has no doubt about Beale's fate: "One thing at least is certain, that of the young and gallant band, whose buoyant spirits led them to seek such a life, and to forsake the comforts of home, with all its enjoyments, for the dangers and privations they must necessarily encounter, not a survivor remains."

Never hearing from his friend again, Morriss also believes that he and his party are dead, as "They were infatuated with the dangers, and with the wild and roving character of their lives, the charms of which lured them farther and farther from civilization, until their lives were sacrificed to their temerity."

Nothing more is ever heard of Beale, though Morriss does receive a letter from St. Louis, Missouri, dated May 9, 1822. In this Beale says, "How long I may be absent I cannot now determine, certainly no less than two years, perhaps longer." The letter carries a bizarre instruction for Morriss. In it, Beale tells him that if he never hears from him or his companions again, then in ten years' time, that is in 1832, Morriss is to open the box he has left behind. Inside he will find papers that are "unintelligible." But the innkeeper is not to worry: at that time Beale will send a friend with another letter, addressed to Morriss, and this will carry the key to unlock the cipher. Morriss is asked to nominate someone in case of sickness or death; meanwhile Beale sends him his best wishes and tells him, "The game is worth the candle."

Needless to say, the friend never turns up, though it subsequently transpires that a letter was left at the New Orleans post office for Morriss in 1832—a letter that was never picked up.

Morriss remains ever hopeful that he will see his friend again. But finally, in 1845, some twenty-three years after he last heard from Beale, Morriss gives up hope and opens the box. Inside, he finds three number-based ciphers. He works on them and keeps their contents secret until 1862, when he finally unburdens his secret to a close friend, who then becomes the anonymous author of the pamphlet and recounts a story that sounds like a classic tale of the Old West.

***

Beale's first letter to Morriss, contained in the box, and dated January 4, 1822, sets the scene. He tells Morriss that, along with a group of friends, he intends to head for the plains "to hunt the buffalo and encounter the savage grizzlies." This is high-risk stuff, and so Beale puts together a party of thirty fellow brave adventurers before setting out from Virginia. They reach Santa Fe in December 1817, where they stay for the winter. Boredom sets in, and the following March, a group of them set off to explore the local area and do some hunting. Two hundred and fifty miles northwest of Santa Fe, they find and follow a huge herd of buffalo, shooting and stampeding them.

That night, while they are camped up, one of them finds "a cleft in the rocks" full of what looks like gold. Two members are sent back to Santa Fe to fetch Beale. For the next year or so they continue to mine the gold, as well as silver, which is also there in prodigious amounts. Being from Virginia, they decide to stick with what they know and what makes them feel secure. They decide therefore that their home state will be the safest place to hide their treasure. They decide to go back east, where they are to bury it in "a cave near Buford's Tavern, in the county of Bedford, which all of us had visited, and which was considered a perfectly safe depository." They travel together for the first 500 miles, after which only ten men continue the journey with Beale back east.

When Beale's party reaches Virginia, they discover that the cave is not suitable, as local farmers use it to store sweet potatoes and vegetables, so they find a better place nearby. Beale and his party then return west for another year's mining before returning once more back east to bury yet more treasure in the same spot.

In the iron box, as well as the three ciphers and the first letter, is another letter, dated January 5, 1822, which tells Morriss that the third of the codes is a list of all those who are entitled to a share, plus details of their addresses and relatives.

* * *

The three ciphers consist of series of numbers.

The first cipher has 520 enciphered entries, each between one and four characters long. The number eighteen is the most common, appearing eight times.

The second cipher has 763 separate entries. The most common is 818, which represents the letter V, one of the most uncommon letters in the language, and appears eighteen times. This makes sense. In a code like this, which is based on a piece of plain text, the letter V does not appear at the beginning of a word very frequently—in fact, in the Declaration of Independence, it only appears once at the beginning of the word "valuable." Even if it appeared more frequently, a clever code-writer would wish to use it often so as to confuse anyone using frequency analysis and looking for the letter E as the most common letter.

The third cipher is 617 entries long. The most common number is ninety-six, which appears thirteen times.

Only the second cipher has ever been broken—by the publisher of the pamphlet, James Ward. The cipher text from the Albany Library version reads:

115, 73, 24, 807, 37, 52, 49, 17, 31, 62, 647, 22,
7, 15, 140, 47, 29, 107, 79, 84, 56, 239, 10, 26,
811, 5, 196, 308, 85, 52, 160, 136, 59, 211, 36,
9, 46, 316, 554, 122, 106, 95, 53, 58, 2, 42, 7,
35, 122, 53, 31, 82, 77, 250, 196, 56, 96, 118,
71, 140, 287, 28, 353, 37, 1005, 65, 147, 807, 24,
3, 8, 12, 47, 43, 59, 807, 45, 316, 101, 41, 78,
154, 1005, 122, 138, 191, 16, 77, 49, 102, 57, 72,
34, 73, 85, 35, 371, 59, 196, 81, 92, 191, 106,
273, 60, 394, 620, 270, 220, 106, 388, 287, 63, 3,
6, 191, 122, 43, 234, 400, 106, 290, 314, 47, 48,
81, 96, 26, 115, 92, 158, 191, 110, 77, 85, 197,
46, 10, 113, 140, 353, 48, 120, 106, 2, 607, 61,
420, 811, 29, 125, 14, 20, 37, 105, 28, 248, 16,
159, 7, 35, 19, 301, 125, 110, 486, 287, 98, 117,
511, 62, 51, 220, 37, 113, 140, 807, 138, 540, 8,
44, 287, 388, 117, 18, 79, 344, 34, 20, 59, 511,
548, 107, 603, 220, 7, 66, 154, 41, 20, 50, 6,
575, 122, 154, 248, 110, 61, 52, 33, 30, 5, 38, 8,
14, 84, 57, 540, 217, 115, 71, 29, 84, 63, 43,
131, 29, 138, 47, 73, 239, 540, 52, 53, 79, 118,
51, 44, 63, 196, 12, 239, 112, 3, 49, 79, 353,
105, 56, 371, 557, 211, 505, 125, 360, 133, 143,
101, 15, 284, 540, 252, 14, 205, 140, 344, 26,
811, 138, 115, 48, 73, 34, 205, 316, 607, 63, 220,
7, 52, 150, 44, 52, 16, 40, 37, 158, 807, 37, 121,
12, 95, 10, 15, 35, 12, 131, 62, 115, 102, 807,
49, 53, 135, 138, 30, 31, 62, 67, 41, 85, 63, 10,
106, 807, 138, 8, 113, 20, 32, 33, 37, 353, 287,
140, 47, 85, 50, 37, 49, 47, 64, 6, 7, 71, 33, 4,
43, 47, 63, 1, 27, 600, 208, 230, 15, 191, 246,
85, 94, 511, 2, 270, 20, 39, 7, 33, 44, 22, 40, 7,

10, 3, 811, 106, 44, 486, 230, 353, 211, 200, 31,
10, 38, 140, 297, 61, 603, 320, 302, 666, 287, 2,
44, 33, 32, 511, 548, 10, 6, 250, 557, 246, 53,
37, 52, 83, 47, 320, 38, 33, 807, 7, 44, 30, 31,
250, 10, 15, 35, 106, 160, 113, 31, 102, 406, 230,
540, 320, 29, 66, 33, 101, 807, 138, 301, 316,
353, 320, 220, 37, 52, 28, 540, 320, 33, 8, 48,
107, 50, 811, 7, 2, 113, 73, 16, 125, 11, 110, 67,
102, 807, 33, 59, 81, 158, 38, 43, 581, 138, 19,
85, 400, 38, 43, 77, 14, 27, 8, 47, 138, 63, 140,
44, 35, 22, 177, 106, 250, 314, 217, 2, 10, 7,
1005, 4, 20, 25, 44, 48, 7, 26, 46, 110, 230, 807,
191, 34, 112, 147, 44, 110, 121, 125, 96, 41, 51,
50, 140, 56, 47, 152, 540, 63, 807, 28, 42, 250,
138, 582, 98, 643, 32, 107, 140, 112, 26, 85, 138,
540, 53, 20, 125, 371, 38, 36, 10, 52, 118, 136,
102, 420, 150, 112, 71, 14, 20, 7, 24, 18, 12,
807, 37, 67, 110, 62, 33, 21, 95, 220, 511, 102,
811, 30, 83, 84, 305, 620, 15, 2, 10, 8, 220, 106,
353, 105, 106, 60, 275, 72, 8, 50, 205, 185, 112,
125, 540, 65, 106, 807, 138, 96, 110, 16, 73, 33,
807, 150, 409, 400, 50, 154, 285, 96, 106, 316,
270, 205, 101, 811, 400, 8, 44, 37, 52, 40, 241,
34, 205, 38, 16, 46, 47, 85, 24, 44, 15, 64, 73,
138, 807, 85, 78, 110, 33, 420, 505, 53, 37, 38,
22, 31, 10, 110, 106, 101, 140, 15, 38, 3, 5, 44,
7, 98, 287, 135, 150, 96, 33, 84, 125, 807, 191,
96, 511, 118, 40, 370, 643, 466, 106, 41, 107,
603, 220, 275, 30, 150, 105, 49, 53, 287, 250,
208, 134, 7, 53, 12, 47, 85, 63, 138, 110, 21,
112, 140, 485, 486, 505, 14, 73, 84, 575, 1005,
150, 200, 16, 42, 5, 4, 25, 42, 8, 16, 811, 125,
160, 32, 205, 603, 807, 81, 96, 405, 41, 600, 136,
14, 20, 28, 26, 353, 302, 246, 8, 131, 160, 140,
84, 440, 42, 16, 811, 40, 67, 101, 102, 194, 138,

205, 51, 63, 241, 540, 122, 8, 10, 63, 140, 47, 48, 140, 288

Ward does not say how the discovery was made that unlocked the second cipher, but it is a book code—a variation on the very popular nomenclator codes of the time. In a book-code encryption system, the sender and recipient both agree on a book or even a specific page as the key text. They then take the first letter of each word in turn and give it a sequential number, usually starting at one. Each number represents the first letter of each word, numbered from the beginning. The key text is the American Declaration of Independence, which reads:

When(1) in(2) the(3) course(4) of(5) human(6) events(7) it(8) becomes(9) necessary(10) for(11) one(12) people(13) to(14) dissolve(15) the(16) political(17) bands(18) which(19) have(20) connected(21) them(22) with(23) another(24) and(25) to(26) assume(27) among(28) the(29) powers(30) of(31) the(32) earth(33) the(34) separate(35) and(36) equal(37) station(38) to(39) which(40) the(41) laws(42) of(43) nature(44) and(45) of(46) nature's(47) god(48) entitle(49) them(50) a(51) decent(52) respect(53) to(54) the(55) opinions(56) of(57) mankind(58) requires(59) that(60) they(61) should(62) declare(63) the(64) causes(65) which(66) impel(67) them(68) to(69) the(70) separation(71) we(72) hold(73) these(74) truths(75) to(76) be(77) self(78) evident(79) that(80) all(81) men(82) are(83) created(84) equal(85) that(86) they(87) are(88) endowed(89) by(90) their(91) creator(92) with(93) certain(94) unalienable(95) rights(96) that(97) among(98) these(99) are(100) life(101) liberty(102) and(103) the(104) pursuit(105) of(106) happiness(107) that(108) to(109) secure(110) these(111) rights(112) governments(113) are(114) instituted(115) among(116) men(117) deriving(118) their(119) just(120) powers(121) from(122) the(123) consent(124) of(125) the(126) governed(127) that(128) whenever(129) any(130) form(131) of(132) government(133) becomes(134) destructive(135) of(136) these(137) ends(138) it(139) is(140) the(141) right(142) of(143) the(144) people(145) to(146) alter(147) or(148) to(149) abolish(150) it(151) and(152) to(153) institute(154) new(155) government(156) laying(157) its(158) foundation(159) on(160) such(161) principles(162) and(163) organizing(164) its(165) powers(166) in(167) such(168) form(169) as(170) to(171) them(172) shall(173) seem(174) most(175) likely(176) to(177) effect(178) their(179) safety(180) and(181) happiness(182) prudence(183) indeed(184) will(185) dictate(186) that(187) governments(188) long(189) established(190) should(191) not(192) be(193) changed(194) for(195) light(196) and(197) transient(198) causes(199) and(200) accordingly(201) all(202) experience(203) hath(204) shown(205) that(206) mankind(207) are(208) more(209) disposed(210) to(211) suffer(212) while(213) evils(214) are(215) sufferable(216) than(217) to(218) right(219) themselves(220) by(221) abolishing(222) the(223) forms(224) to(225) which(226) they(227) are(228) accustomed(229) but(230) when(231) a(232) long(233) train(234) of(235) abuses(236) and(237) usurpations(238) pursuing(239) invariably(240) the(241) same(242) object(243) evinces(244) a(245) design(246) to(247) reduce(248) them(249) under(250) absolute(251) despotism(252) it(253) is(254) their(255) right(256) it(257) is(258) their(259) duty(260) to(261) throw(262) off(263) such(264) government(265) and(266) to(267) provide(268) new(269) guards(270) for(271) their(272) future(273) security(274) such(275) has(276) been(277) the(278) patient(279) sufferance(280) of(281) these(282) colonies(283) and(284) such(285) is(286) now(287) the(288) necessity(289) which(290) constrains(291) them(292) to(293) alter(294) their(295) former(296) systems(297) of(298) government(299) the(300) history(301) of(302) the(303) present(304) king(305) of(306) great(307) Britain(308) is(309) a(310) history(311) of(312) repeated(313) injuries(314) and(315) usurpations(316) all(317) having(318) in(319) direct(320) object(321) the(322)

establishment(323)   of(324)   an(325)   absolute(326)
tyranny(327)   over(328)   these(329)   states(330)   to(331)
prove(332)   this(333)   let(334)   facts(335)   be(336)
submitted(337)   to(338)   a(339)   candid(340)   world(341)
he(342)   has(343)   refused(344)   his(345)   assent(346)   to(347)
laws(348)   the(349)   most(350)   wholesome(351)   and(352)
necessary(353)   for(354)   the(355)   public(356)   good(357)
he(358)   has(359)   forbidden(360)   his(361)   governors(362)
to(363)   pass(364)   laws(365)   of(366)   immediate(367)   and(368)
pressing(369)   importance(370)   unless(371)   suspended(372)
in(373)   their(374)   operation(375)   till(376)   his(377)
assent(378)   should(379)   be(380)   obtained(381)   and(382)
when(383)   so(384)   suspended(385)   he(386)   has(387)
utterly(388)   neglected(389)   to(390)   attend(391)   to(392)
them(393)   he(394)   has(395)   refused(396)   to(397)   pass(398)
other(399)   laws(400)   for(401)   the(402)   accommodation(403)
of(404)   large(405)   districts(406)   of(407)   people(408)
unless(409)   those(410)   people(411)   would(412)
relinquish(413)   the(414)   right(415)   of(416)
representation(417)   in(418)   the(419)   legislature(420)   a(421)
right(422)   inestimable(423)   to(424)   them(425)   and(426)
formidable(427)   to(428)   tyrants(429)   only(430)   he(431)
has(432)   called(433)   together(434)   legislative(435)   bodies(436)
at(437)   places(438)   unusual(439)   uncomfortable(440)
and(441)   distant(442)   from(443)   the(444)   depository(445)
of(446)   their(447)   public(448)   records(449)   for(450)   the(451)
sole(452)   purpose(453)   of(454)   fatiguing(455)   them(456)
into(457)   compliance(458)   with(459)   his(460)   measures(461)
he(462)   has(463)   dissolved(464)   representative(465)
houses(466)   repeatedly(467)   for(468)   opposing(469)   with(470)
manly(471)   firmness(472)   his(473)   invasions(474)   on(475)
the(476)   rights(477)   of(478)   the(479)   people(480)   he(481)
has(482)   refused(483)   for(484)   a(485)   long(486)   time(487)
after(488)   such(489)   dissolutions(490)   to(491)   cause(492)
others(493)   to(494)   be(495)   elected(496)   whereby(497)
the(498)   legislative(499)   powers(500)   incapable(501)   of(502)

annihilation(503) have(504) returned(505) to(506) the(507) people(508) at(509) large(510) for(511) their(512) exercise(513) the(514) state(515) remaining(516) in(517) the(518) meantime(519) exposed(520) to(521) all(522) the(523) dangers(524) of(525) invasion(526) from(527) without(528) and(529) convulsions(530) within(531) he(532) has(533) endeavored(534) to(535) prevent(536) the(537) population(538) of(539) these(540) states(541) for(542) that(543) purpose(544) obstructing(545) the(546) laws(547) for(548) naturalization(549) of(550) foreigners(551) refusing(552) to(553) pass(554) others(555) to(556) encourage(557) their(558) migration(559) hither(560) and(561) raising(562) the(563) conditions(564) of(565) new(566) appropriations(567) of(568) lands(569) he(570) has(571) obstructed(572) the(573) administration(574) of(575) justice(576) by(577) refusing(578) his(579) assent(580) to(581) laws(582) for(583) establishing(584) judiciary(585) powers(586) he(587) has(588) made(589) judges(590) dependent(591) on(592) his(593) will(594) alone(595) for(596) the(597) tenure(598) of(599) their(600) offices(601) and(602) the(603) amount(604) and(605) payment(606) of(607) their(608) salaries(609) he(610) has(611) erected(612) a(613) multitude(614) of(615) new(616) offices(617) and(618) sent(619) hither(620) swarms(621) of(622) officers(623) to(624) harass(625) our(626) people(627) and(628) eat(629) out(630) their(631) substance(632) he(633) has(634) kept(635) among(636) us(637) in(638) times(639) of(640) peace(641) standing(642) armies(643) without(644) the(645) consent(646) of(647) our(648) legislatures(649) he(650) has(651) affected(652) to(653) render(654) the(655) military(656) independent(657) of(658) and(659) superior(660) to(661) the(662) civil(663) power(664) he(665) has(666) combined(667) with(668) others(669) to(670) subject(671) us(672) to(673) a(674) jurisdiction(675) foreign(676) to(677) our(678) constitution(679) and(680) unacknowledged(681) by(682) our(683) laws(684) giving(685)

his(686) assent(687) to(688) their(689) acts(690) of(691)
pretended(692) legislation(693) for(694) quartering(695)
large(696) bodies(697) of(698) armed(699) troops(700)
among(701) us(702) for(703) protecting(704) them(705)
by(706) a(707) mock(708) trial(709) from(710)
punishment(711) for(712) any(713) murders(714) which(715)
they(716) should(717) commit(718) on(719) the(720)
inhabitants(721) of(722) these(723) states(724) for(725)
cutting(726) off(727) our(728) trade(729) with(730) all(731)
parts(732) of(733) the(734) world(735) for(736)
imposing(737) taxes(738) on(739) us(740) without(741)
our(742) consent(743) for(744) depriving(745) us(746) in(747)
many(748) cases(749) of(750) the(751) benefits(752) of(753)
trial(754) by(755) jury(756) for(757) transporting(758)
us(759) beyond(760) seas(761) to(762) be(763) tried(764)
for(765) pretended(766) offenses(767) for(768) abolishing(769)
the(770) free(771) system(772) of(773) English(774) laws(775)
in(776) a(777) neighboring(778) province(779)
establishing(780) therein(781) an(782) arbitrary(783)
government(784) and(785) enlarging(786) its(787)
boundaries(788) so(789) as(790) to(791) render(792) it(793)
at(794) once(795) an(796) example(797) and(798) fit(799)
instrument(800) for(801) introducing(802) the(803) same(804)
absolute(805) rule(806) into(807) these(808) colonies(809)
for(810) taking(811) away(812) our(813) charters(814)
abolishing(815) our(816) most(817) valuable(818) laws(819)
and(820) altering(821) fundamentally(822) the(823)
forms(824) of(825) our(826) governments(827) for(828)
suspending(829) our(830) own(831) legislature(832) and(833)
declaring(834) themselves(835) invested(836) with(837)
power(838) to(839) legislate(840) for(841) us(842) in(843)
all(844) cases(845) whatsoever(846) he(847) has(848)
abdicated(849) government(850) here(851) by(852)
declaring(853) us(854) out(855) of(856) his(857)
protection(858) and(859) waging(860) war(861) against(862)
us(863) he(864) has(865) plundered(866) our(867) seas(868)

ravaged(869) our(870) coasts(871) burnt(872) our(873) towns(874) and(875) destroyed(876) the(877) lives(878) of(879) our(880) people(881) he(882) is(883) at(884) this(885) time(886) transporting(887) large(888) armies(889) of(890) foreign(891) mercenaries(892) to(893) complete(894) the(895) works(896) of(897) death(898) desolation(899) and(900) tyranny(901) already(902) begun(903) with(904) circumstances(905) of(906) cruelty(907) and(&)(908) perfidy(909) scarcely(910) paralleled(911) in(912) the(913) most(914) barbarous(915) ages(916) and(917) totally(918) unworthy(919) the(920) head(921) of(922) a(923) civilized(924) nation(925) he(926) has(927) constrained(928) our(929) fellow(930) citizens(931) taken(932) captive(933) on(934) the(935) high(936) seas(937) to(938) bear(939) arms(940) against(941) their(942) country(943) to(944) become(945) the(946) executioners(947) of(948) their(949) friends(950) and(951) brethren(952) or(953) to(954) fall(955) themselves(956) by(957) their(958) hands(959) he(960) has(961) excited(962) domestic(963) insurrections(964) amongst(965) us(966) and(967) has(968) endeavored(969) to(970) bring(971) on(972) the(973) inhabitants(974) of(975) our(976) frontiers(977) the(978) merciless(979) Indian(980) savages(981) whose(982) known(983) rule(984) of(985) warfare(986) is(987) an(988) undistinguished(989) destruction(990) of(991) all(992) ages(993) sexes(994) and(995) conditions(996) in(997) every(998) stage(999) of(1000) these(1001) oppressions(1002) we(1003) have(1004) petitioned(1005) for(1006) redress(1007) in(1008) the(1009) most(1010) humble(1011) terms(1012) our(1013) repeated(1014) petitions(1015) have(1016) been(1017) answered(1018) only(1019) by(1020) repeated(1021) injury(1022) a(1023) prince(1024) whose(1025) character(1026) is(1027) thus(1028) marked(1029) by(1030) every(1031) act(1032) which(1033) may(1034) define(1035) a(1036) tyrant(1037) is(1038) unfit(1039) to(1040) be(1041) the(1042) ruler(1043) of(1044) a(1045) free(1046) people(1047)   nor(1048)   have(1049)   we(1050)   been(1051) wanting(1052)   in(1053)   attention(1054)   to(1055)   our(1056) British(1057)   brethren(1058)   we(1059)   have(1060) warned(1061)   them(1062)   from(1063)   time(1064)   to(1065) time(1066)   of(1067)   attempts(1068)   by(1069)   their(1070) legislature(1071)   to(1072)   extend(1073)   an(1074) unwarrantable(1075)   jurisdiction(1076)   over(1077)   us(1078) we(1079)   have(1080)   reminded(1081)   them(1082)   of(1083) the(1084)   circumstances(1085)   of(1086)   our(1087) emigration(1088)   and(1089)   settlement(1090)   here(1091) we(1092)   have(1093)   appealed(1094)   to(1095)   their(1096) native(1097)   justice(1098)   and(1099)   magnanimity(1100) and(1101)   we(1102)   have(1103)   conjured(1104)   them(1105) by(1106)   the(1107)   ties(1108)   of(1109)   our(1110) common(1111)   kindred(1112)   to(1113)   disavow(1114) these(1115)   usurpations(1116)   which(1117)   would(1118) inevitably(1119) interrupt(1120) our(1121) connections(1122) and(1123)   correspondence(1124)   they(1125)   too(1126) have(1127)   been(1128)   deaf(1129)   to(1130)   the(1131) voice(1132)   of(1133)   justice(1134)   and(1135)   of(1136) consanguinity(1137)   we(1138)   must(1139)   therefore(1140) acquiesce(1141)   in(1142)   the(1143)   necessity(1144) which(1145)   denounces(1146)   our(1147)   separation(1148) and(1149)   hold(1150)   them(1151)   as(1152)   we(1153) hold(1154)   the(1155)   rest(1156)   of(1157)   mankind(1158) enemies(1159)   in(1160)   war(1161)   in(1162)   peace(1163) friends(1164)   we(1165)   therefore(1166)   the(1167) representatives(1168)   of(1169)   the(1170)   united(1171) states(1172)   of(1173)   America(1174)   in(1175)   general(1176) congress(1177)   assembled(1178)   appealing(1179)   to(1180) the(1181)   supreme(1182)   judge(1183)   of(1184)   the(1185) world(1186)   for(1187)   the(1188)   rectitude(1189)   of(1190) our(1191)   intentions(1192)   do(1193)   in(1194)   the(1195) name(1196)   and(1197)   by(1198)   authority(1199)   of(1200) the(1201)   good(1202)   people(1203)   of(1204)   these(1205) colonies(1206)   solemnly(1207)   publish(1208)   and(1209)

declare(1210)   that(1211)   these(1212)   united(1213)
colonies(1214) are(1215) and(1216) of(1217) right(1218)
ought(1219)   to(1220)   be(1221)   free(1222)   and(1223)
independent(1224)   states(1225)   that(1226)   they(1227)
are(1228)   absolved(1229)   from(1230)   all(1231)
allegiance(1232) to(1233) the(1234) British(1235) crown(1236)
and(1237)   that(1238)   all(1239)   political(1240)
connection(1241) between(1242) them(1243) and(1244)
the(1245) state(1246) of(1247) great(1248) Britain(1249)
is(1250)   and(1251)   ought(1252)   to(1253)   be(1254)
totally(1255) dissolved(1256) and(1257) that(1258) as(1259)
free(1260)   and(1261)   independent(1262)   states(1263)
they(1264) have(1265) full(1266) power(1267) to(1268)
levy(1269)   war(1270)   conclude(1271)   peace(1272)
contract(1273)   alliances(1274)   establish(1275)
commerce(1276) and(1277) to(1278) do(1279) all(1280)
other(1281) acts(1282) and(1283) things(1284) which(1285)
independent(1286)   states(1287)   may(1288)   of(1289)
right(1290)   do(1291)   and(1292)   for(1293)   the(1294)
support(1295)   of(1296)   this(1297)   declaration(1298)
with(1299) a(1300) firm(1301) reliance(1302) on(1303)
the(1304)   protection(1305)   of(1306)   divine(1307)
providence(1308) we(1309) mutually(1310) pledge(1311)
to(1312)   each(1313)   other(1314)   our(1315)   lives(1316)
our(1317) fortunes(1318) and(1319) our(1320) sacred(1321)
honor(1322).

Once Ward discovered that this was the key text, he was able to go through the laborious process of taking the first letter from each word to assemble the plain text and break the second cipher, which then reads:

I have deposited in the county of Bedford, about four miles from Buford's, in an excavation or vault, six feet below the surface of the ground, the following articles, belonging jointly to the parties whose names are given in number three herewith.

The first deposit consisted of ten hundred and fourteen pounds of gold, and thirty-eight hundred and twelve pounds of silver, deposited Nov. eighteen nineteen.

The second was made Dec. eighteen twenty one and consisted of nineteen hundred and seven pounds of gold, and twelve hundred and eight-eight of silver also jewels obtained in St. Louis in exchange to save transportation and valued at thirteen thousand dollars.

The above is securely packed in iron pots, with iron covers. The vault is roughly lined with stone and the vessels rest on solid stone and are covered with others. Paper number one describes the exact locality of the vault so that no difficulty will be had in finding it.[5]

This form of encryption was instantly recognizable to anyone at the time, though Thomas Beale had the good sense to adapt it from its original pure form.

The original form of this sort of encryption was a book code. Benedict Arnold, a man who is both American hero and traitor, used this code system in his plan to surrender West Point to the British. During the American War of Independence, he had shown himself to be both resourceful and courageous, every inch a revolutionary hero. But he had exactly the right profile that any counter-intelligence officer seeks in a traitor: Arnold was disaffected with the American strategy of allying forces with the French, he was under investigation for corruption and was under a financial squeeze from his young wife. He was recruited to the British side by a smart young major, ironically with a French name, John André. The code system they used was initially based on a book that was a standard legal handbook but would not have been on many bookshelves, Blackstone's *Commentaries*, Volume One, fifth Oxford edition. They used three numbers to make up each word, the first number represented the page, the second the line, and the third the actual word itself. The key text was a poor choice and all concerned struggled to find the right codes. For example, the sender had to wade through 331 pages of turgid legal prose before he found the word "militia." They then switched to the *Universal Etymological English Dictionary*, which at least gave them the words but was a dead giveaway as the middle number represented the column on the page. To disguise this, they added seven to the numbers, but the plot was uncovered. Major André was hanged, but Arnold escaped. For once, the British did not double-cross someone who had betrayed his own side, and Arnold became a general in the Colonial Army.

Cryptographers then adapted this failed system and used only the first letter of each word, which had the extra advantage of being polyalphabetic. Any rich piece of prose would offer many words beginning with the common letters, like E, R and T, and so the smart compiler of the cipher text could use a different one each time to defeat any attempt at letter-frequency analysis.

The compiler of cipher two had to make some clever changes. He did not need to, but at the ninety-fifth word, he uses "unalienable" rather than "inalienable." There is no word beginning with X, which he needs for "six," so he uses word 994, "sexes," and takes the middle letter. Similarly, there are no words in the American Declaration of Independence beginning with Y, so he uses word 822, "fundamentally," and then takes the last letter rather than the first. He also does something else rather clever: he uses the cipher number 844 for the word "inn." In theory, 844 should stand for the letter A, as this is the first letter of the word "all," but here it stands for the word "inn." He has cleverly concatenated 8=I, 4=N, 4=N, which breaks the rules of the cipher, but it's the sort of small trick that will derail an amateur nineteenth-century code-breaker.

Cipher one refers to the locality of the vault. The Albany Library version reads:

71, 194, 38, 1701, 89, 76, 11, 83, 1629, 48, 94, 63, 132, 16, 111, 95, 84, 341, 975, 14, 40, 64, 27, 81, 139, 213, 63, 90, 1120, 8, 15, 3, 126, 2018, 40, 74, 758, 485, 604, 230, 436, 664, 582, 150, 251, 284, 308, 231, 124, 211, 486, 225, 401, 370, 11, 101, 305, 139, (130), 189, 17, 33, 88, 208, 193, 145, 1, 94, 73, 416, 918, 263, 28, 500, 538, 356, 219, 27, 176, 130, 10, 460, 25, 485, 18, 436, 65, 84, 283, 118, 320, 138, 36, 416, 280, 15, 71, 224, 961, 44, 16, 401, 39, 88, 61, 304, 12, 21,

24, 283, 134, 92, 63, 246, 486, 682, 7, 219, 184,
360, 780, 18, 64, 463, 474, 131, 160, 79, 73, 440,
95 18, 64,581, 34, 69, 128, 367, 460, 17, 81, 12,
103, 820, 62, 116, 97, 103, 862, 70, 60, 1317,
471, 540, 208, 121, 890, 346, 36, 150, 59, 568,
614, 13, 120, 63, 219, 812, 2160, 1780, 99, 35,
18, 21, 136, 872, 15, 28, 170, 88, 4, 30, 44, 112,
18, 147, 436, 195, 320, 37, 122, 113, 6, 140, 8,
120, 305, 42, 58, 461, 44, 106, 301, 13, 408, 680,
93, 86, 116, 530, 82, 568, 9, 102, 38, 416, 89,
71, 216, 728, 965, 818, 2, 38, 121, 195, 14, 326,
148, 234, 18, 55, 131, 234, 18, 55, 131, 234, 361,
824, 5, 81, 623, 48, 961, 19, 26, 33, 10, 1101,
365, 92, 88, 181, 275, 346, 201, 206, 86, 36, 219,
320, 829, 840, 68, 326, 19, 48, 122, 85, 216, 284,
919, 861, 326, 985, 233, 64, 68, 232, 431, 960,
50, 29, 81, 216, 321, 603, 14, 612, 81, 360, 36,
51, 62, 1.84, 78, 60, 200, 314, 676, 112, 4, 28,
18, 61, 136, 247, 819, 921, 1060, 464, 895, 10, 6,
66, 111, 38, 41, 49, 602, 423, 962, 302, 294, 875,
78, 14, 23, 111, 109, 62, 31, 501, 823, 216, 280,
34, 24, 150, 1000, 162, 286, 19, 21, 17, 340, 19,
242, 31, 85, 234, 140, 607, 115, 33, 191, 67, 104,
86, 52, 88, 16, 80, 121, 67, 95, 122, 216, 548,
96, 11, 201, 77, 366, 218, 65, 667, 890, 236, 154,
211, 10, 98, 34, 119, 56, 216, 119, 71, 218, 1164,
1496, 1817, 51, 39, 210, 36, 3, 19, 540, 232, 22,
141, 617, 84, 290, 80, 46, 207, 411, 150, 29, 38,
46, 172, 85, 194, 36, 261, 543, 897, 62, 18, 212,
416, 127, 931, 19, 4, 63, 96, 12, 101, 418, 16,
140, 230, 460, 538, 19, 27, 88, 612, 1431, 90,
716, 275, 74, 83, 11, 426, 89, 72, 84, 1300, 1706,
814, 221, 132, 40, 102, 34, 858, 975, 1101, 84,
16, 79, 23, 16, 81, 122, 324, 403, 912, 227, 936,
447, 55, 86, 34, 43, 212, 107, 96, 314, 264, 1065,

324, 428, 601, 203,213, 71, 87, 96, 202, 35, 10,
2, 41, 17, 85, 221, 736, 820, 214, 11, 60, 760

The third cipher carries the names of the rest of Beale's hunting party, who are described as the "joint owners of the fund deposited," together with the names of the nearest relatives and their last known addresses. The Albany Library version reads:

317, 8, 92, 73, 112, 89, 67, 318, 28, 96, 107, 41,
78, 146, 397, 118, 98, 114, 246, 348, 116, 74, 88,
12, 65, 32, 14, 81, 19, 76, 121, 216, 85, 33, 66,
15, 10×, 68, 77, 43, 24, 122, 96, 117, 36, 211,
301, 15, 44, 11, 46, 89, 18, 136, 68, 317, 28, 90,
82, 304, 71, 43, 221, 198, 176, 310, 319, 81, 99,
264, 380, 56, 37, 319, 2, 44, 53, 28, 44, 75, 98,
102, 37, 85, 107, 117, 64, 88, 136, 48, 151, 998,
175, 89, 315, 326, 78, 96, 214, 218, 311, 43, 89,
51, 90, 75, 128, 96, 33, 28, 103, 84, 65, 26, 41,
246, 84, 270, 98, 116, 32, 59, 74, 66, 69, 240,
15, 8, 121, 20, 77, 89, 31, 11, 106, 81, 191, 224,
328, 18, 75, 52, 82, 117, 201, 39, 23, 2.17, 27,
21, 84, 35, 54, 109, 128, 49, 77, 86, 1, 81, 217,
64, 55, 83, 116, 251, 269, 311, 96, 54, 32, 120,
18, 132, 102, 219, 211, 84, 150, 219, 275, 312,
64, 10, 106, 87, 75, 47, 21, 29, 37, 81, 44, 18,
126, 115, 132, 160, 181, 203, 76, 81, 299, 314,
337, 351, 96, 11, 28, 97, 318, 238, 106, 24, 93,
3, 19, 17, 26, 60, 73, 88, 14, 126, 138, 234, 286,
297, 321, 365, 264, 19, 22, 84, 56, 107, 98, 123,
111, 214, 136, 7, 33, 45, 40, 13, 28, 46, 42, 107,
196, 227, 344, 198, 203, 247, 116, 19, 8, 212,
230, 31, 6, 328, 65, 48, 52, 59, 41, 122, 33, 117,
11, 18, 25, 71, 36, 45, 83, 76, 89, 92, 31, 65, 70,
85, 96, 27, 33, 44, 50, 61, 24, 112, 136, 149,
176, 180, 194, 143, 171, 205, 296, 87, 12, 44, 51,
89, 98, 34, 41, 208, 173, 66, 9, 35, 16, 95, 8,
113, 175, 90, 56, 203, 19, 177, 183, 206, 157,

200, 218, 260, 291, 305, 618, 951, 320, 18, 124,
78, 65, 19, 32, 124, 48, 53, 57, 84, 96, 207, 244,
66, 82, 119, 71, 11, 86, 77, 213, 54, 82, 316,
245, 303, 86, 97, 106, 212, 18, 37, 15, 81, 89,
16, 7, 81, 39, 98, 14, 43, 216, 118, 29, 55, 109,
138, 172, 213, 64, 8, 227, 304, 611, 221, 364,
819, 375, 128, 296, 11, 18, 53, 76, 10, 15, 32,
19, 71, 84, 120, 134, 68, 73, 89, 96, 230, 48, 77,
26, 101, 127, 936, 218, 439, 178, 171, 6v, 226,
313, 215, 102, 18, 167, 262, 114, 216, 66, 59, 48,
27, 19, 13, 82, 48, 162, 34, 127, 139, 34, 127,
139, 34, 128, 129, 74, 63, 120, 11, 54, 61, 73,
92, 180, 66, 75, 101, 124, 265, 89, 96, 126, 274,
896, 917, 434, 461, 235, 890, 312, 413, 328, 381,
96, 105, 217, 66, 118, 22, 77, 64, 42, 12, 7, 55,
24, 83, 67, 97, 109, 121, 135, 181, 203, 219, 228,
256, 21, 34, 77, 319, 374, 382, 675, 684, 717,
864, 203, 4, 18, 92, 16, 63, 82, 22, 46, 55, 69,
74, 112, 135, 186, 175, 119, 213, 416, 312, 343,
264, 119, 186, 218, 343, 417, 845, 951, 124, 209,
49, 617, 856, 924, 936, 72, 19, 29, 11, 35, 42,
40, 66, 85, 94, 112, 65, 82, 115, 119, 236, 244,
186, 172, 112, 85, 6, 56, 38, 44, 85, 72, 32, 47,
73, 96, 124, 217, 314, 319, 221, 644, 817, 821,
934, 922, 416, 975, 10, 22, 18, 46, 137, 181, 101,
39, 86, 103, 116, 138, 164, 212, 218, 296, 815,
380, (390?), 4, 2, 460, 495, 675, 820, 952

The codes themselves consist of one- to four-digit numbers, separated by commas. There are plenty of details here to entice any cryptanalyst. A preliminary analysis of the distribution of the numbers produces an immediate insight: cipher two is much flatter than ciphers one or three, which are much closer to each other in style. It is assumed therefore that they are similar to each other but different from cipher two. On the face of it, this looks like common sense, but this cannot be assumed for certain.

The most likely explanation is that ciphers one and three are not book codes but nomenclator codes. These had been the dominant form of encryption used by governments and religious institutions since they were first introduced in the early fourteenth century by papal secretaries, who used simple abbreviations, such as A for "king" and D for "pope." This simple encryption system, which would have only fooled the dim-witted, was very quickly developed by Italian city states, and by the nineteenth century, these codes were sophisticated vehicles used for transmitting long and complex messages. By this time, they consisted of long lists of letters, commonly used syllables and whole words, and some of the dictionaries contained thousands of entries. In this system, each item of text is assigned a discrete number, which is only shared by those in the know. The great advantage for the nineteenth-century users of this type of code was that it offered a relatively high level of security, provided the code books were kept within the circle of those who wished to keep their secrets safe. They were even more secure when the key codes were changed on a regular basis. If a code book was stolen or broken, then the damage was limited to the time it was in use.

One American enthusiast of nomenclator codes was Robert Livingstone, the secretary of foreign affairs. In 1781, he had forms printed with the numbers up to 1,700, against which were assigned letters, syllables and words. A more public version appeared a little later, a small cipher handbook called *A Dictionary: to Enable Any Two Persons to Maintain a Correspondence, With a Secrecy, Which is Impossible for Any Other Person to Discover.*[6] Instead of forms, this was a small book that again listed words and syllables in alphabetical order, which could then be numbered randomly. If two people bought copies of the book and then gave all the text entries random but identical numbers, they could be reasonably assured that their enciphered communications would be secure. To defeat frequency analysis, which by this time was well developed, common letters (E, T, A, O, I, N, S, H, R, D, L and U) and popular words like "the" and "and" were given many different numbers.

The profile chart for cipher one fits a nomenclator very well. The total text consists of 520 separate numerical entries, within which there are 179 unique elements that appear only once. These single elements are scattered throughout. The numbers used in the cipher text tend to be concentrated below 1,000. The cipher-setter does use numbers above 1,000, but there are far fewer taken from here. One interesting point to note straight away is the fourth element, number 1,701, appears just once. The previous number in the series is 1,629 and the subsequent one is 1,780. This might well be the name of a person or place, which would only be significant to the sender and the receiver. Cipher two, which has been decoded, consists of 763 entries, of which 263 are different, and it shakes down to 158 words, which calculates as about one word for every four items of number code. If the same proportions are applied to cipher one, then the 520 separate elements would be decoded into a text of about 130 words. This is certainly enough words to provide a detailed description of exactly where to find the treasure.

Cipher three also fits a nomenclator, almost exactly. It consists of 617 distinct numerical entries, of which 183 are only used once. Applying the same formula as cipher two (one word for every four entries), this comes out as a plain text of 183 words. According to Beale's letter, this cipher consists of the names and addresses of the thirty men who were his companions in the great adventure and who are co-owners of the treasure. Each entry averages out at six words. The 183 unique entries could easily be their names, each person having a first and second name. This would leave an average four words per person, which would be just about right to name the town or village where they lived. At this time, there were smallish towns, not major cities, and the name and county would be enough for them to be found.

***

Over the years, like other historical codes, there has been no shortage of suggested solutions, exotic and otherwise. There is a serious overlap between Masonic language and the vocabulary of both mystery and cryptography, and so, inevitably, the Freemasons pop up in many of the other unsolved codes and related mysteries. In the case of *The Beale Papers*, it is not just a matter of suggestion or conspiracy theory. Masonic provenance is everywhere at work here. Any crypt-analyst looking for clues as to the likely plain text has to start with the Freemasons.

For a start, the publisher of the pamphlet, James B. Ward, was a Freemason, a member of Dove Lodge No. 51, which he joined in 1862 but was then "suspended" from in 1867, for reasons that are not known. The pamphlet is riddled with Masonic references.

Famously, the Freemasons are a fraternal but clandestine organization. Not so much a secret organization as a society with secrets. Masons "hele" their secrets, which means to cover them up, conceal them from the common light. Secret matters are said to be so "abstruse" or "profound" that it is hard for outsiders to understand. Secrets are described as "cryptic," which in Freemasonry is a word often associated with a crypt or vault, a hiding place. In cipher two, this relatively unusual word (which I have set in italics) is used twice to describe the Beale treasure: "I have deposited in the county of Bedford, about four miles from Buford's, in an excavation or *vault*, six feet below the surface of the ground [...] The *vault* is roughly lined with stone, and the vessels rest on solid stone." The writer of the pamphlet then uses the word "vault" twice more. This is an odd word to use, as Beale originally tells Morriss that they came back to find a "cave" they all knew. When this was discovered to be not suitable, they "selected a better place." No mention of a vault at this stage until the ciphers are decrypted, which, when taken together, is highly suggestive of a Masonic link.

The vaulted crypt is hugely important in Masonic legend and carries several layers of highly charged symbolic meaning, as it is believed there were several vaults on the site of King Solomon's Temple. Many Masons believe there was a vault under the Sanctum Sanctorum, the Holy of Holies. This blessed sanctuary consisted of the innermost chamber of the Tabernacle in Solomon's Temple and was the resting place of the Ark of the Covenant. Vaults also carry a secondary symbolic meaning as an entrance through the grave into eternal life. There is a further huge clue in the cipher text, which helps solidify the Masonic connection. The highest number in the cipher text is 2,906,[7] a hugely significant number in Masonic lore.

There are only two other numbers that are above 2,000—2,018 and 2,160—so it is fair to assume that it was chosen deliberately rather than randomly. The number 2,906 would have been known instantly to Ward—as it is to all Freemasons—because it is the number of pilasters (square pillars) in Solomon's Temple.

There is a further link. It is tangential but intriguing—and certainly enough to get the Masonic-watchers overexcited. The writer of the letters signs himself "Thos Jeffn Beale," the assumption being that his middle name is Jefferson, after Thomas Jefferson, the author of the American Declaration of Independence. If you remove the capital letters of each name (T)homas (J)efferson (B)eale, the residue of letters left over—HOMASEFFERSONEALE—is an anagram of "Freemason safe house," though, as any cryptographer knows, short-string anagrams such as these are relatively easy to construct.

***

In the absence of a solution, there are three basic theories.

The first is that this is a hoax, pure and simple. The unsolved codes are nothing more than random numbers. The purpose of the pamphlet was purely commercial. Having enticed readers and purchasers of his pamphlet with the partially solved code and a wild tale of a lifetime's riches to the lucky person who cracked it, Ward then guaranteed his future sales by ensuring that the remaining lines of code could never be solved. Even at the time, the pamphlet suggests the buried treasure is worth $750,000—a fortune.

The second theory is a variation on the first: that this was a hoax but the motive was not just commercial. It was a classic nineteenth-century practical joke. Under this scenario, the most likely prankster is Edgar Allan Poe, the great nineteenth-century American master-spinner of mysteries.

The third theory is that the kernel of the story is true: there was (and maybe still is) treasure buried somewhere in Bedford County. The mistakes in the ciphers and the anomalies in language are all deliberate—further pointers to the underlying truth buried deep in this little pamphlet.

Attached to this theory is the even more exotic notion that the gold referred to is not the proceeds of a mine in California but a much more substantial haul: the Confederate gold, that enormous pile secreted away when the South was defeated by the North—to be accessed one glorious day when the southern forces would rise again and defeat the North. Many still believe in this today. It is one of the great and most recycled beliefs of modern American history, all the more powerful because it cannot be proved or disproved.

The brilliance of Ward's pamphlet is that there is just enough evidence to support each theory but not enough to be completely convincing. In turn, each theory has plenty of evidence to contradict it, but not enough to deliver what might be regarded as a knockout blow.

***

One of the modern advocates of the hoax theory is Jim Gillogly, the cryptanalyst who subsequently cracked the *Kryptos* code using a sophisticated computer program.[8] Twenty years before getting to grips with *Kryptos*, he tackled the Beale ciphers. He assumed that the Declaration of Independence is the key text and applied it to cipher one. This is what he produced:

SCS?E TFA?G CDOTT UCWOT WTAAI WDBII DTT?W TTAAB
BPLAA ABWCT LTFIF LKILP EAABP WCHOT OAPPP MORAL
ANHAA BBCCA CDDEA OSDSF HNTFT ATPOC ACBCD DLBER
IFEBT HIFOE HUUBT TTTTI HPAOA ASATA ATTOM TAPOA AAROM
PJDRA??TSB COBDA AACPN RB**ABF DEFGH IIJKL MMNOH PP**AWT
ACMOB LSOES SOAVI SPFTA OTBTF THFOA OGHWT ENALC
AASAA TTARD SLTAW GFESA UWAOL TTAHH TTASO TTEAF
AASCS TAIFR CABTO TLHHD TNHWT STEAI EOAAS TWTTS OITSS
TAAOP IWCPC WSOTT IOIES ITTDA TTPIU FSFRF ABPTC COAIT
NATTO STSTF??ATD ATWTA TTOCW TOMPA TSOTE CATTO
TBSOG CWCDR OLITI BHPWA AE?BT STAFA EWCI? CBOWL
TPOAC TEWTA FOAIT HTTTT OSHRI STEOO ECUSC?RAIII RLWST
RASNI TPCBF AEFTB

The following string appears 187 numbers into the code: ABF DEFGH IIJKL MMNOH PP, which I have underlined and marked in bold. The odds against this are many millions to one against. But Jim Gillogly does not conclude that this confirms—beyond doubt—that the Beale ciphers are a hoax:

> Among the possibilities is that it is a random event, and "just happened" in a cryptogram enciphered using another document. This is quite unlikely [...] Another possibility is that the *Declaration of Independence* is in fact the key, but that another level of encryption (e.g. elimination of nulls) must be stripped away. My investigations do not preclude this possibility, although I have been unable to extract any intelligible plain text from it.

As he remarked, rather ruefully, "It is often much more difficult, if not impossible, to prove that a document is meaningless than to extract the sense from a meaningful one." Though Jim Gillogly is circumspect, for many others this whole story is so highly improbable that it cannot be anything other than a commercial hoax, the motive being to sell a cheap pamphlet that could sit easily alongside the trashy novels of adventure in the West. Many of these share common themes with *The Beale Papers*: tall, swarthy men of mystery, hunting excitement, treasure and brave adventurers pitting their wits and their lives against a cruel and unyielding landscape. Ward's apologists argue that his motive may well have been entirely benign. In May 1883, two years before *The Beale Papers* were published, a fire destroyed several buildings in Lynchburg; five men died trying to put it out. As a good local citizen, Ward used the pamphlet to raise money for their relatives. An interesting proposition, but as with much about this code, there is little firm evidence for this and it can be filed as supposition.

Regardless of whether Ward was a clandestine philanthropist or not, his critics highlight further glitches in the story, which point to it being fiction. For a start, there is no trace of a Thomas J. Beale at this time in Virginia, but this does not necessarily mean he did not exist.[9] He was a drifter, though a well-heeled one, who arrived with no past and left without a future. There were no formal records at this time, and even now it is relatively easy for people to disappear in the United States and start new lives with new identities.

The skeptics also argue that there is a problem with the language used, citing three of the words in *The Beale Papers* that—it is said—did not exist at the time the letters were allegedly written. The argument is that the letters were supposedly written in 1822 but these words were not recorded elsewhere until 1826. The words are captured in just two sentences, which I have set in italics: "Keeping well together they followed their trail for two weeks or more, securing many, and *stampeding* the rest." The second sentence is "Everyone was diligently at work with such tools and *appliances* as they had *improvised*, and quite a little pile had already accumulated." But this is not really a sustainable argument that is strong enough to destroy the credibility of *The Beale Papers*. "Stampeding" and "improvised" both appear elsewhere in Virginia in 1826. At this time, the eastern states of the United States were the proverbial melting pot, with many immigrant groups coming from Europe, bringing with them their own languages, traditions and cultures. Though English was the dominant tongue, words from other languages were constantly added. Some stuck, others disappeared, and the compilers of dictionaries were always out of sync and slightly behind. A four-year gap between the use of these words here and elsewhere is therefore relatively insignificant, a meaningless piece of pedantry. "Appliances" may or may not have been in widespread use in Virginia at this time, but as a word it had a long history, first being used in England in 1561 and then, fifty years later, by Shakespeare.

Much more important, however, are the references to Morriss. The pamphlet quotes him as saying, "It was in the month of January, 1820, while keeping the Washington Hotel, that I first became acquainted with Beale." But the skeptics point to records showing that Morriss did not become the proprietor until more than three years later, in December 1823. This could be explained by arguing that Ward's source was interviewing Morriss, who by this time was a very old man of eighty-four who was trying to recall events of sixty years before. These are then transcribed by Ward's source, adding further to the possibility of error. But there is a problem with the sequence of events: the two Beale letters are dated 1822, a year before Morriss becomes the proprietor.

All this points to something much more intriguing: the author of the Beale letters is also Ward's source, the anonymous person who wrote the manuscript. The entire pamphlet is written by one hand, which is either Ward's anonymous source or, more likely, Ward himself.[10] And there is no shortage of clues, all of which point to a single hand for the entire pamphlet, which means that whoever wrote it also set the ciphers.

Though there can be much argument about the many areas of the whole Beale story, this—at least—is one area where the evidence appears compelling.

For a start, there are plenty of words that are common to both the writer of the Beale letters and the anonymous author of the rest of the pamphlet. Many of these are common words ("success," "pursuit," "enterprise," "commence," "latter," "systematize," "afford," "ascertain," "unintelligible," "ultimate," "contingency," "engage," "understand," "fully" and "encounter"), but taken as a whole, they suggest one writer sharing a single lexicon.

Both Beale in his letters and the writer of the pamphlet are very fond of beginning sentences with the phrase "It was ... ." This could be explained away by two arguments: Ward's source was transcribing a series of lengthy interviews with Morriss and—like police officers taking statements from witnesses—it always ends up in their language rather than that of the person they are interviewing. The second argument is that anyone writing about another's work can easily fall into the trap of using their words, especially if they appear to be an unconfident writer like the person who Ward claims is his source.

However, there is further evidence that points to a single author and that is something few writers are aware of: their sentence length. The average length of a Beale sentence is 28.75 words, whereas the rest of the pamphlet is 28.82,[11] a coincidence maybe, but one that provides further reinforcement to the idea that there was a single hand at work here.

This style of analysis—called stylometrics—is a relatively new tool both for cryptanalysts and anyone wanting to locate those otherwise invisible clues left by writers. At its simplest, it means analyzing and comparing texts and looking for those patterns that are not immediately obvious to the naked eye and can be easily missed. At its best, it can prove that two texts share the same author, as no matter how hard the writer might try to disguise their style, there are some fundamentals that will always be there. It is as if writers leave fingerprints in the text, though instead of being shown by dusting on powder, they are revealed by computer analysis. Readers who wish to practice some stylometrics analysis themselves can download a brilliant piece of freeware called Signature, written by Dr. Peter Millican, a fellow and tutor in philosophy at Hertford College, Oxford University.[12]

Using this, it is possible to carry out a fascinating analysis that compares *The Beale Papers* (which are supposed to be written by Ward's anonymous source) and the letters written by Beale himself.

The first comparison is word length, which compares the frequency with which words containing the same number of letters are used. The result looks extraordinary. There is an almost perfect match:

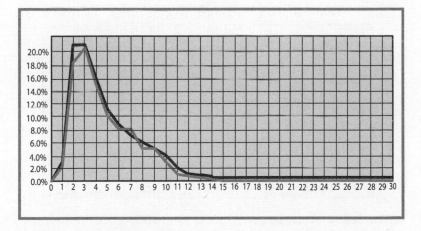

Millican's software also allows you to compare the number of times each letter in the alphabet is used. Again, there is what looks like remarkable overlap:

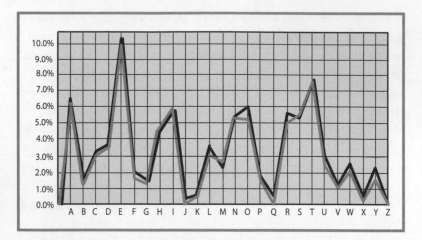

Another really interesting clue to authorship is to look at punctuation marks, such as periods, exclamation marks, question marks, commas, etc.—and even rarer items such as semicolons, colons, dashes and brackets, which are more significant, as letter frequency patterns will tend to be similar anyway. Again, it is one of those key indicators that can give away a writer's hand. As with the other graphs, the results look conclusive:

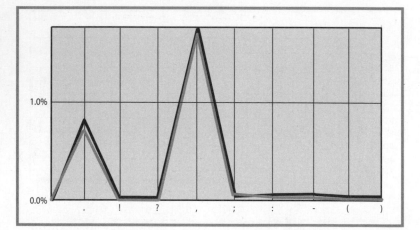

A discordant note is struck by comparing the sentence lengths. Though the average is the same, the distribution of sentence lengths is very different:

However, this can be explained by the argument that a series of personal letters and what is essentially a story written in prose would inevitably have a different rhythm, even if they were written by the same hand.

Though this looks pretty convincing overall, there is one further piece of analysis that needs to be carried out before any conclusions can be drawn. The Signature software program has another built-in statistical test called chi-square distribution, which provides a more precise analysis. This comes from probability theory and is used to measure statistical probability distributions and provide a guide as to whether they are significant or not. Chi-square measures two things and then compares them. The first is the sample text measured against a reference text. The second is the second sample also measured against the same reference text. Basically, if the two samples have the same author, they will differ from all other texts in a similar way. The results are inconclusive.[13] But as Millican points out, "The problem is that this sort of significant difference can easily occur, even with texts by the same author, especially if the samples are short, or if there is any systematic difference between them—e.g. prose style, dialog content, repeated use of specific names."

So those hoping for the clinching piece of evidence that will clearly demonstrate that Ward's anonymous source is the same hand as the man who wrote the Beale letters will be disappointed.[14] Even though *The Beale Papers* are reasonably long and have just over eleven thousand words, the letters themselves are less than three thousand words, and the mathematical problem is that there is simply not enough text to draw a reliable conclusion.

However, there is one clinching argument that gives the game away and confirms *The Beale Papers* as having a single author, and that is the use of the key text. In Morriss's account, the contents of the box consisted of the three ciphers but no key text. It is not explained anywhere how Morriss discovered that the American Declaration of Independence was the text that would unlock cipher two. But—and this is the crucial point—it is not the correct version. The original Declaration of Independence has 1,327 words; the one

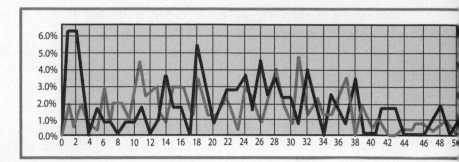

used in *The Beale Papers* only has 1,322. What is more, *The Beale Papers*'s version of the Declaration of Independence is only ever used here; this is the only place it appears.

When the anonymous writer of the pamphlet decrypted cipher two, he used the Beale version of the Declaration of Independence, not the correct one. According to the pamphlet, this was done forty years later. The anonymous writer should be using a different version of the Declaration of Independence, but he does not. Whoever it was (either Ward or his anonymous source) was a poor cryptographer, and he makes the same mistakes as Beale did when he first enciphered the plain text. There are so many mistakes that it is inconceivable that both men could have made the same ones. The odds against this are millions to one, and the common-sense explanation is that both writers are working from the same version. But according to the pamphlet, there was no copy of the Declaration of Independence in the box Beale left behind. The conclusion therefore has to be that one man wrote the code and then produced the decrypt.

***

Ultimately, whether the Beale ciphers are a genuine code written by Thomas Beale, Ward's anonymous source, Ward himself or a single hand may not be that important. More intriguing is the question, who was behind this? Was it just a hoax by an impoverished publisher who wanted to separate the credulous from their cash, and make himself some easy money, or is there something much more interesting going on here?

One favorite theory is that the author is none other than the great nineteenth-century American story writer and chronicler of the

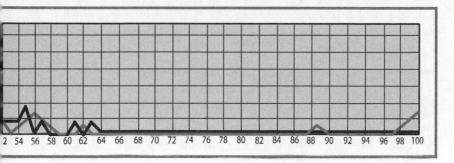

macabre, Edgar Allan Poe. There is plenty here to fuel such a theory. For a start, there is no shortage of superficial similarities between the writing styles he used and that of the author of *The Beale Papers*.[15]

Poe loved to show off his knowledge of foreign languages and he makes such references in sixty-four of his seventy tales. Poe's favorite foreign language was French, and in *The Beale Papers* Morriss is described as being "*sans peur et sans reproche.*" Poe's favorite foreign phrase was *par excellence,* which appears in six of his stories and once in *The Beale Papers.* Poe was prone to using indefinite measurements, such as "about six inches," "two or three men," "a week or two" or "nearly three miles." *The Beale Papers* have thirty-two such references, though this was common amongst nineteenth-century writers. Another common nineteenth-century writing style that Poe was also prone to using was never using one adjective when two would do: "shadowy and vague," "spectral and ominous," "bitter and serious." *The Beale Papers* are guilty of this on sixty-six occasions, but then, in a pre-TV age, this was very common. Poe often referred to "iron" in his short stories, and this is done three times in *The Beale Papers*, but as it was the most common cheap metal in use at the time, this may not be significant. He had something of a fetish about eyes and teeth and he often used these to define his characters. The same pattern is seen in *The Beale Papers*, particularly in the description of the hero, Thomas J. Beale: "He was about six feet in height, with jet-black eyes and hair of the same color, worn longer than was the style at that time."

As we saw earlier, the writer of *The Beale Papers* shares another stylistic habit with Poe, which is to begin sentences with the phrase "It was ... ." This appears six times in the Beale letters, eight times in the rest of the pamphlet and twelve times in the Poe short story *The*

Gold Bug, which is often assumed to be Poe's public version of his interest in codes and treasure. Both Poe and the anonymous writer of the pamphlet use reflexive pronouns, especially "myself," but again, this is a characteristic of nineteenth-century literature.

Poe liked to use an unnamed narrator, but this too is a common literary device and not one confined to nineteenth-century dime novels. There are a whole series of words ("peculiar," "excite," "scarcely," "interest," "wealth," "poverty," "loss of wealth," "singular," "design," "accident," "intense" and "anxiety") that both Poe and the author of *The Beale Papers* use. As well as single words, there are a series of phrases—e.g. "delicacy of feeling," "sense of delicacy," "nothing of importance/interest/consequence," "throw light upon the subject," "bring to light," "Virginia gentleman," "my dear friend" and "barely perceptible"—loved both by Poe and the author of *The Beale Papers*.

Though all these are intriguing clues and pointers that might excite and interest the reader, in the end they are all a bit shadowy and vague, and there is no solid and overwhelming iron bond to link the two writers. Besides, Poe's writing style is easy to pastiche, as the previous sentence shows.

That said, there is no shortage of fans for the Poe-Ward thesis.

Two key sources are often quoted. The first is *The Gold Bug*, which is a short story about the discovery of some treasure and the cracking of a code. The anonymous narrator of the story, which is told in the first person and clearly modeled on Poe himself, gives a short account of how to crack a simple code using character-frequency analysis, though this is of little value in trying to crack the codes in *The Beale Papers*. The other text is a great hoax Poe perpetrated on the gullible readers of *Burton's Gentlemen's Magazine*, in 1840. *The Journal of Julius Rodman* was billed as "an account of the first passage across the Rocky Mountains of North America ever achieved by civilized man." It ran for six months and fooled everyone until Poe stopped writing it when he did not get paid. Again, there are similarities between the apparent tale of a group of bold adventurers pitting themselves against the untamed wilderness of nineteenth-century America and the plucky band of heroes who went out west with Thomas Beale, but there the similarities end. There are no obvious sentences, or even clauses, that suggest any sort of overlap of authorship other than the themes; but then these were the common themes of the cheap and popular adventure fiction of the time.

Again, stylometrics is a useful tool here. If you compare the text from *The Journal of Julius Rodman*, *The Beale Papers* and the Beale letters, there are many similarities. If you compare word length, the result is striking:

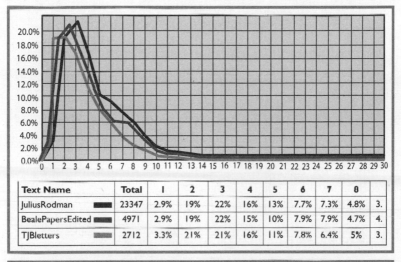

Text Name		Total	1	2	3	4	5	6	7	8	
JuliusRodman	▬	23347	2.9%	19%	22%	16%	13%	7.7%	7.3%	4.8%	3.
BealePapersEdited	▬	4971	2.9%	19%	22%	15%	10%	7.9%	7.9%	4.7%	4.
TJBletters	▬	2712	3.3%	21%	21%	16%	11%	7.8%	6.4%	5%	3.

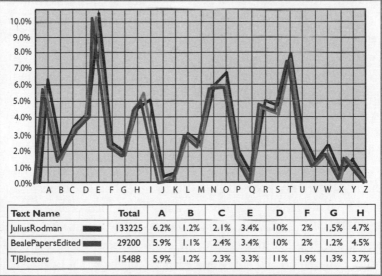

Text Name		Total	A	B	C	E	D	F	G	H
JuliusRodman	▬	133225	6.2%	1.2%	2.1%	3.4%	10%	2%	1.5%	4.7%
BealePapersEdited	▬	29200	5.9%	1.1%	2.4%	3.4%	10%	2%	1.2%	4.5%
TJBletters	▬	15488	5.9%	1.2%	2.3%	3.3%	11%	1.9%	1.3%	3.7%

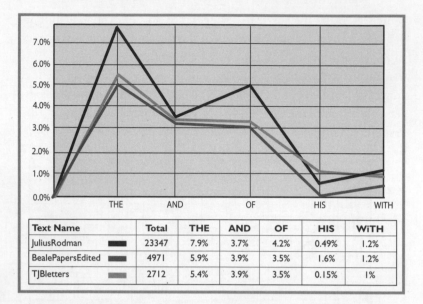

Text Name		Total	THE	AND	OF	HIS	WiTH
JuliusRodman	■■■	23347	7.9%	3.7%	4.2%	0.49%	1.2%
BealePapersEdited	■■■	4971	5.9%	3.9%	3.5%	1.6%	1.2%
TJBletters	■■■	2712	5.4%	3.9%	3.5%	0.15%	1%

If you strip out the texts and break them down by the frequency of each letter, the overlap is extraordinary.

The frequency with which several common words—"the," "and," "of," "his" and "with"—are used shows a similar pattern. The frequency of letters, length of sentences and use of common words are not matters over which a writer has a great deal of conscious control.

Dr. Millican remarks that "It is tempting to look at these graphs, conclude they are virtually identical, and hence that Poe wrote *The Beale Papers*."

However, there are two glitches. The first is demonstrated in the graph on page 185, which compares sentences by the pattern created by their length. Here, the three texts are not so rigid and there are wide variations between both parts of *The Beale Papers* and Edgar Allan Poe's story.

For the passionate advocates of the theory that Poe is the author, the results are disappointing. If you assume that *The Beale Papers* and the Beale letters had just one author and then compare them with *The Journal of Julius Rodman* and run the chi-square test, the results are not significant.[16] As Dr. Millican says, "There are too many assumptions and not enough data to conclude that Edgar Allan Poe is, or is not, the author of *The Beale Papers*."

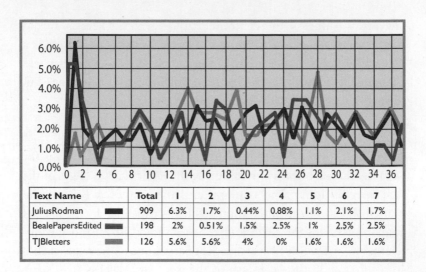

Text Name		Total	1	2	3	4	5	6	7
JuliusRodman		909	6.3%	1.7%	0.44%	0.88%	1.1%	2.1%	1.7%
BealePapersEdited		198	2%	0.51%	1.5%	2.5%	1%	2.5%	2.5%
TJBletters		126	5.6%	5.6%	4%	0%	1.6%	1.6%	1.6%

***

Of course, it could be that the two undeciphered codes are genuine ciphers that, when deciphered, will reveal that this was a hoax all along.

Nineteenth-century America was a golden age of mining scams. Historically, whenever the price of precious metals goes up, the number of scams increases; market demand is met by the creativity of the fraudster. As scams go, this one was fairly harmless.

Customers only lost 50¢, though the obsessive lost much more: their sanity. Knowing how gold fever can infect the gullible, the pamphlet does carry a clear warning, which is also a giveaway as to the true nature of *The Beale Papers*:

> Never, as I have done, sacrifice your own and your family's interests to what may prove an illusion; but, as I have already said, when your day's work is done, and you are comfortably seated by your good fire, a short time devoted to the subject can injure no one, and may bring its reward. By pursuing this policy, your interests will not suffer, your family will be cared for, and your thoughts will not be absorbed to the exclusion of other important affairs. With this admonition, I submit to my readers the papers upon which this narrative is founded.

Ward warns, "A short time devoted to the subject can injure no one," but cautions against devoting any more. This is as close to a lawyer's warning as any customer will ever get. There is an old American saying—often attributed to Mark Twain—that a mine is a hole in the ground with a liar at the top. In this case, the liar was charging 50¢ a time. The question is, which lies was he telling? But to answer that means cracking the code.

**

The third theory is that the mistakes are deliberate: there really is (or was) treasure and it was buried during the latter chaotic stages of the American Civil War. The assumption is that *The Beale Papers* were written shortly before publication (which is explained by the alleged anachronisms in the text) and that the gold, silver and jewelry referred to in *The Beale Papers* are just part of one of the many caches secreted away in the final days of the war. The belief is that many rich Confederates—fearful of losing out to the North—buried much of their wealth underground. Their motives were twofold. Like the rich in every war, they believed that their class would survive even if their side lost and they needed instantly available assets (gold, silver and jewelry) to start again. A more charitable explanation is that they were stashing funds to finance an ongoing war against the North. There is a potential third source for the gold—the theft and robbery that always takes place in the murderous chaos that forms the texture of everyday life in the dying days of any war. Whatever the motive or the source, the belief is that the anonymous writer of *The Beale Papers* was a key member of the Confederate cause and therefore wanted his fellow southerners to find the gold. It is an intriguing theory, but there is no real evidence to support it.

**

Over the decades, there have been several claims by people who believe they have found the treasure site. The most recent was a group who also say they located it having decoded the remaining ciphers.[17]

The plain text they get from cipher one is:

Last request of Thomas Jefferson Beale. Keep on persevering, the rewards awaiting you are so vast that you will find it hard to comprehend.

I know this final paper contradicts one prior, instructions are the entire amount in the vaults yours. All others have taken their shares, everyones in harmony. We will make this trip our final undertaking, We have been reassured by the President we will bring back an amount equal or better already shared. I leave no keys to unlock the three papers, it will take hard work to find the treasure. I've tried to make it impossible. Have given the Government and delivered amount same as we have taken.[18]

A thank you handshake is our receipt, the Treasurer of the United States accepted as taxes paid. Concluding: I have no living heirs.

The problem with this is that it does not fit in with any of the story that surrounds the original cipher, and there has to be a basic expectation that both the plain text and the rest of the narrative would at least match each other in content. Quite simply, it does not make any sense in the context of the story for Beale to have sent this letter.

And as for the location, they get a plain text that is significantly shorter than the cipher text and reads:

> Nineteen is the distance south, Left onto second point. Two's on first part of main rock south in east wall, Ground on souths six feet deep. Open front side of point straight down the point in front upper part. Remove rocks, Then with them remove dirt five feet down and round. On Now, Open point two's wall straight in, Now open south side, Now On down under point.

When they located the site (though I don't see quite how that is possible from this description), they found a cave with the remains of iron pots. Close, but no cigar. There are hundreds of caves all over the United States used over the last few hundred years by those seeking shelter in the wilderness.

The final word should go to the first man who used computers to try and crack these ciphers, Dr. Carl Hammer, who in 1971 was the vice-president of research at Sperry Rand UNIVAC. His position gave him access to what were then the world's most powerful computers. He concluded that there were cyclic patterns in the numbers, they were not random, but most likely text-encoded in the same manner as the decoded cipher two. Though he never broke the code, he had grim news for the army of treasure-hunters, saying that the name of the first one to crack the Beale code will never be known: "We will learn only the name of the second person to crack it—the one who follows directions to Beale's underground vault, and finds it empty."

The original treasure-hunter in *The Beale Papers* remarked, as he gave up, that he had no doubt that "Someone, through fortune or accident, will speedily solve their mystery and secure the prize which has eluded him."

This will not stop the continual caravan of treasure-hunters making the pilgrimage to the Blue Ridge Mountains, Virginia, all convinced that they will be the chosen one who will succeed where all have failed before.

CHAPTER 6

Dorabella "Ah, That Is Telling!" Number 36

> "The Enigma I will not explain—its 'dark saying' must be left unguessed."
>
> —Sir Edward Elgar, composer

July 14, 1897, "Forli," Malvern, Worcestershire

No major composer in the history of music was more interested in codes, ciphers and puzzles than Sir Edward Elgar. It is not just that he lived and breathed them. They informed every aspect of his life and his music. He is the enigma, a living cryptogram, always teasing and puzzling everyone who engaged with him—whether they were his close friends or his huge audience of listeners. He was his own score, setting himself, his life and his friends to music. His *Variations on an Original Theme (Enigma)* is *the* single composition that defines the fertile area where music and mathematics collide, with cryptography as the spice in the mix, holding it all together. For him, everything was redolent with meaning. The surface and the apparent, the clandestine and the encoded were all variations on the same interlocking theme.

Typical of the man is the address of one of the houses where he lived with his wife, Caroline Alice, and his daughter, Carice (Elgar's encoded amalgam of "Caroline Alice"). They lived in Wells Road, Malvern, and he called their house "Craeg Lea," a typical faux-Celtic, twilight-sounding name much loved by the owners of houses in

English lace-curtained suburbia, both then and now. But even this is not what it seems, being both an abbreviation and an anagram-based code for the people who live there: A (Alice), C (Carice) and E (Edward) plus ELGAR form the letters that make up "Craeg Lea." Here is a man who obsessively composes every detail of his life, always driven relentlessly on by a febrile mind that never does anything in half measures, least of all language, where he is often at his most playful. Typical is a letter he wrote to Ivor Atkins: "Mark ye, Firapeel, I waxe olde & dulle & glumme & sourmooded, bilious, excursive and dispertinent." As well as: "I wot well you are in merrie wise fallen on yr feste in Rams-hys-gate: albeit a fear, a parlous fear, holdes me, yr. true Friend, that you behave not altogether seemly in ye town. I finde ye annciente moode wearinge to ye penne, ye braine & to ye reader."

A huge and commanding figure, Edward Elgar never settles for the safe or the predictable. He is always craving the cerebral challenge, with cryptography giving him the intellectual excitement and mental fun he needs every day. This desperate need for wordplay is everywhere. On his manuscript for *The Dream of Gerontius*, instead of writing "DoG" as the shorthand, he writes "Dan," this being the name of the bulldog owned by George Sinclair that appears as a character in the "Eleventh Enigma Variation."

Edward Elgar was born in 1857, the fourth child of six, with three brothers and two sisters. This was stuffy Victorian England; his life mapped out for him from childhood. He was brought up in a village, Broadheath, three miles from Worcester in the West Midlands. His father owned a small music shop and supplemented his relatively meager income by tuning pianos, which in a pre-television era were widely owned in working-class and lower-middle-class families. Widespread ownership meant there was no shortage of work, but few of his customers were rich, so none of it paid well. In time, the young Edward could have expected to inherit the shop and continue Elgar & Sons but for his spectacular and incandescent musical ability, which catapulted him out of the rural backwaters of Midlands mediocrity on to the international stage. He started to learn the piano aged seven and then wrote his first piece—some incidental music called "Humoreske Broadheath"—for the school play when he was ten. He took up the violin two years later and wrote his first full composition, *Chantant*, when he was fifteen, before starting on his first symphony when he was twenty-one. Not quite Mozart but very impressive nonetheless.

Like many other composers, there were melodies and themes, sequences of notes and sounds in his head all the time, he himself remarking, "There is music in the air, music all around us, the world is full of it and you simply take as much as you require." In his pictures, he looks every inch the Edwardian gentleman, beautifully cut suit, stiff collar, handkerchief in his top pocket, huge mustache and clear, bright, twinkly eyes. Later in life, his neck is slightly bowed and he has the mournful, jowly appearance of one of his dogs, a classic example of the owner beginning to resemble the pet.

His mother converted to Catholicism shortly before he was born and he was brought up as a Roman Catholic in a rigidly dominant Protestant society, acutely aware that from birth he was blighted as an outsider. Truly gifted, he was an enigmatic blend of personality. He could be charismatic, charming and a fabulous friend, but he was also prone to self-doubt, intense shyness and feelings of being inept. He was often insecure in public situations and could be prickly, never forgetting his humble origins and once turning down an invitation to a very posh lunch with the brush-off line "You would not wish your board to be disgraced with the presence of a piano tuner's son and his wife."

He lived through two great eras of English history, the Victorian and then the Edwardian, both times of huge technological change but when the social order was buttoned down with a heavy reinforcement of social convention. The class structure was ironclad. Few married above or beneath them. Edward Elgar's wife, Alice, the daughter of a distinguished major general in the British Army, was one of the very few exceptions and had to resist the huge family pressure not to marry a shopkeeper's son, a man many rungs below her on the very carefully defined social ladder. Ironically, of course, he subsequently leapfrogs well above her in the social rankings, becoming England's greatest composer and a baronet, though for many this would still not have been enough. He would always be new money, easily dismissed by the aristocracy as a man who buys his own furniture.

He was also something of a non-conformist, who loved to tease and shock and ask the awkward questions, especially if there was a great joke to be had, knowing that with one outrageous remark or prank he could burst the over-inflated bubble of a pompous, thin-lipped, self-regarding society where place, perceived status and convention were more important than talent or ability.

Typical is a visit to the Worcester Dog Show, which has cleverly been sited in a hollow shortly before a huge thunderstorm so that when Elgar arrives with a friend, it is more like a shallow, muddy lake than a field. They pad round the duckboards before finding a tent full of handbag-sized dogs—those tiny bundles of wheezing fur that have long been the pet of choice for the airhead, whether it is supermodels today or, back in Edward Elgar's time, ladies who lunch and disapprove. Elgar spots a couple of society ladies, prim, perfect and proper, always on camera and consumed by a desire to be seen and admired by all decent people everywhere. From the moment he sees them, he has about as much control as a heat-seeking missile. He takes his friend, sidles over to them and, once within earshot, announces in a loud voice, "What a place to hold a dog show! Why don't they hold it in the cathedral and make *some* use of the place?" In a world where the Church and the local cathedral are at the apex of the social pecking order, this is a face-slapping remark, carrying a potency and irreverence barely imaginable today. He then saunters away, knowing he leaves them both scandalized and paralyzed.

Oh, the horror, the horror!

On the face of it, this sacrilegious behavior looks bizarre: after all, this was the man who wrote an oratorio about the Twelve Apostles and was inspired by them from an early age, believing that their faith was a model for him and that their inspiration would help him prevail. However, although he loved choral music, his faith slowly ebbed away and in later years he was at the agnostic end of the religious scale.

Edward Elgar is the quintessential English composer, whose *Pomp and Circumstance March No. 1*, better known as "Land of Hope and Glory," is the ultimate patriotic English stadium anthem, always sung with huge gusto at the Last Night of the Proms at the Royal Albert Hall. The tune will also be instantly recognizable to thousands of American graduates. In the U.S., it is known as "The Graduation Song," and hundreds of thousands have collected their degrees to its uplifting refrain. Elgar himself knew he had a tune that was going to be performed as long as there are musical instruments and people who wish to celebrate, saying, "I've got a tune that will knock 'em flat, knock 'em flat, a tune like that comes once in a lifetime!"

Initially, he was shunned by a rigid, class-shackled home audience who could not see what a gem they had in their midst. Ironically, it was a German, Richard Strauss, then regarded as the world's greatest living composer, who toasted him in 1902 as "one of the leaders of musical art of modern times, the first English progressive musician."

***

This, then, is the man who, aged forty, composes a short cipher to a young woman, Dora Penny. She is never able to decipher the letter. He never reveals the meaning and then takes the secret with him to his grave. The letter is dated July 14, 1897 and is one of two sent that day.

This is what the cipher looks like:

There are eighty-seven characters in all, and after the fifth character on the third line is a dot, which is so prominent it appears to be deliberate. This cryptogram looks like a simple substitution cipher, but it defies any classical letter-frequency analysis. The intriguing clue is the signature. His normal one looks like this:

Even more bewildering, the signature at the bottom of the Dorabella cipher is opened with what looks like a capital T, which is then followed by two very strange symbols: one of which looks like July and then what looks like "14.97." It looks remarkably like the number two in the signature below, from 1928, in which the two has an extra flourish on top. It is also very similar to the symbol that appears fifth from the right-hand side on the top row of the cipher.

Quite what all this means is not clear, but it does suggest that this may be some kind of alphanumeric cipher, one composed of letters and numbers, with the numbers then deciphering into letters.

One thing is certain: it is not chance. Elgar was a composer, precise in every detail. This is the man who wrote a part for a bass clarinet marked "*pp*," in which the player of this instrument matches, note for note, the brass and the woodwind for twenty bars or more but has to play it so softly that it cannot possibly be heard. When challenged, he pointed out that the player had a solo coming up and he wanted the instrument to be fully warmed up before taking center stage. Now that is the mark of a man obsessed with minutiae.

Edward Elgar is the man who propelled the word "enigma" into the national consciousness. His life and works are defined by the word "enigmatic," but there is so much about this tale of a middle-aged composer and a glamorous woman almost half his age that intrigues. In major part, this is because their relationship is so opaque and much of the story, as generally agreed, does not make much coherent sense.

The facts, as commonly presented, are these: Miss Dora Penny is the twenty-two-year-old daughter of the Reverend Alfred Penny, Rector of St. Peter's Church, Wolverhampton. She first meets the Elgars when her father marries Mary Frances Baker, of Hasfield, near Gloucester. Clearly a woman of some wealth, with her comes "a very substantial addition to the furniture line to our large rectory" and some new friends, including Edward and Alice Elgar.

This is Dora's account of their first meeting:

> Picture us now, my stepmother and me, tramming up to the station at Wolverhampton to meet them, on Friday, December 6, 1895. The train came in and, of course, not having seen one another for an age, the two friends fell upon each other and Mr. Elgar was left for me to look after. I quickly found out that music was the last thing he wanted to talk about. I think we talked about football. He wanted to know if I ever saw the Wolverhampton Wanderers play, and when he heard that our house was a stone's throw from their ground he was quite excited.

Wolverhampton Wanderers was one of the twelve founding clubs in the new Football League in 1888, mostly based in the northwest of England and the Midlands. Football (known as soccer in the U.S.) was just beginning, a working-class sport in which the players came from and genuinely represented their local areas.

Elgar, who is passionate about the area where he was born and brought up, has clearly got the football bug. Even better for him, he now has his wife and an attractive young woman to go to the matches with and a house nearby to visit for refreshments before and after the game. It's a wonderful image. England's greatest ever composer cheering on young men from his area as they represent their town, civic pride and regional spirit—all a far cry from the teams of overpaid mercenaries who today make up most professional football teams.

As well as football, Edward Elgar, Alice and the young Dora walk on the Malvern Hills, discuss map-reading, go horse-racing, attend concerts and fly kites. She becomes the official Elgar archivist and remains a close friend with both Edward and his wife until 1913, when she marries Richard Powell and the Elgars move to London. Throughout this period, the relationship is close, but she does not write about it until much later, in 1937. By this time, both Edward and his wife, Alice, are dead. He for three years, and she for seventeen.

Edward Elgar sends her the enciphered note on July 14, 1897, eighteen months after their first meeting, but she does not reveal it to the world until she includes a copy of it as an appendix to her book, where she added:

> It is well known that Elgar was always interested in puzzles, ciphers, cryptograms and the like. The cipher here reproduced—the third letter I had from him, if indeed it is one—came to me enclosed in a letter from Alice [Elgar's wife] to my stepmother. On the back of it is written "Miss Penny." It followed upon their visit to us at Wolverhampton in July 1897.
>
> I have never had the slightest idea what message it conveys; he never explained it and all attempts to solve it have failed. Should any reader of this book succeed in arriving at a solution, it would interest me very much to hear of it.[1]

In the second edition of the book, which was published ten years later in an extensively revised and enlarged version, there is an additional footnote: "Since the first edition of this book appeared, the cipher has, I know, been examined by a good few people skilled in such matters. Nobody, so far as I am aware, has yet succeeded in reading it." Had she been psychic, she would have added, "not now and not in the future."

As time goes by, a year after sending this letter to the young Dora, Elgar comes home one Friday night after teaching all day, something which is definitely not his favorite occupation. He does not mind it so much if the pupils are good, but when they are not he says it is like "turning a grindstone with a dislocated shoulder." To relax, he lights a cigar and sits down at the piano to play his wife a piece of music. In the finest tradition of appreciative listeners, she tells him to play it again, which he does, though this time changing it slightly. The "Enigma Variations" are born and will be performed two years later, establishing him as the preeminent composer of his generation.

The big question for everyone trying to break the eighty-seven symbols of the Dorabella cipher is whether this is a stand-alone or merely the overture to a much greater symphonic puzzle, the elusive meaning behind the "Enigma Variations," which form the second great mystery of Elgar's life.

Given his great love of practical jokes, there is always the possibility (as there is with all the unsolved codes and ciphers in this book) that this cipher is meaningless gibberish. But this possibility can be quickly discounted. His jokes had a purpose and to send out a series of scribbles to a young woman of whom he was clearly very fond, if not besotted, would not have had any value. There would have been no fun in it, either for him or her—only a huge face-losing let-down if he had to reveal to her that it was without meaning. Apart from anything else, in his own mind at least, he had given her all the clues she needed to solve it, but she did not realize what he was telling her.

Even more baffling is that though he was adept at puzzles, she was not. At the time Edward Elgar sent it, he was forty years old and Dora Penny was twenty-three. She died in 1964, but that does not mean that the key that unlocks the Dorabella cipher necessarily went with her to her grave. In theory, there must be something in their time together or something about her life that will provide the crucial leverage.

The relationship he had with the young Dora Penny is a real mystery. Elgar enjoyed the company of young women, and today, this sort of close friendship between a very prominent public figure and an attractive, much younger woman would not survive the crucible of the tabloid press. Having been seen at the football game with

Dora Penny, he would then be an easy paparazzi target when they were out flying kites or walking the Malvern Hills together.

Elgar clearly doted on his young female companion. He obviously wanted—maybe even needed—to send her a private message. Elsewhere, he was very flirtatious with her, sending her this message, enough to excite a prurient press, had it been made public. "Being a pennytential week [...] This is Xmas sirloinidly frivolous [...] & it put Dorabellissima so sweetly prettily." Subsequently, he also complained, "Oh! the fickleality of you," and in a letter of October 25, 1901, he asked her:

Whether you are as nice as

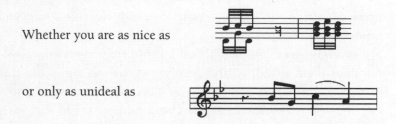

or only as unideal as

Two weeks later, he signed another letter to her using this as his signature, all of which suggests a far greater level of intimacy (at least on his part) than she owns up to in her account. Elgar clearly loved his wife, but this was a tough time for them both. They had gone to London so he could establish himself, but he had failed to make his mark and they had to return to Malvern. A humiliation for him and no doubt a triumph for her friends and relatives who had warned her against the marriage. They had one daughter, who by this time, 1899, was nine years old, but there had been no more children after her. Socially, Alice Elgar was trapped. If the close relationship her husband was enjoying with the young Dora Penny was anything more than friendship, then she would have been obliged to look the other way and be as brave as she could in public. This was a repressive era when women did not have the vote and divorce meant social ostracism. In 1920, there were less than six hundred divorces a year. To get divorced meant a public trial, with the tabloids relishing every gory detail. Regardless of who was guilty and who was innocent, it was a brutal ordeal, humiliating, expensive and terrifying. It was only for the truly desperate. If Dora Penny was his only such relationship, then it would not have aroused as much suspicion, but Elgar had similar liaisons with women both throughout his marriage and after the death of his wife. In the language of the time, they would be called his "muses"—close relationships with women that today would be regarded as affairs.

Before he was married, he was engaged to Helen Weaver, who broke off the engagement and emigrated to New Zealand, breaking his heart. He wrote to his friend, Charles Buck:

> I will not sorry you with particulars but must tell you that things have not prospered with me this year at all, my prospects are worse than ever & to crown my miseries my engagement is broken off & I am lonely. Perhaps at some future time I may come out of my shell again but at present I remain here; I have not the heart to speak to anyone.

Though he is always portrayed as a devoted husband, after he was married he was very close to a local teacher in Malvern called Rosa Burley. As well as Dora Penny, there was Lady Alice Stuart-Wortley (the "Windflower"), Lady Mary Lygon, an American woman called Julia Worthington and others. His love for younger women persisted into old age. Eleven years after the death of his wife, when he was well into his seventies, he took up with a young violinist in her thirties, Vera Hockman. They became delightfully close. He described her as "my mother, my child, my lover and my friend." In that charming way he had of immortalizing his intimates and his friends by their initials, she is V.H. in his sketches for his Third Symphony.

In Dora Penny's account, theirs was an entirely innocent relationship, but clearly it meant more to him than that. If it was just a casual social acquaintance, why go to the trouble of constructing a cipher that has defeated the best of the world's cryptographers since it was first published in 1937? The fact is that—apart from his wife and daughter—she was one of the most important women in his life.

***

The Enigma I will not explain—its "dark saying" must be left unguessed, and I warn you that the apparent connexion between the

Variations and the Theme is often of the slightest texture; further, through and over the whole set another and larger theme "goes," but is not played. So the principal theme never appears, even as in some late dramas, e.g. Maeterlinck's L'Intruse and Les Sept Princesses [...] the chief character is never on the stage.

The "Enigma Variations" was first played at St. James's Hall in London on June 19, 1899. The conductor was Dr. Hans Richter, and it was dedicated "to my friends pictured within." Elgar's program notes, which outlined the characters by initials only (C.A.E., H.D.S-P., R.B.T., W.M.B. and so on), did nothing to explain but plenty to excite a turn-of-the-century audience, for whom he was rapidly becoming the English composer of choice. In a single paragraph in the concert program, he launched a whole new branch of musicology, a place where historical detectives, gossips, treasure-hunters, cryptographers, musicians, critics and anyone else with a love of mystery can roam free.

This was his break-out hit, which plucked him from relative obscurity and set him on the road to becoming an international superstar. For some, the expression "dark saying" was a covert reference to his self-doubt. For others, this is Elgar at his most playful, anticipating that this short phrase was the hook into the popular imagination. Whatever his motivation or mental state, he did what every successful code- or cipher-creator did, before or since: when asked, he became ever more elliptical about the meaning of the "Enigma Variations." The more brittle his behavior and the ruder he became toward anyone who interrogated him on the subject, the more it excited the public's interest. As the gaps were slowly filled in, the premature claims of success were never far away and newspaper headlines proclaiming, "'Enigma Variations': Mystery Solved!" only served to ramp up the excitement and propel both the piece and Edward Elgar farther into the public imagination. As a piece of marketing it has rarely been surpassed. From the first time it was played, the speculation was intense. Even now, over a century later, it is still as strong.

Initially, *The Times*, the ultimate house newspaper for the movers rather than the shaken, moaned that they did not know the names behind the initials and the hunt was on. Elgar wrote to one of them, his publisher, August Jaeger, who features in the "Variations," telling him that he had written the "Variations" as he imagined his friends might have done "if they were asses enough to compose," a classically self-deprecating piece of English humor.

Finally, in 1928, Elgar himself went public, giving a partial account of the "friends pictured within," though he did not identify them all so that even now the enigma still manages to entice musical historians and critics, all with their eyes on the two elusive prizes: the meaning of the "Enigma Variations" and the plain text behind the letter to Dora Penny.

Elgar himself told Dora Penny that she above all should be able to decipher the code. The search for clues has therefore focused on these two areas, the letter and the "Enigma Variations," with the latter offering potentially the richest seam. What was it about Dora Penny that made her so important to him that he celebrated her in the same élite group that made up his most intimate friends? If there is a key to understanding the enigma, then this is the most likely place where it will be concealed.

In all, fourteen people and a dog are featured in the "Variations," including the young woman who had received the ciphered letter two years before. In order to decipher the covert meaning behind the "Enigma Variations," it is first necessary to see who is included and why.

The "First Variation" is C.A.E. This is Caroline Alice Elgar, his greatest supporter and about whom he wrote, "There is no break between the theme and this movement. The variation is really a prolongation of the theme with what I wished to be romantic and delicate additions; those who knew C.A.E. will understand this reference to one whose life was a romantic and delicate inspiration." She was not only a devoted Edwardian wife, but his greatest supporter and the one who constantly pushed him out of his bleak periods of self-doubt.

The "Second Variation" is H.D.S.-P. Hew David Steuart-Powell was an early friend when Elgar was learning his craft playing in small orchestras and ensembles in his home area. He was a well-known local amateur pianist who would "warm up" before a performance with finger-loosening exercises, which Elgar parodies saying, "His characteristic diatonic run over the keys before beginning to play is here humorously travestied in the semi-quaver passages; these should suggest a Toccata, but chromatic beyond H.D.S.-P.'s liking."

The "Third Variation" is R.B.T., Richard Baxter Townsend, an old friend and one of several eccentrics in Elgar's life who brought out the most playful aspects of his character. He was distinctive-looking, with bright-red cheeks, turquoise-blue eyes and gray hair. He rode everywhere on a bike, but being slightly deaf, he invented a continuously ringing bell to warn others of his approach. His life was rich and full, one of those empire-building Englishmen who do not understand the concept of a problem but see only a series of character-building challenges. He was a cattle rancher and gold prospector in Texas and Colorado, where he became a first-class rifle shot and met Billy the Kid in New Mexico. His life on the range is recorded in great detail in the very popular *Tenderfoot* books, which are now something of a collector's item.[2] He was a fanatical golfer and played with Elgar. He was an actor and great mimic, with a very high-pitched speaking voice, parodied here. As Elgar put it, "the low voice flying off occasionally into 'soprano' timbre. The oboe gives a somewhat pert version of the theme, and the growing grumpiness of the bassoons is important."

The "Fourth Variation" is W.M.B., William Meath Baker. In Elgar's words, he was "a country squire, gentleman and scholar." He was a compulsive organizer, and this variation "was written after the host had, with a slip of paper in his hand, *forcibly* read out the arrangements for the day and hurriedly left the music-room with an inadvertent bang of the door. In bars 15—24 are some suggestions of the teasing attitude of the guests."

The "Fifth Variation," R.P.A., is Richard Penrose Arnold, the son of the poet and historian Matthew Arnold. He was, like Elgar, self-taught and a great wit, represented here by "much light-hearted badinage among the wind instruments."

The "Sixth Variation," Ysobel, is Isabel Fitton, a viola player and one of Elgar's pupils. Her variation is based on a beginner's exercise called crossing the strings, "a pensive and, for a moment, romantic movement."

The "Seventh Variation," Troyte, is Arthur Troyte Griffith, a local architect and largely failed pianist, who believed his variation depicted a time when he and Elgar were caught in a thunderstorm. Sadly for him, it was much less fun:

> The uncouth rhythm of the drums and lower strings was really suggested by some maladroit essays to play the pianoforte; later the strong rhythm suggests the attempts of the instructor (E.E.) to make something like order out of chaos, and the final despairing "slam" records that the effort proved to be in vain.

The "Eighth Variation," W.N., is Winifred Norbury, one of Elgar's neighbors and, unlike Troyte, a very good pianist. He would often try out his compositions with her; she would play the piano, and he the violin. To use Elgar's word, she was "gracious."

The "Ninth Variation," Nimrod, is named after August Johannes Jaeger, one of his closest friends and an editor at his music publisher, Novello. The name "Nimrod" is a classic Elgar pun. In biblical and ancient myth, he is a mighty hunter and "Jaeger" is German for "hunter." Here, the variation is based on a specific event, a summer walk one evening when they discussed how Beethoven was the best at the slow movement.

The "Tenth—and cryptologically most significant—Variation" is Dorabella, which is Dora Penny, here nicknamed "Dorabella" after the character from Mozart's *Così fan Tutte*. According to Elgar's notes, it is an intermezzo, a transition piece between two others. "The movement suggests a dance-like lightness" to which he added, ever mysteriously, "The inner sustained phrases at first on the viola and later on the flute should be noted." Once again, he was enigmatic about the nature of their relationship and what she meant to him.

The "Eleventh Variation" is G.R.S., George Robertson Sinclair, the organist at Hereford Cathedral. Initially, there was much speculation that this was about his style of playing, but Elgar dismissed this, saying it had "nothing to do with organs or cathedrals." It was all about his bulldog, Dan. The first bar is him falling down the bank into the River Wye, the next two bars are him paddling upstream to find a landing place, followed by his rejoicing bark. Sinclair had challenged Elgar to set this incident to music, so he did. An alternative view is that Elgar, who loved the coded pun, was alluding here to the German composer Johann Sebastian Bach.

The "Twelfth Variation," B.G.N., is Basil G. Nevinson, one of Elgar's lifelong and closest friends, and a cellist who played in the same trio with Elgar on violin and Steuart-Powell on piano.

With the final two variations, Elgar takes us back into an opaque world of code and mystery.

The "Thirteenth Variation" is represented by *** and he declined ever to name her directly. All he said was that "The asterisks take the place of the name of a lady who was, at the time of the composition, on a sea voyage. The drums suggest the distant throb of the engines of a liner, over which the clarinet quotes a phrase from Mendelssohn's *Calm Sea and Prosperous Voyage*."

Various candidates have been suggested. Lady Mary Lygon is one favorite, along with Helen Weaver, his ex-fiancée. Another suggestion is his American friend Julia Worthington. This variation is warm and romantic, and hints at another side of Elgar and his clandestine feelings for women outside his marriage. Writing something like this for a former lover shows that he was relatively insensitive to his wife's feelings and adds to the circumstantial evidence that his relationship with Dora Penny was more than just social acquaintance.

The "Fourteenth Variation," E.D.U., is Elgar himself; "Edoo" being his wife's nickname for him. In his words it is:

> bold and vigorous in general style. Written at a time when friends were dubious and generally discouraging as to the composer's musical future, this variation is merely to show what E.D.U. (a paraphrase of a fond name) intended to do. References made to Var. I (C.A.E.) and to Var. IX (Nimrod), two great influences on the life and art of the composer, are entirely fitting to the intention of the piece.

The great mystery, the hidden Elgar code, is what is the clandestine enigma that lurks somewhere here? Ever since it was first performed, there have been many suggestions.

Inevitably, some have argued that it was yet another of Elgar's practical jokes and there is nothing hidden here—what better tease could there be than to send people looking for something that does not exist? This can be discounted. Troyte Griffith, one of those featured, guessed that it was "God Save the King" but was sharply rebuffed by Elgar in 1924, who told him, "No, of course not, but it is so well known that it is extraordinary that no one has found it." Troyte was one of his best friends, and though Elgar liked to tease, there is nothing in his history that suggests he would tell a lie directly to someone this close to him. More important, he told his daughter, Caroline Alice, that there was a tune, which she confirmed in a letter to Dora Penny in 1942. Dora Penny's husband, Richard Powell, suggested "Auld Lang Syne" as the hidden melody and "friendship" as the theme.

Throughout the 1950s, the Americans joined the hunt for the tune, suggesting, "Una Bella Serenata" from *Così fan Tutte*, Bach's "Agnus Dei," Beethoven's Piano Sonata Op. 13 (Pathétique), Purcell's "When I Am Laid In Earth" and Sullivan's "None Shall Part Us From Each Other." Yet more suggestions include "Home Sweet Home," "All Through the Night," "For He's a Jolly Good Fellow," "Pop Goes the Weasel," "Ta-ra-ra-boom-de-ay" and Chopin's G minor Nocturne.

Anyone wishing to break this code should consider a couple of clues. The first is that there are only thirteen friends represented, not fourteen, the final one being Elgar himself. The other is the program note itself. Though Elgar made up nonsense words, he was very precise in his public utterances, especially anything written down in his name. This was his great marketing moment, and like any great advertising slogan, every word counts. In the introduction, he writes not of a tune or melody but of a "larger theme" in counterpoint with the musical theme *and* with each of the variations. Some argue that the enigma here is not a tune but something else in his life—and if this is the case, then the most obvious question is whether the "Enigma Variations" are in fact him and his life.

In the end, we ourselves are the sum of the people we are close to. Elgar recognized this and chose those people who had most informed his everyday existence. In this scenario, the "Thirteenth

Variation," ***, would not be one but all the women he loved. As he says in the final sentence of the program, "The whole of the work is summed up in the triumphant, broad presentation of the theme in the major."

This would explain why he could not bear to reveal the secret to anyone, why it was so obvious to him but not to any of them—not even to his wife, his daughter or to Dora Penny, the three women he was closest to for longest. Many years later, Dora asked him about the secret of the "Enigma Variations." His reply was predictably enigmatic: "I thought that you, of all people, would guess it."

CHAPTER 7

"This Is the Zodiac Speaking ... "

"So now I have a little list."

—Gilbert and Sullivan, *The Mikado*

Southern California, June 4, 1963

A sweltering-hot summer day, tempered only by the sea breezes from the Pacific Ocean. On a remote beach in Gaviota Park (meaning "seagull," a name given to the area by the Spanish in 1769), two students from nearby Lompoc High School are taking part in Senior Ditch Day, an annual ritual of lazing about on the beach for a day before graduation.

The young couple are straight from the central casting department of every Hollywood nostalgia movie trying to recapture a previous golden age. This is the early 1960s, and America has a glamorous young president, Jack Kennedy, in the White House. The Korean War is a convenient memory, and few have yet heard of Vietnam. Though it is already costing U.S. taxpayers over $1 million a day, the war has not really registered on the domestic radar. For most young Americans, it is still just a small country far away. By the time the Zodiac finishes his killing spree, the war in Southeast Asia will have tainted every U.S. community. Over fifty thousand young American men will be dead, and seventy thousand will be severely crippled.

Their school photographs are the epitome of early-1960s, pre-hippy, high-school America. Robert Domingos, eighteen, is a classic-looking all-American college boy. He is handsome, strong-jawed and has the contemporary fashionable hairstyle of choice, a flat-top crew-cut. His clothes are smart—neat jacket, white shirt, dark tie, a uniform of respectability and reassurance ready to take him into the adult word. His fiancée, Linda Kaye Edwards, seventeen, carries the regulation beehive haircut loved by teenage girls across America. Her clothes are smart and preppy, her smile demure but knowing. For everyone who knows them, they are an idyllic teenage couple, laughing together, carefree and very much in love.

That afternoon, they separate themselves from the others, finding a remote spot along the rocky beach where they can be alone and unseen. With eyes only for each other, they lie in the soft sand, enjoying the afternoon heat, as the waves come into shore.

But they are not alone.

As they walk down to the beach, a hunter is following them.

In the bushes above, a heavily armed man is looking for human prey.

His weapons of choice are a knife and a .22-caliber semi-automatic, loaded with his favorite ammunition—Super X copper-coated bullets. Apart from his killing weapons, he also carries some pre-cut pieces of rope; crucial accoutrements for the humiliating ritual he is about to force on his young victims. The plan is detailed, precise. He has gone through it over and over in his head a hundred times or more and knows exactly what he is going to do. He sneaks up on them and confronts them at gunpoint, giving Linda Edwards some rope. He orders her to tie her boyfriend. But as her hands are shaking, he escapes and they run.

But this is exactly what the hunter wants.

He shoots Domingos in the back, eleven times in all, and then shoots Edwards nine times, each bullet fired into her chest. He drags the bodies about 11 yards to a makeshift shack. He pulls Linda Edwards's body on top of Domingos's, cutting the shoulder straps to her bathing suit and baring her breasts. He then collects the bullet casings and places them with the bodies, along with the rope. The final stage in his plan is to set fire to the shack using matches, but—and this will not be the only time—his planning fails. He has not brought any fuel to ignite the fire and he cannot get the flames started.

He then leaves.

***

Ever since 1963, this murder has baffled successive generations of police detectives and other investigators. It remains unsolved, even though the murderer left plenty of clues. What makes it even more chilling is that this killing on a Californian beach in broad daylight is not an isolated incident. It was followed by a string of similar murders over the next ten years. The killer was obsessed with his brand image, giving himself a name, the Zodiac (beginning his letters, "This is the Zodiac speaking ..."), and a logo—a circle with larger lines through it, like the crosshairs of a rifle sight:

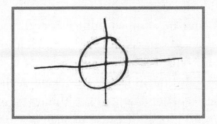

As with other unprosecuted serial killers, his legend has grown ever since he first terrorized southern California in the 1960s and early 1970s. Inevitably, there are other murders attributed to him, as well as killings he claimed but which he may not have committed, and this makes the total body count difficult to state with any certainty. The total death toll from his murder spree is at least seven, probably nine, but could be any number between ten (a number he claimed early on in his killing spree) and several dozen—thirty-seven being his final claim. This final figure is plausible as there were a large number of similar but unsolved murders and unexplained disappearances in California during the period in which the Zodiac was operating. However, some of these may be copycat killings. For the millions who are interested in serial killers, the Zodiac has some tantalizing links to another, even more gruesome psychopath who was killing at the same time: Charles Manson. Such is the potency of the Zodiac brand—and plagiarism being the sincerest form of flat-tery—that he has twice been copied by other serial killers, both of whom took his name and logo.

The first copyist began killing more than twenty years after the Zodiac had begun to terrorize southern California. The second was on the other side of the world.

In November 1989, the New York Police received a letter with the Zodiac's familiar call sign ("This is the Zodiac speaking ...") warning that he would kill twelve times, once for each sign of the zodiac. Seven years later, he had killed three and went on to shoot a further six before he was arrested after an armed siege at the home of his half-sister, Gladys "Chachi" Reyes. Heriberto "Eddie" Seda con-fessed and was sentenced to eighty-three and a half years in prison.[1] But this is not the same Zodiac who had terrorized southern California three decades earlier.

In the years after he stopped killing, the Zodiac's reputation grew. By the late 1990s he was not just a national brand. He had gone global. While Seda was awaiting trial in New York, another Zodiac popped up, this time in Japan. This being the home of *manga* comics and hyper-realistic violence, the killings were shocking in their brutality, even more so because of their location—Kobe, an attractive and prosperous city on the coast, west of Tokyo.

In February 1997, a sadistic killer starts mutilating cats. But these are just a taste of what is to come. He leaves their bodies at the same locations where he then brutally attacks young girls with a hammer. In March, he repeatedly stabs a ten-year-old girl in the head before killing her with a length of steel pipe. Less than an hour later, he stabs a nine-year-old boy, who survives, though he nearly bleeds to death. The crime scene is daubed with the familiar circle and cross, first seen in California over thirty years before. Two months later, a janitor finds a plastic bag at the gates to the school where he works. Inside is the severed head of a local eleven-year-old mentally retarded boy. Stuffed in his mouth is a message written in red ink, along with the Zodiac's icon. Later that day, the boy's headless body is found under a house in the woods near the school. The police subsequently catch a fifteen-year-old youth. In his room, they find weapons, a journal and "a book about the San Francisco killings."[2]

The original Zodiac has cast a very long shadow, which is not that surprising as he was guaranteed immortality through the film *Dirty Harry*, released in 1971.

One of the Zodiac's real-life letters carried a truly chilling threat: "School children make nice targ-ets, I think I shall wipe out a school bus some morning, just shoot out the frunt tire + then pick off the kiddies as they come bouncing out." This threat is then used to brilliant and frightening cinematic effect by the actor Andrew Robinson before he is brought to justice by Inspector Harry Callahan, played by Clint Eastwood, with one of the most famous speeches in any cop movie:

> I know what you're thinking: "Did he fire six shots or only five?" Well, to tell you the truth, in all this excitement I've kinda lost track myself. But being this is a .44 Magnum, the most powerful handgun in the world, and would blow your head clean off, you've got to ask yourself one question: "Do I feel lucky?" Well, do ya, punk?[3]

Typical of other serial killers, the Zodiac loved to taunt the authorities, using his letters to the newspapers as a platform for his routine denigration of the police and their inability to catch him ("Hey pig doesnt it rile you up to have your noze rubed in your boo-boos?"). But in one aspect he is unique among serial killers: he also sent ciphers to the newspapers. The Zodiac was a man obsessed with codes and hidden meanings. He planned his killings with meticulous care and no doubt chose his name with the same diligence. He was also interested, if not obsessed, with all matters astrological. His encryption system was unique, a mixture of English capital letters, some of which were reversed, plus other symbols. He also employed a series of strange symbols as cipher-text representations of plain-text letters, some of which (the inverted V and a V filled in) were in common use by American newspaper typesetters at the time. He numbered his pages in the manner used in print works. The first page in a sequence of three is numbered "1/3," the second "2/3" and so on, a common technique used at the time by newspaper typesetters so they would not miss any pages in the sequence.[4] One of the ciphers sent by the Zodiac to newspapers has been solved, but three have not.

As with the other unsolved ciphers, any attempt to solve them will require an all-encompassing holistic approach. More than any other cipher, this is about the mental state of the man who sent them, and to solve them means sifting every area of his activities for clues. The ciphers themselves are fascinating and reveal much of the man, though here—again, as with many unsolved ciphers—the raw evidence is often contradictory, which just serves to make them even more treacherously seductive.

The Zodiac's writings are laced with spelling mistakes, both in the ciphers themselves ("forrest," "dangeroue," "experence," "thae," "paradice" and "sloi") as well as in the letters he writes in plain text ("origionaly," "frunt," "fireing," "thashing," "cene," "raceing," "shabbly," "christmass," "epasode," "silowets," "pencel" and "darck"). Are these evidence of dyslexia, low intelligence, poor education, a combination of these, or are they a deliberate ploy to confuse investigators? Even more exotic, can the extra and the missing letters be taken together to mean something new?

The Zodiac's first cipher was cracked in a few days by a pair of gifted amateurs, but the subsequent encoded messages got increasingly fiendish to solve as his behavior became more erratic, almost schizophrenic. On the one hand, he took ever bigger risks and left ever more clues behind, such as fingerprints. But on the other, he used more and more complex code systems to cover his identity. However, they do have one thing in common: they served to humiliate his enemies, "the blue pigs" as he called the police.

The murders—especially those that are definitely his and those he claims to have carried out—need to be scoured in detail for clues. Even those killings that are only on the "possible" list deserve some examination. Lurking in the fine detail may be a crucial clue—both as to the meaning of the ciphers and the psychological profile of the man who wrote them.

The double murders in 1963 of the young lovers Robert Domingos and his fiancée, Linda Kaye Edwards, set the tone of much that is to follow, which is why many investigators suspect that this was the first murder carried out by the Zodiac.

There are several key characteristics that define it as the work of the Zodiac. First, there is the choice of victims—two young lovers in a remote spot where they are especially vulnerable. They choose this spot so they cannot easily be seen, a double-edged sword as it means that the Zodiac is unlikely to be seen either. Second, this appears to be a motiveless killing. He does not steal from them and, apart from cutting Edwards's bathing-suit straps, there is nothing of a sexual nature here. This pattern is repeated in all the killings attributed to him. Third, he stalks his victims. This killing is essentially opportunistic. Had the young lovers not separated themselves from the others, he could not have risked shooting them. And fourth, there is meticulous planning: the pieces of rope are pre-cut, he has both a gun and a knife, and he is heavily armed, in all hitting them with twenty bullets, a very high number for any murder. He may well have fired more rounds and missed. And finally, though the planning is meticulous and he has clearly rehearsed it many times in his head beforehand, things go wrong. He probably intended to burn the bodies, but he had not brought enough material to make a fire.

Less than a year after he killed Domingos and Edwards, there was another, remarkably similar double murder.

February 5, 1964. Joyce and Johnny Swindle, a young couple, both twenty, go for an early-evening walk by the Pacific Ocean near their home in San Diego. He is training to be a radio operator at the nearby U.S. Navy base, and they tend to keep to themselves, spending much of their days alone in their apartment, apart from a regular early-evening walk to get a cup of coffee each at a local café called the Sandy Dollar. As with the double murder the previous year, the Zodiac's planning is meticulous. He hides in darkness behind some concrete. The caliber of weapon used is the same and may well be the same gun, a .22 Remington rifle model 550-1. He fires two shots into Joyce Swindle's chest. After she has fallen and Johnny Swindle is leaning over her, he fires two more rounds, hitting him in the leg and then in the head. He fires twice more, missing both times. He then walks over and shoots them both in the head at very close range.

More than two years pass before there is another murder linked to the Zodiac, this time a single woman.

October 30, 1966. Cheri Jo Bates is a pretty eighteen-year-old student who works at the local bank to pay her way through college. Late that Sunday afternoon, she goes to the college library. At 5 feet 3 inches and weighing just 108 pounds, she is tiny, just half the weight of the man tampering with her car. While she is in the library, her killer removes the leads to the distributor cap, making it impossible for her to start her car and giving him the perfect excuse to talk to her. Who could resist the offer of help from a kindly stranger? She leaves the library at 9 p.m. and is dead within hours. As with the other killings, there is no motive, either financial or sexual. Though the killer stabs her repeatedly, she puts up a terrific fight. The following morning, the area where she was killed looks like a plowed field and the local pathologist finds fragments of the killer's hair and skin under her fingernails.

Though this murder is now often considered to be the Zodiac, the local police do not attribute it to him, remaining convinced that it is a local boy who knows her. But despite taking him in for questioning, they never manage to build a credible case—a typical pattern of police behavior in murder cases worldwide. They get an *idée fixe* and nothing—certainly not anything as old-fashioned as evidence—will shake them.

A month after Cheri Jo Bates's death, the *Riverside Press-Enterprise* received a letter, dated November 29, 1966, which was clearly written either by her killer or by someone very close to the case. Whichever it was, the writer had detailed and intimate knowledge of the incident ("I first cut the middle wire from the distributor") that was not in the public domain. The letter had been rendered untraceable by a simple but clever ruse. In an age before computers, typists made multiple copies by putting a sheet of paper under the original with a sheet of carbon paper in between. Several copies could be made at the same time, but each successive layer becomes more smudged and more indistinct, making it impossible to identify the specific typewriter used. Many investigators doubt that this letter is the work of the killer who will emerge later as the

Zodiac: it is typed and his subsequent letters are handwritten, and there are relatively few spelling mistakes. The alternative view is that this is the Zodiac in his original and coherent manifestation: the subsequent spelling mistakes are deliberate, and the progressive deterioration in his communications reflects the growing imbalance of his already fragile sanity.

The letter read:

> SHE WAS YOUNG AND BEAUTIFUL BUT NOW SHE IS BATTERED AND DEAD. SHE IS NOT THE FIRST AND SHE WILL NOT BE THE LAST I LAY AWAKE NIGHTS THINKING ABOUT MY NEXT VICTIM. MAYBE SHE WILL BE THE BEAUTIFUL BLOND THAT BABYSITS NEAR THE LITTLE STORE AND WALKS DOWN THE DARK ALLEY EACH EVENING ABOUT SEVEN. OR MAYBE SHE WILL BE THE SHAPELY BRUNETT THAT SAID XXX NO WHEN I ASKED HER FOR A DATE IN HIGH SCHOOL. BUT MAYBE IT WILL NOT BE EITHER. BUT I SHALL CUT OFF HER FEMALE PARTS AND DEPOSIT THEM FOR THE WHOLE CITY TO SEE. SO DON'T MAKE IT TO EASY FOR ME. KEEP YOUR SISTERS, DAUGHTERS, AND WIVES OFF THE STREETS AND ALLEYS. MISS BATES WAS STUPID. SHE WENT TO THE SLAUGHTER LIKE A LAMB. SHE DID NOT PUT UP A STRUGGLE. BUT I DID. IT WAS A BALL. I FIRST CUT THE MIDDLE WIRE FROM THE DISTRIBUTOR. THEN I WAITED FOR HER IN THE LIBRARY AND FOLLOWED HER OUT AFTER ABOUT TWO MINUTES. THE BATTERY MUST HAVE BEEN ABOUT DEAD BY THEN. I THEN OFFERED TO HELP. SHE WAS THEN VERY WILLING TO TALK TO ME. I TOLD HER THAT MY CAR WAS DOWN THE STREET AND THAT I WOULD GIVE HER A LIFT HOME. WHEN WE WERE AWAY FROM THE LIBRARY WALKING, I SAID IT WAS ABOUT TIME. SHE ASKED ME, "ABOUT TIME FOR WHAT?" I SAID IT WAS ABOUT TIME FOR HER TO DIE. I GRABBED HER AROUND THE NECK WITH MY HAND OVER HER MOUTH AND MY OTHER HAND WITH A SMALL KNIFE AT HER THROAT. SHE WENT VERY WILLINGLY. HER BREAST FELT WARM AND VERY FIRM UNDER MY HANDS, BUT ONLY ONE THING WAS ON MY MIND. MAKING HER PAY FOR ALL THE BRUSH OFFS THAT SHE HAD GIVEN ME DURING THE YEARS PRIOR. SHE DIED HARD. SHE SQUIRMED AND SHOOK AS I CHOCKED HER, AND HER

LIPS TWICHED. SHE LET OUT A SCREAM ONCE AND I KICKED
HER IN THE HEAD TO SHUT HER UP. I PLUNGED THE KNIFE
INTO HER AND IT BROKE. I THEN FINISHED THE JOB BY CUT-
TING HER THROAT. I AM NOT SICK. I AM INSANE. BUT THAT
WILL NOT STOP THE GAME. THIS LETTER SHOULD BE PUB-
LISHED FOR ALL TO READ IT. IT JUST MIGHT SAVE THAT GIRL
IN THE ALLEY. BUT THAT'S UP TO YOU. IT WILL BE ON YOUR
CONSCIENCE. NOT MINE. YES, I DID MAKE THAT CALL TO
YOU ALSO. IT WAS JUST A WARNING. BEWARE ... I AM STALK-
ING YOUR GIRLS NOW.

> CC. CHIEF OF POLICE
> ENTERPRISE

The envelope was written by hand with a felt-tip pen in a style
that the Zodiac would later use. It read:

> Daily Enterprise
> Riverside Calif
> Attn: Crime

Five months later, a poem was found in a desk in the storage
area of the college that Cheri Jo Bates had attended. It was signed
"r h," all lower-case lettering. The poem read:

> Sick of living/unwilling to die
> cut.
> clean.
> if red /
> clean.
> blood spurting,
> dripping,
> spilling;
> all over her new
> dress
> oh well
> it was red
> anyway.
> life draining into an
> uncertain death.
> she won't

die.
this time
someone ll find her.
just wait till
next time

Four years later, after the police in California had amassed a small collection of Zodiac correspondence, a handwriting expert at the California Bureau of Criminal Identification said it was a match: this brutal piece of verse was written by the same hand who wrote the Zodiac letters and killed at least seven more. And just to close the circle, the Zodiac then linked himself with this murder when he wrote to the *San Francisco Chronicle*, telling them, "I do have to give them [the police and journalists who had worked on this case] credit for stumbling across my riverside activity, but they are only finding the easy ones, there are a hell of a lot more down there."

Less than two years after the Cheri Jo Bates murder, the Zodiac struck again. This time it was a double killing, which resonated with the early double homicide of Robert Domingos and Linda Edwards some five years before.

December 20, 1968. Betty Lou Jensen, aged just sixteen, is out on her first date with a local boy, David Arthur Faraday, who is a year older. They drive in a brown two-ton Rambler station wagon to a remote spot at a gravel parking area on Lake Herman Road, just outside Vallejo, California. Vallejo has the west coast's first shipyard, the souvenirs of which are to be found even today in the attractive Victorian houses lining the waterfront shoreline. The community is assured and prosperous, and even today, many are still shocked about what happened next.

At about 11:15 p.m., the killer approaches. He fires a single shot, hitting Faraday in the back of the head. It does not kill him instantly; he dies subsequently in the hospital. As with the previous murder on the beach, the woman runs, and he shoots her five times in her upper back, the bullets hitting her in a close pattern. She dies immediately. The bullets are the same as those used in the Domingos-Edwards murder—Super X copper-coated bullets—and the weapon is a J. C. Higgins semi-automatic.

As with the other double murders, there is no sexual or financial motive—other than the obvious one of raw, mind-bending, soul-destroying jealousy that others are enjoying what (presumably) he cannot. There is no mocking phone call afterward (a sometime Zodiac trait), but years later, when he claims credit for this double murder, he provides much detail that is not in the public domain and could only be known by the killer.[5]

The following summer, the Zodiac struck again at what is by now a familiar target—young lovers, parked in the sort of remote spot that is generally nicknamed "Lovers' Lane."

July 4, 1969. Darlene Ferrin, aged twenty-two, is a waitress, married for a second time after divorcing her first husband, who she said was lazy and violent toward her. But the man in the car is not her second husband. Instead, it is a nineteen-year-old local laborer, Mike Mageau. It is just after 11 p.m., roughly the same time as the killing the year before. The young couple stop in a secluded area of Blue Rock Springs Park ("to talk"). A light-brown car approaches (similar to the vehicle seen leaving previous murder scenes). Thinking it is the police, they get their identification cards ready, but instead the man in the dark opens fire, shooting five times into the car before returning to his vehicle. Though he has proved to be a deadly shot in the past, on this occasion his marksmanship is not as good. As he walks away, he hears moaning from the car. He returns, shooting each of them twice more, killing Darlene Ferrin, but amazingly, Mike Mageau survives.

This murder is the pivotal event in the Zodiac series. Forty minutes afterward, the Zodiac calls the local police. The detail is precise and accurate: he correctly describes the weapon used (a 9-millimeter handgun), the location and the number of victims, and he also claims credit for the Jensen-Faraday murders. Despite claiming four murders, the police report puts the motive down as "Jealousy/Revenge," but after a few weeks, there are no arrests and the police investigation is going nowhere until there is the breakthrough, which will take these murders from the status of local murders to ones that achieve international status in the annals of modern crime.

On July 31, 1969, the Zodiac writes three linked letters to the newspapers, using a similar code system. Much of the detail in them was not in the public domain at this time, confirming him as the killer. But this is not all: each letter has a cipher attached. The first is to the local paper, the *Vallejo Times Herald*, the second to the *San Francisco Examiner*, and the third to the *San Francisco Chronicle*. The local police send them off to the professionals at the National Security Agency, Naval Intelligence, the CIA and the FBI.

The basic letter reads:

> Dear Editor
>
> I am the killer of the 2 teenagers last Christmass at Lake Herman and the Girl last 4th of July. [This would be Darlene Ferrin. By now the killer would have known that Mike Mageau had survived despite being shot four times at relatively close range.] To Prove this I shall state some facts which only I + the police know.
>
> Christmass
> 1 Brand name of ammo Super X
> 2 10 shots fired
> 3 Boy was on back feet to car
> 4 Girl was lyeing on right side feet to west
>
> 4th of July
> 1 Girl was wearing patterned pants
> 2 Boy was also shot in knee
> 3 Brand name of ammo was Western
> Here is a cyipher or that is part of one. The other 2 parts of this cipher have been mailed to the S.F. Examiner + the S.F. Chronicle.
>
> I want you to print this cipher on your frunt page by Fry Afternoon Aug 1-69, If you do not do this I will go on a kill rampage Fry night that will last the whole week end. I will cruse around and pick off all stray people or coupples that are alone then move on to kill some more untill I have killed over a dozen people.

The letter to the *Examiner* is similar, but the one to the *Chronicle* also raises the level of the challenge, claiming that "In this cipher is my identity." Interestingly, he correctly uses the word "cipher" rather than the more common "code," suggesting at least a passing understanding of the dark arts.

Taken together, the ciphers read:

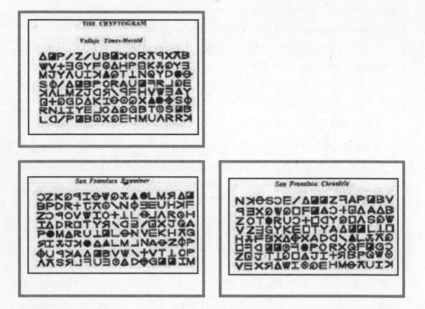

The local police then set a classic trap. The Vallejo police chief, Jack Stiltz, challenges him, "We're not satisfied that the letter was written by the murderer, but it could have been," saying he wants another letter "with more facts to prove it." The killer responds with a three-page letter to the *San Francisco Examiner*—and now he has a name. He calls himself "the Zodiac." His letter opens (as they do from now on) with the chilling sentence "This is the Zodiac speaking ...," taunting them with the ciphers that are still unsolved: "By the way, are the police having a good time with the code? If not, tell them to cheer up; when they do crack it, they will have me." In a grim warning of what will follow, he ended his letter by saying:

> When taped to a gun barrel, the bullet will strike in the center of the black dot in the light. All I had to do was spray them as if it was a water hose; there was no need to use the gun sights. I was not happy to see that I did not get front page coverage.

Interestingly, the opening and closing sentences are crisp, concise, grammatically correct and read like the work of someone who is well educated, thoughtful and knows what he is doing. The rest of the letter is a grammatical mess and littered with spelling mistakes, more evidence of the Zodiac's ever-growing schizophrenic outlook on the world, one in which his relationship with reality becomes ever more fractured. The spelling mistakes are in italics:

On the 4th of July: I did not open the car door. The window was rolled down *all ready*. The boy was *origionaly* sitting in the *frunt* seat when I began *fireing*. When I fired the first shot at his head, he leaped backwards at the same time, thus spoiling my aim. He ended up on the back seat then the floor in back *thashing* out very violently with his legs; that's how I shot him in the knee. I did not leave the *cene* of the killing with squealing tires + *raceing* engine as described in the Vallejo paper. I drove away quite slowly so as not to draw attention to my car. The man who told police that my car was brown was a negro about 40-45 rather *shabbly* dressed. I was in this phone booth having some fun with the Vallejo cop when he was walking by. When I hung the phone up the damn thing began to ring & that drew his attention to me + my car.

Last *Christmass* In that *epasode* the police were wondering how I could shoot + hit my victims in the dark. They did not openly state this, but implied this by saying it was a well lit night + I could see *silowets* on the horizon. Bullshit that area is *srounded* by high hills + trees. What I did was tape a small *pencel* flash light to the barrel of my gun. If you notice, in the center of the beam of light if you aim it at a wall or ceiling you will see a black or *darck* spot in the center of the circle of light about 3 to 6 inches across.

In all, there are fourteen spelling mistakes in fourteen sentences, but none in the six sentences that bracket this central portion of the letter. It is as if there are two distinct voices or even personalities at work here. When he is in killer mode, describing what he did and the preparations he made, the spelling mistakes are frequent. When he is communicating directly with the authorities or being more reflective, there are no mistakes and the quality of the writing is markedly different. Of course, it may be that this is one voice that is then disguised—an explanation that would be very useful in understanding the mind of the man who set the codes.

While he is having fun and pampering his ego by teasing the police, two local amateur cryptanalysts, Donald Gene Harden, a forty-one-year-old local high-school teacher, and his wife, Bettye June, are busy working on the three ciphers. In less than a week they decrypt all three, correctly identifying them as a polyalphabetic code, in which more than one symbol is used for the same letter in the plain text. Having followed the case, they realized that they were dealing with an egomaniac and that the first symbol would stand for the letter I. As with the open text of his letter, it is littered with spelling and grammatical mistakes.

The plain text as deciphered by the Hardens reads:

> I like killing people because it is so much fun it is more fun than killing wild game in the forrest because man is the most dangeroue animal of all to kill something gives me the most thrilling experence it is even better than getting your rocks off with a girl the best part is thae when I die I will be reborn in paradice and all the I have killed will become my slaves I will not give you my name because you will try to sloi down or stop my collecting of slaves for my afterlife.

As for his identity (if that was actually concealed in the cipher) the last seventeen letters are deciphered as "EEORIFTEMETHHPITI."

Though the ciphers were broken, the key issue of his identity was not resolved, and less than two months later, he struck again. This time, it was early evening on the shoreline of Lake Berryessa, a 22-mile-long artificial lake in Napa, California, formed when the Bureau of Reclamation built the spectacular Monticello Dam in 1957.

Of all the Zodiac killings, this is easily the most bizarre. By this time, it is clear that there was huge confusion in his mind between himself as a person and himself as a persona, who he was and who he identified with. He no longer knew where one ended and the other began. To all intents, they were a blur, one and the same.

September 27, 1969. Cecelia Ann Shepard is just twenty-two years old. Her boyfriend, Bryan Hartnell, is also twenty-two. Shortly after 6 p.m., they are lying on a blanket by the shore when the

Zodiac approaches them, armed with an automatic handgun. He is wearing a hooded mask, which looks as if it is made from the sort of four-cornered paper bags used by grocery stores. It has slots for his eyes, over which he wears clip-on sunglasses. The mask goes down over his chest and back, with the distinctive Zodiac symbol sewn on to it. His sleeves are tied to his wrists, his trousers tucked into his boots. On his belt is a holder for a knife, which looks more like a bayonet. It is complete with wooden handle, held together by brass rivets and surgical tape. He is somewhere between 5 feet 8 inches and 6 feet tall. A footprint suggests a man with size 10 shoes, possibly over 200 pounds in weight, which matches the description given by the survivor.[6] The man in the mask tells them he has just escaped from prison[7] and needs money and a car to drive over the border to Mexico. The two students keep talking, trying to keep calm and reason with him, but he instructs Cecelia Shepard to tie her boyfriend's wrists. In a vain attempt to appease him, she tosses her wallet to the man, but he declines it.

Once Hartnell is tied, the Zodiac stabs him repeatedly in the back. As he falls and plays dead, the killer turns to Cecelia, who has been screaming at him to stop. He then stabs her ten times—five in the front, and five in the back—before casually strolling off. This time, his planning works. In his pocket is a large black Magic Marker pen. He walks over to Hartnell's car, and on the door, he draws the familiar Zodiac logo and then writes:

Vallejo
12-20-68
7-4-69
Sept 27-69-6:30
by knife

Though he was stabbed six times in all, Bryan Hartnell survives the attack, but Cecelia Shepard does not. With a cut to her aorta, she dies in the hospital two days later. Later, Hartnell said that his first thought was that they were dealing with "a sluggish, slow, rather stupid individual," though he tempered this by adding, "I have been able to see by the way he operates that he is neither of these. Not that he is a genius, but he is definitely not stupid. He's got plans."[8]

Less than an hour later, the police get a call. A calm voice says, "I want to report a murder, no, a double murder. They are two miles north of Park Headquarters. They were in a white Volkswagen Karmann Ghia." The switchboard operator asks where he is calling from, but all he says is, "I'm the one that did it." Then he drops the receiver and walks away, leaving a fingerprint on the receiver.[9] The phone booth is 27 miles from the murder scene, but just 5 miles from the police station.

The Zodiac never again referred directly to this attack, which at least must raise the possibility that this was a copycat killing, but there seems little doubt that it is an authentic Zodiac murder. Engaging them in conversation and then stabbing his victims was very different from shooting them when they were either in their cars or running away,[10] though the killer had done exactly this in the Domingos-Edwards double homicide six years before. On balance, it is the Zodiac. First, there is the uniform, though this could have been copied. Second, there is the handwriting on the car door, which is a pretty good match with the handwriting in the letters. This was in the public domain and therefore relatively easy to replicate, but not perhaps when you are trying to leave the scene of a double murder.

The list on the car door can easily be decoded and was clearly written by the man who had just killed Cecelia Shepard and stabbed Bryan Hartnell.

> Vallejo = Domingos/Edwards
> 12-20-68 = Faraday/Jensen
> 7-4-69 = Ferrin/Mageau
> Sept 27-69-6:30 = Hartnell/Shepard
> by knife = Hartnell/Shepard

A month later, there was another killing, not of a courting couple this time, but of a single man. For anyone looking at the Zodiac ciphers, this single murder is the hinge, linking the killings with which he establishes his reputation and his brand image and everything that follows. But this murder is completely unlike any of the previous killings, even though the killer claims to be the Zodiac. It is also followed by the three ciphers that remain unsolved to this day.

October 11, 1969, 9:55 p.m. Paul Stine, a cab driver, is hailed at the corner of Mason and Geary streets in San Francisco. His passenger tells him to go to the corner of Washington and Maple, by the Presidio, one of America's most famous military landmarks, near the Golden Gate Bridge. Stine is 5 feet 9 inches tall, twenty-nine years old, married and weighs 180 pounds. As a lone white male, he is therefore completely unlike any previous Zodiac target. When the taxi stops a block away, the Zodiac shoots Stine in the side of the head at almost point-blank range. He then gets into the front seat, carefully removes a piece of Stine's bloodstained shirt, but leaves behind his Timex watch, his checkbook, a ring and just over $4. He then wipes down the interior of the cab, the dashboard and the passenger's door with a white cloth, before getting out. He walks round to the driver's door, which he also wipes, before calmly strolling away.

The whole scene is witnessed by three teenagers looking down from a second-floor window, who subsequently describe a white male, in his early forties, 5 feet 8 inches tall, heavily built, with "reddish-blond" crew-cut hair, wearing glasses, dark-brown trousers, a dark navy-blue or black parka-style jacket and dark shoes.[11] In the minutes between the shooting and the time when the police patrol cars arrive, the message is garbled and the officers are told to look for a black man. As they drive up, they approach the killer, who is casually walking away from the scene. He has no problem telling them that an armed man has just left in the other direction—and off they go. In the dark evening light, they missed the bloodstains on his jacket. And this is the closest the police ever knowingly get to the Zodiac.

Initially, the police believe this is a simple murder, with robbery as the motive. They therefore start looking for an armed robber who targets cab drivers, not a serial killer who attacks courting couples after dark. Their first poster describes a man they want for robbing taxi drivers, whose *modus operandi* is to direct the driver to take him into or near a park, where he robs them at gunpoint. The poster notes, "In one case victim was shot in head at contact."[12] Their reasoning was that there had been a couple of recent similar incidents, including the robbery of a cab driver, less than a fortnight before, on September 30, 1969, at 11 p.m.

Paul Hom had collected a fare who wanted to go to the junction of Washington and Cherry streets. He then told the driver to continue on to the Presidio, where he pulled out a long-barreled revolver and robbed him of $35 in cash. The driver pleaded for his life and the robber spared him, bundling him into the trunk of the yellow cab.

The only hole in this theory was the cab driver's description of the man who had robbed him. The description is precise; after all, Paul Hom had spent several terrifying minutes up close with him. He tells the police that his attacker was a twenty-four-year-old man, weighing "135 pounds with black hair and eyes" wearing a "blue denim jacket and dark slacks." This did not match the description of Stine's killer. All three teenage witnesses, as well as the two police officers who had seen him lumbering away, had described a man who was much older and heavier. According to one of the police officers, "The individual I saw that night was a white male adult approximately thirty-five to forty-five years of age, 5 feet 10 inches, 180 to 210 pounds." Though the physical description was fairly precise, some of his statement was bizarre, including this gem of police deductive reasoning: "Subject at no time appeared to be in a hurry, walking with a shuffling lope, slightly bent forward. The subject's general appearance—Welsh ancestry."[13]

While the police flounder about, the killer sets the pace, calling the shots as he has done since the start. They have little idea what they are doing, but he does. The same day that the police put out their "wanted" poster, he writes to his journal of choice, the *San Francisco Chronicle*. On the night of the Stine murder, the police had called out the dog teams from the base at the Presidio and seven of them had searched the area. As the Zodiac had escaped, he clearly felt that he had earned his bragging rights:

> This is the Zodiac speaking. I am the murderer of the taxi driver over by Washington St. + Maple St. last night, to prove this here is a blood stained piece of his shirt. I am the same man who did in the people in the north bay area. The S.F. Police could have caught me last night if

they had searched the park properly instead of holding road races with their motorcicles seeing who could make the most noise. The car drivers should have just parked their cars and sat there quietly waiting for me to come out of cover.

He ended the letter with his most famous threat: "School children make nice targ-ets, I think I shall wipe out a school bus some morning, just shoot out the frunt tire + then pick off the kiddies as they come bouncing out."

Five days later, the San Francisco Police altered their "wanted" poster, using virtually the same identikit picture as before, though they were now calling him Zodiac, aged thirty-five to forty-five and heavily built.

Three weeks went by and the trail got very cold until another letter arrived—and just to raise the ante, it carried the first of the three ciphers. As with the previous letters, it carried two stamps and the instruction "Please Rush to Editor" written twice on the envelope.

Once again, this letter was sent to the *San Francisco Chronicle*, on November 8, 1969, but it is very different from the previous ones, being in the form of a "Jesters" card. It begins, predictably enough, with the phrase "This is the Zodiac speaking ... "

The card is macabre and reads:

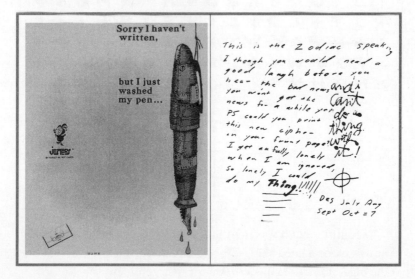

In the same envelope was something else—a cipher written in the same strange symbol system that the Zodiac had used on previous occasions. It has never been cracked and reads:

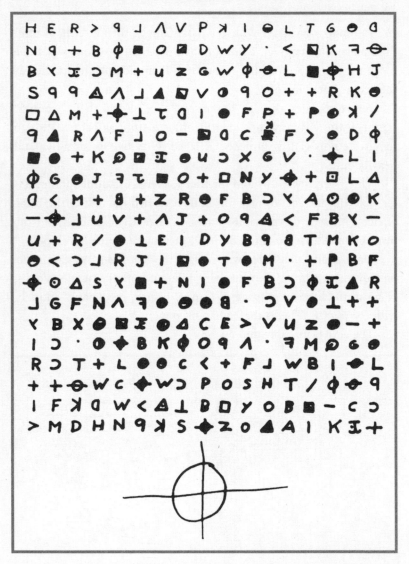

To confirm that it was from him, the Zodiac included a fragment of Stine's bloodstained shirt.[14] Whoever can decipher it will win one of the biggest prizes in modern American cryptology.

Apart from the symbols used, it is significantly different from the other codes. In all, the Zodiac used sixty-five symbols, flattening out the distribution pattern and making it much less vulnerable to attack by traditional letter-frequency analysis. Despite this, some cryptanalysts claim to have broken parts of the code, finding phrases, like "on weekdays," "teens are dead and more," "I need kids," "do insane," "ritual needs holes," "wait and see," "stayed no darn"—all standard Zodiac stuff.

There are several partial solutions, one of which was suggested to the police. It reads:

> Herb Caen: I give them hell too
> to deed hell is a clue.
> There some see a name below
> a killer's game is pills, parole
> me. Cops met to talk to me.
> Such time. These fools helpd me.
> Mad killer places a mask
> bull s.

> Alone, pleasured I'd like to kill.
> Scared I eat a pill.
> Assh-le I plan to harm, phone, ask.
> CB sells slaves because all
> collection either pleased to lie in hell.
> He's me. Toschi the pig leads me.
> Collects eighth, some mail K.T.

Herb Caen was a columnist for the *San Francisco Chronicle* who had written on the Zodiac, though he was not the most prominent journalist to do so. Toschi was the flamboyant, bow-tie wearing, publicity-seeking police officer who became (in part) the inspiration for Clint Eastwood's character in *Dirty Harry*.

Another version reads:

> Herb Caen I give them
> hell too blast these
> lies sleuth sheolh
> see a name below kill-

leers film a pills ga-
me pardon me agcept t-
o blast ne bullshie
these fools shall me-
et killer pleas ask
lunblad sole at plsd
ul clear it lake it so
stare I eat a pillll
assholle I plant mr
ah phane lake b alll
slaves because deal
willl stolen eithe-
r late tea spall I he-
ll slash toschi the
pig m stalls a o deal
c eighth sole m slain

Before the murder of the cab driver, those murders that had been definitely attributed to the Zodiac had shared many similar characteristics. His victims had almost always been in pairs, and he had shot or stabbed courting couples after sunset or late at night. They had all been shot on weekends. He had sometimes goaded his victims to flee and then shot them while they were escaping, and he had chosen his killing fields with care, always attacking in areas that were both remote and near large expanses of water, either the ocean or a vast lake. But suddenly, with the murder of Paul Stine, he had done what no psychological profiler would have predicted. He had shot a single, twenty-nine-year-old male in a heavily populated area of San Francisco, rather than choosing a remote spot.

However, there is a consistent pattern here. In all the killings, he exercises power over his victims before he kills them. He wants them to know that they are about to die at his hands. Sending coded letters to newspapers and then taunting them is part of the same pattern of exercising power—showing not only to his victims but to the wider world that he is a superior being.

What was even more baffling was that the day after he sent the card, the Zodiac wrote another letter to the *San Francisco Chronicle*.

Again, the envelope carried two stamps and the double instruction "Please Rush to Editor."[15] In it, he claimed to have killed seven, though it is very difficult see how he reached this figure. By this time, the murders that were possibly attributable to him were: Domingos-Edwards, Joyce-Johnny Swindle, Bates, Jensen-Faraday, Ferrin, Shepard and Stine, which makes ten in all. A total of seven can only be reached if one of the early pairs is removed plus a single. Either of the first two pairs could be removed, but then a single one has to be removed. The only candidates are Bates (a murder he claims later), Ferrin (the deceased in a pair he tried to kill and which he claimed at the time), Shepard (again, the deceased in a pair that he claimed) or Stine (a murder he definitely committed). The only explanations are that he was deliberately trying to mislead or that his mind was already showing signs of major damage.

His frustration was beginning to creep in as he railed against "the police for their telling lies about me." He said that in the future he would no longer announce to anyone when he committed his murders, instead making them look like "routine robberies, killings of anger, + a few fake accidents, etc."

Once again, he taunted the police, saying they "shall never catch me, because I have been too clever for them." He described how he used airplane cement on his fingertips to avoid leaving prints behind. He also provided a lot of chilling detail of how he had outwitted the police on the night of the Stine killing and then—just to raise the collective blood pressure—he described his "death machine," which he said was "all ready made."

Just before Christmas, December 20, 1969, there was a "Zodiac" letter sent to a well-known lawyer called Melvyn Belli, asking for help as he did not believe he could control himself much longer. The typeface and writing style is very different from the others and there must be doubts about its authenticity, though according to one account, he included a swatch from Stine's bloodstained shirt.

Over the winter and into the following spring, police forces all over California continued to squander their leads. There was a possible near miss on Highway 132 in March 1970, involving Kathleen Johns and her daughter. A thirty-year-old, dark-haired man came close to abducting them, but they escaped. The case is a mess, as Kathleen Johns has consistently changed her story, though the Zodiac subsequently claimed credit for this incident in another letter to the *San Francisco Chronicle* in July.

But then, a month after the Johns incident, on April 20, 1970, there was another letter and another cipher, which, like the preceding one, remains unsolved. Though it carried the usual pair of stamps, it was simply addressed to the editor of the *San Francisco Chronicle*, which may or may not be significant.

It started as always with his catchphrase, and then it was straight into a full-frontal taunt against the authorities:

The letter then continued:

> I am mildly cerous as to how much money you have on my head now. I hope you do not think that I was the one who wiped out that blue meannie with a bomb at the cop station. Even though I talked about killing school children with one. It just wouldnt doo to move in on someone elses teritory. But there is more glory in killing a cop than a cid because a cop can shoot back. I have killed ten people to date. It would have been a lot more except that my bus bomb was a dud. I was swamped out by the rain we had a while back.

The reference to "blue meannie" was lifted from the Beatles' animated film *Yellow Submarine* and was widely used at the time for all things music-hating and evil, especially the police. In this case, it was a twenty-five-year-old police officer, Richard Radetich, who was shot in the head by a driver while he was writing out a parking ticket against him. His denial was a mark of his inflated view of himself, as all the witnesses to the Radetich shooting described an African-American who the police had little problem tracing as he already had a criminal record.

In this letter, he had increased his death toll to ten, though it is difficult to know which, if any, murders he was referring to as he had stopped calling the police after he had committed them and there were no specific letters containing discrete details that only the killer could know.

This was the penultimate unbroken cipher. There was just one more to come, a couple of months later. By this time, he was claiming a murder toll of twelve, though the only detail he provided was a claim to "have shot a man in a car with a .38," though he provided no details as to who, when or where. Instead, there was a map, marking a place where a bomb would be buried—and a cipher. The letter ended:

The Map coupled with this code will tell you who-e the bomb is set. You have untill next Fall to dig it up.

The best route toward a solution to the ciphers is to try to identify their writer, to see if there are some clues in his life that can provide a key or set of keys to unlock the mystery of his encryption system—though with the provision that the cryptographer at work here may not be the same person who committed all of the murders.

The unsolved cipher letters could well have been written by someone with an obsessive interest in the case. However, even if they turn out to be two different people, it is still a legitimate exercise for anyone trying to break these ciphers—after all, if the writer was not the killer, it was someone who was very close to the case, or even a prankster who wanted to get into the head of the killer and in some way emulate or be an extension of him. At the very least, it was someone who knew enough to pass themselves off as the killer.

This is a perfectly feasible scenario. Unlike the first three letters with the cipher that was cracked, the subsequent letters with the unsolved puzzles do not contain any information that was not already in the public domain. The plain text attached is very much in the Zodiac style, but this is easy to copy—a mixture of self-righteous hurt at the hands of the authorities, coupled with a desperate need to threaten and brag—which any competent writer who had read the California papers could have copied.

The various California police forces interviewed at least two thousand possible suspects. Top of the list in this case—with no other possible suspect even close—is a local misfit, convicted pedophile and venomous misogynist, Arthur Leigh Allen.[16] According to those who knew him well, he always went out armed, had an arsenal of weapons at his home that in type and caliber matched those used in the murders, and crucially, he had cipher papers in his house that used the same symbol set as that used by the Zodiac. His life pattern constantly intersects with the Zodiac's activities, and there are substantial overlaps between his movements and several of the murders. In the end, though he was a long-term favorite for many of the police departments who dealt with him over the years, he was never charged. The evidence against him was substantial, but it was never tested in court. One of the most telling aspects of this case is the spectacular incompetence of the police and authorities, and the failure to build a water-tight case against him is just one of them. It has to be said that many other murder suspects have been dragged into court—and convicted—on much less evidence, though they have tended to be black.

The circumstantial evidence is clearly enough to put Allen in the frame. The first letter written to the police after the Bates murder was written on a make of typewriter called a Royal, which had the Elite font for its typeface, a model Allen owned. He also had a Zodiac watch, which was given to him as a Christmas present by his mother in December 1967. The company symbol was then used by the Zodiac killer from August 1969 onward. Interestingly, Allen lied about when he received the watch, giving a much later date. And physically—220/250 pounds in weight, heavily built, size 10-1/2 shoes—he matched both survivors' descriptions, and his feet were the same size as the prints left at the scene.

More specifically, the evidence of his few friends brings him into much greater focus as the prime suspect. In January 1968, he told a friend, Donald Cheney, that he was going to write a novel, the key elements of which will be gruesomely familiar to anyone who knows this case. By the time he spoke to Cheney, there were three dead linked to the man who would become known as the Zodiac (Robert Domingos and Linda Edwards from June 1963, and Cheri Jo Bates from October 1966), though his identity, logo and brand name were not yet established. According to Cheney, Allen said that in his novel (which certainly sounds very autobiographical in the way he described it to his friend), he would call himself Zodiac, adopting the symbol from his watch as his logo. He would then stalk and kill young lovers in remote spots ("people in Lovers' Lane") and shoot them at night using a rifle with a torch attached to the sights. He would then write letters to the police, taunting them when they failed to catch him. He also said that he would entrap his victims by flagging them down when they were driving and telling them that they had a problem with the wheels of their car. He would offer to fix it but would in fact loosen the nuts so that they would crash and he could then offer them a lift, at which point they would be in his control and he could kidnap them. The Zodiac subsequently used exactly this method in March 1970, when he kidnapped Kathleen Johns, then aged twenty-two, and her baby daughter as they were on their way to visit a sick relative. And just to complete the sequence, the Zodiac then boasted of this in a letter to the *San Francisco Chronicle*, saying he gave "a rather intersting ride to a coupple howers one evening a few months back."

He also told Cheney that he would shoot children as they alighted from their school bus, an image that even now chills every parent, whether American or not. Again, the Zodiac subsequently boasted of this in a letter.

The year after the Cheney conversation, the Zodiac killer shot Darlene Ferrin and Mike Mageau as they chatted late one night in their car at a remote spot, then sent letters to the papers, the first step to launching himself as an international brand, ready to be admired and copied by psychopaths everywhere. More than twenty years later, in 1992, Mageau (who survived the shooting, though Ferrin did not) was shown some pictures and immediately picked out Allen as his killer. When asked why he had not done so before, he said that this was the first time he had been shown pictures of potential suspects—an astonishing claim if true. What is even more extraordinary is that the year before, in February 1991, the police had searched Allen's house and taken away a large amount of highly suspicious evidence—pipe bombs, bomb-making equipment, enough weaponry to start a small-scale gang war, flashlight, papers and news cuttings relating to the Zodiac, a knife and typewriters. Yet despite this and Mageau's positive identification of him, he was never charged with this or any of the other murders. Given the repeated incompetence of the various police forces who dealt with this case over the years, it is not that surprising.

Mageau was not the only person to positively identify Allen. In the mid-1970s, a Department of Justice investigator took Bryan Hartnell (who, like Mageau, had survived a double-murder attempt even though the woman he was with had been killed) to the shop where Allen was working behind the counter. Though Hartnell had not seen the face of his attacker, as the Zodiac was wearing a bag covering his head at the time, he told the investigators that Allen's body was the same size and shape and his voice was a perfect match.

In one of his longest letters to the papers, posted in September 1969, the Zodiac described making a bomb made of ammonium nitrate, stove oil and gravel to blow up a school bus. When Allen's house was searched in February 1991 the police found completed pipe bombs as well as bomb-making formulas that used ammonium nitrate and stove oil.

The ciphers, letters and handwriting all point toward Allen and further help to triangulate him as the Zodiac. The Zodiac letters are full of spelling mistakes, which was something Allen did in his everyday life. According to his brother, Ron, he loved to misspell words for "fun" as this confused others. When the police searched his house, they took away papers with the word "eggs" spelled as "aigs." Both Allen and the Zodiac wrote "Merry Xmass." Allen said "trigger mech" for "trigger mechanism," a phrase that the Zodiac wrote. Any attempt to decipher the remaining uncracked codes must include the assumption that both the cipher text and the plain text may contain deliberate spelling mistakes.

If this is the case, then the plain-text letter sent to the papers after the Cheri Jo Bates murder takes on an extra significance for any cryptanalyst trying to break these codes. This is a man who can spell properly and whose grammar is at least adequate, which means that the spelling mistakes are deliberate, as is the flexible attitude to basic grammar. This is a man who is hiding himself from the world, communicating in code and even then the code contains further levels of encryption within.

His handwriting is not a perfect match but close and this can be explained by the fact that he was ambidextrous. Naturally left-handed, he was forced (like many others in the 1940s and 1950s) to write with his right hand, which was regarded as "normal." Allen denied that he could write with both hands to the police, but his brother confirmed that he was ambidextrous.

For cryptanalysts, there are a series of numerical coincidences, which may or may not be significant. The letters were initially signed with a poorly constructed symbol, which looks like thirty-two. He was thirty-two years old at the time of the Bates murder. He lived at 32 Fresno Street in Vallejo, California, and his code contains thirty-two symbols. Highway 132 is where he picked up Kathleen Johns and her daughter.

There is also something else about him that would have to be taken into account by any cryptographer and it is something that no profiler could ever have predicted: he was a Gilbert and Sullivan fan, identifying himself, inevitably, with Ko-Ko, the Lord High Executioner from the opera *The Mikado*. In his letter to the *San Francisco Chronicle* on July 24, 1970, he complained that he was "rather unhappy because you people will not wear some nice [Zodiac] buttons." The letter goes on, "So now I have a little list ..."

The verse it comes from is:

As some day it may happen that a victim must be found,
I've got a little list—I've got a little list
Of society offenders who might well be underground,
And who never would be missed—who never would be missed!

Two days later, he writes again to the *San Francisco Chronicle*, in what is his longest letter. In it, he quotes at length from *The Mikado*. By now, he claims a death toll of thirteen and goes into great detail about the tortures that he will have waiting for his slaves in the afterlife.

As his reputation grew, he became more grandiose in his view of himself and this is reflected in his letters, which become increasingly eccentric. By 1971, he claims to have killed seventeen, a figure that more than doubles over the next three years. In a letter sent to the *San Francisco Chronicle* at the end of January 1974, the Zodiac writes, "I saw and think 'the Exorcist' the best satirical comidy that I have ever seen." There at the bottom of the single sheet is the score "ME—37 SFPD—0." SFPD is the San Francisco Police Department, though this was only one among many police forces scattered all over California trying to get a grip on the Zodiac and several other serial killers who were plying their trade in California at this time.

Though boastful, the figure of thirty-seven may just be plausible.

Between 1970 and 1974, Allen went to Sonoma State College, and during this time, seven female students were murdered, a pattern of killing that stopped when he finished his course and left. Though they were not killings of courting couples, they all resonate with the murder of Cheri Jo Bates, one of the very first killings linked to the Zodiac.

Like Cheri Jo Bates, these murders are muscular and brutal. The women are strangled, smothered and, in one case, dispatched with a broken neck. The killer also keeps souvenirs, which though common among serial killers, had begun to emerge in the Zodiac killings in the 1960s and early 1970s.

In all, the police looked at the murders of fifteen young women in this area between February 1972 and September 1974, killings that stopped when Allen was arrested for child molestation.

He pleaded guilty and was sent to Atascadero Prison from March 1975 to August 1977. His Crime Investigation and Identification (CII) number was 1311511, and his Social Security number was 576-44-8882. Here, he was given a polygraph (lie-detector) test, which—by some accounts—he passed, though others are doubtful, arguing that his results showed strong evidence of the extensive use of tranquilizers, which would not be that surprising. Allen was a big man, with a foul temper, and it would have been common practice then (and now) to keep him in a pacified state through the regular use of what was nicknamed the "liquid cosh" by prison staff. Allen clearly felt he had failed the polygraph and that this test was very damaging to him, because while he was in prison he wrote a letter that exonerated himself and confirmed that he was not the Zodiac.

In July 1992, Mike Mageau positively identified Arthur Leigh Allen as the man who had shot him over two decades earlier. The time gap is immense, and the human memory is notoriously unreliable, but you are hardly ever likely to forget the face of someone who shoots you at close range. On August 26, 1992, after being overweight for much of his adult life, Arthur Leigh Allen died from heart disease as well as diabetes. The police searched his house two days later.

The Vallejo Police Department has never released the full details of this search, but there is one intriguing entry in their report—"Item 7a. Strips of paper with math"—the traditional tool of amateur cryptographers throughout the ages.

Appendix: Internet Version of the Beale Ciphers

The Internet version of cipher one is substantially different from the Albany Library version and reads:

71, 194, 38, 1701, 89, 76, 11, 83, 1629, 48, 94, 63, 132, 16, 111,
95, 84, 341, 975, 14, 40, 64, 27, 81, 139, 213, 63, 90, 1120, 8,
15, 3, 126, 2018, 40, 74, 758, 485, 604, 230, 436, 664, 582, 150,
251, 284, 308, 231, 124, 211, 486, 225, 401, 370, 11, 101, 305,
139, 189, 17, 33, 88, 208, 193, 145, 1, 94, 73, 416, 918, 263, 28,
500, 538, 356, 117, 136, 219, 27, 176, 130, 10, 460, 25, 485, 18,
436, 65, 84, 200, 283, 118, 320, 138, 36, 416, 280, 15, 71, 224,
961, 44, 16, 401, 39, 88, 61, 304, 12, 21, 24, 283, 134, 92, 63,
246, 486, 682, 7, 219, 184, 360, 780, 18, 64, 463, 474, 131, 160,
79, 73, 440, 95, 18, 64, 581, 34, 69, 128, 367, 460, 17, 81, 12,
103, 820, 62, 116, 97, 103, 862, 70, 60, 1317, 471, 540, 208,
121, 890, 346, 36, 150, 59, 568, 614, 13, 120, 63, 219, 812,
2160, 1780, 99, 35, 18, 21, 136, 872, 15, 28, 170, 88, 4, 30, 44,
112, 18, 147, 436, 195, 320, 37, 122, 113, 6, 140, 8, 120, 305,
42, 58, 461, 44, 106, 301, 13, 408, 680, 93, 86, 116, 530, 82,
568, 9, 102, 38, 416, 89, 71, 216, 728, 965, 818, 2, 38, 121, 195,
14, 326, 148, 234, 18, 55, 131, 234, 361, 824, 5, 81, 623, 48,
961, 19, 26, 33, 10, 1101, 365, 92, 88, 181, 275, 346, 201, 206,
86, 36, 219, 324, 829, 840, 64, 326, 19, 48, 122, 85, 216, 284,
919, 861, 326, 985, 233, 64, 68, 232, 431, 960, 50, 29, 81, 216,
321, 603, 14, 612, 81, 360, 36, 51, 62, 194, 78, 60, 200, 314,
676, 112, 4, 28, 18, 61, 136, 247, 819, 921, 1060, 464, 895, 10,
6, 66, 119, 38, 41, 49, 602, 423, 962, 302, 294, 875, 78, 14, 23,

111, 109, 62, 31, 501, 823, 216, 280, 34, 24, 150, 1000, 162,
286, 19, 21, 17, 340, 19, 242, 31, 86, 234, 140, 607, 115, 33,
191, 67, 104, 86, 52, 88, 16, 80, 121, 67, 95, 122, 216, 548, 96,
11, 201, 77, 364, 218, 65, 667, 890, 236, 154, 211, 10, 98, 34,
119, 56, 216, 119, 71, 218, 1164, 1496, 1817, 51, 39, 210, 36, 3,
19, 540, 232, 22, 141, 617, 84, 290, 80, 46, 207, 411, 150, 29,
38, 46, 172, 85, 194, 39, 261, 543, 897, 624, 18, 212, 416, 127,
931, 19, 4, 63, 96, 12, 101, 418, 16, 140, 230, 460, 538, 19, 27,
88, 612, 1431, 90, 716, 275, 74, 83, 11, 426, 89, 72, 84, 1300,
1706, 814, 221, 132, 40, 102, 34, 868, 975, 1101, 84, 16, 79, 23,
16, 81, 122, 324, 403, 912, 227, 936, 447, 55, 86, 34, 43, 212,
107, 96, 314, 264, 1065, 323, 428, 601, 203, 124, 95, 216, 814,
2906, 654, 820, 2, 301, 112, 176, 213, 71, 87, 96, 202, 35, 10, 2,
41, 17, 84, 221, 736, 820, 214, 11, 60, 760

The Internet version of cipher two, the solved cipher, reads:

115, 73, 24, 807, 37, 52, 49, 17, 31, 62, 647, 22, 7, 15, 140, 47,
29, 107, 79, 84, 56, 239, 10, 26, 811, 5, 196, 308, 85, 52, 160,
136, 59, 211, 36, 9, 46, 316, 554, 122, 106, 95, 53, 58, 2, 42, 7,
35, 122, 53, 31, 82, 77, 250, 196, 56, 96, 118, 71, 140, 287, 28,
353, 37, 1005, 65, 147, 807, 24, 3, 8, 12, 47, 43, 59, 807, 45,
316, 101, 41, 78, 154, 1005, 122, 138, 191, 16, 77, 49, 102, 57,
72, 34, 73, 85, 35, 371, 59, 196, 81, 92, 191, 106, 273, 60, 394,
620, 270, 220, 106, 388, 287, 63, 3, 6, 191, 122, 43, 234, 400,
106, 290, 314, 47, 48, 81, 96, 26, 115, 92, 158, 191, 110, 77, 85,
197, 46, 10, 113, 140, 353, 48, 120, 106, 2, 607, 61, 420, 811,
29, 125, 14, 20, 37, 105, 28, 248, 16, 159, 7, 35, 19, 301, 125,
110, 486, 287, 98, 117, 511, 62, 51, 220, 37, 113, 140, 807, 138,
540, 8, 44, 287, 388, 117, 18, 79, 344, 34, 20, 59, 511, 548, 107,
603, 220, 7, 66, 154, 41, 20, 50, 6, 575, 122, 154, 248, 110, 61,
52, 33, 30, 5, 38, 8, 14, 84, 57, 540, 217, 115, 71, 29, 84, 63, 43,
131, 29, 138, 47, 73, 239, 540, 52, 53, 79, 118, 51, 44, 63, 196,
12, 239, 112, 3, 49, 79, 353, 105, 56, 371, 557, 211, 505, 125,
360, 133, 143, 101, 15, 284, 540, 252, 14, 205, 140, 344, 26,
811, 138, 115, 48, 73, 34, 205, 316, 607, 63, 220, 7, 52, 150, 44,
52, 16, 40, 37, 158, 807, 37, 121, 12, 95, 10, 15, 35, 12, 131, 62,

115, 102, 807, 49, 53, 135, 138, 30, 31, 62, 67, 41, 85, 63, 10,
106, 807, 138, 8, 113, 20, 32, 33, 37, 353, 287, 140, 47, 85, 50,
37, 49, 47, 64, 6, 7, 71, 33, 4, 43, 47, 63, 1, 27, 600, 208, 230,
15, 191, 246, 85, 94, 511, 2, 270, 20, 39, 7, 33, 44, 22, 40, 7, 10,
3, 811, 106, 44, 486, 230, 353, 211, 200, 31, 10, 38, 140, 297,
61, 603, 320, 302, 666, 287, 2, 44, 33, 32, 511, 548, 10, 6, 250,
557, 246, 53, 37, 52, 83, 47, 320, 38, 33, 807, 7, 44, 30, 31, 250,
10, 15, 35, 106, 160, 113, 31, 102, 406, 230, 540, 320, 29, 66,
33, 101, 807, 138, 301, 316, 353, 320, 220, 37, 52, 28, 540, 320,
33, 8, 48, 107, 50, 811, 7, 2, 113, 73, 16, 125, 11, 110, 67, 102,
807, 33, 59, 81, 158, 38, 43, 581, 138, 19, 85, 400, 38, 43, 77,
14, 27, 8, 47, 138, 63, 140, 44, 35, 22, 177, 106, 250, 314, 217,
2, 10, 7, 1005, 4, 20, 25, 44, 48, 7, 26, 46, 110, 230, 807, 191,
34, 112, 147, 44, 110, 121, 125, 96, 41, 51, 50, 140, 56, 47, 152,
540, 63, 807, 28, 42, 250, 138, 582, 98, 643, 32, 107, 140, 112,
26, 85, 138, 540, 53, 20, 125, 371, 38, 36, 10, 52, 118, 136, 102,
420, 150, 112, 71, 14, 20, 7, 24, 18, 12, 807, 37, 67, 110, 62, 33,
21, 95, 220, 511, 102, 811, 30, 83, 84, 305, 620, 15, 2, 10, 8,
220, 106, 353, 105, 106, 60, 275, 72, 8, 50, 205, 185, 112, 125,
540, 65, 106, 807, 138, 96, 110, 16, 73, 33, 807, 150, 409, 400,
50, 154, 285, 96, 106, 316, 270, 205, 101, 811, 400, 8, 44, 37,
52, 40, 241, 34, 205, 38, 16, 46, 47, 85, 24, 44, 15, 64, 73, 138,
807, 85, 78, 110, 33, 420, 505, 53, 37, 38, 22, 31, 10, 110, 106,
101, 140, 15, 38, 3, 5, 44, 7, 98, 287, 135, 150, 96, 33, 84, 125,
807, 191, 96, 511, 118, 40, 370, 643, 466, 106, 41, 107, 603,
220, 275, 30, 150, 105, 49, 53, 287, 250, 208, 134, 7, 53, 12, 47,
85, 63, 138, 110, 21, 112, 140, 485, 486, 505, 14, 73, 84, 575,
1005, 150, 200, 16, 42, 5, 4, 25, 42, 8, 16, 811, 125, 160, 32,
205, 603, 807, 81, 96, 405, 41, 600, 136, 14, 20, 28, 26, 353,
302, 246, 8, 131, 160, 140, 84, 440, 42, 16, 811, 40, 67, 101,
102, 194, 138, 205, 51, 63, 241, 540, 122, 8, 10, 63, 140, 47, 48,
140, 288

And using the Declaration of Independence as the key text, the plain text reads as follows:

When(1) in(2) the(3) course(4) of(5) human(6) events(7) it(8) becomes(9) necessary(10) for(11) one(12) people(13) to(14) dissolve(15) the(16) political(17) bands(18) which(19) have(20) connected(21) them(22) with(23) another(24) and(25) to(26) assume(27) among(28) the(29) powers(30) of(31) the(32) earth(33) the(34) separate(35) and(36) equal(37) station(38) to(39) which(40) the(41) laws(42) of(43) nature(44) and(45) of(46) nature's(47) god(48) entitle(49) them(50) a(51) decent(52) respect(53) to(54) the(55) opinions(56) of(57) mankind(58) requires(59) that(60) they(61) should(62) declare(63) the(64) causes(65) which(66) impel(67) them(68) to(69) the(70) separation(71) we(72) hold(73) these(74) truths(75) to(76) be(77) self(78) evident(79) that(80) all(81) men(82) are(83) created(84) equal(85) that(86) they(87) are(88) endowed(89) by(90) their(91) creator(92) with(93) certain(94) unalienable(95) rights(96) that(97) among(98) these(99) are(100) life(101) liberty(102) and(103) the(104) pursuit(105) of(106) happiness(107) that(108) to(109) secure(110) these(111) rights(112) governments(113) are(114) instituted(115) among(116) men(117) deriving(118) their(119) just(120) powers(121) from(122) the(123) consent(124) of(125) the(126) governed(127) that(128) whenever(129) any(130) form(131) of(132) government(133) becomes(134) destructive(135) of(136) these(137) ends(138) it(139) is(140) the(141) right(142) of(143) the(144) people(145) to(146) alter(147) or(148) to(149) abolish(150) it(151) and(152) to(153) institute(154) new(155) government(156) laying(157) its(158) foundation(159) on(160) such(161) principles(162) and(163) organizing(164) its(165) powers(166) in(167) such(168) form(169) as(170) to(171) them(172) shall(173) seem(174) most(175) likely(176) to(177) effect(178) their(179) safety(180) and(181) happiness(182) prudence(183) indeed(184) will(185) dictate(186) that(187) governments(188) long(189) established(190) should(191) not(192) be(193) changed(194) for(195) light(196) and(197) transient(198)

causes(199)   and(200)   accordingly(201)   all(202)
experience(203)   hath(204)   shown(205)   that(206)
mankind(207) are(208) more(209) disposed(210) to(211)
suffer(212) while(213) evils(214) are(215) sufferable(216)
than(217) to(218) right(219) themselves(220) by(221)
abolishing(222) the(223) forms(224) to(225) which(226)
they(227) are(228) accustomed(229) but(230) when(231)
a(232) long(233) train(234) of(235) abuses(236) and(237)
usurpations(238) pursuing(239) invariably(240) the(241)
same(242) object(243) evinces(244) a(245) design(246) to(247)
reduce(248)   them(249)   under(250)   absolute(251)
despotism(252) it(253) is(254) their(255) right(256) it(257)
is(258) their(259) duty(260) to(261) throw(262) off(263)
such(264) government(265) and(266) to(267) provide(268)
new(269) guards(270) for(271) their(272) future(273)
security(274) such(275) has(276) been(277) the(278)
patient(279) sufferance(280) of(281) these(282) colonies(283)
and(284) such(285) is(286) now(287) the(288) necessity(289)
which(290) constrains(291) them(292) to(293) alter(294)
their(295) former(296) systems(297) of(298) government(299)
the(300) history(301) of(302) the(303) present(304) king(305)
of(306) great(307) Britain(308) is(309) a(310) history(311)
of(312) repeated(313) injuries(314) and(315) usurpations(316)
all(317) having(318) in(319) direct(320) object(321) the(322)
establishment(323)   of(324)   an(325)   absolute(326)
tyranny(327) over(328) these(329) states(330) to(331)
prove(332)   this(333)   let(334)   facts(335)   be(336)
submitted(337) to(338) a(339) candid(340) world(341)
he(342) has(343) refused(344) his(345) assent(346) to(347)
laws(348) the(349) most(350) wholesome(351) and(352)
necessary(353) for(354) the(355) public(356) good(357)
he(358) has(359) forbidden(360) his(361) governors(362)
to(363) pass(364) laws(365) of(366) immediate(367) and(368)
pressing(369) importance(370) unless(371) suspended(372)
in(373)   their(374)   operation(375)   till(376)   his(377)
assent(378) should(379) be(380) obtained(381) and(382)

when(383) so(384) suspended(385) he(386) has(387) utterly(388) neglected(389) to(390) attend(391) to(392) them(393) he(394) has(395) refused(396) to(397) pass(398) other(399) laws(400) for(401) the(402) accommodation(403) of(404) large(405) districts(406) of(407) people(408) unless(409) those(410) people(411) would(412) relinquish(413) the(414) right(415) of(416) representation(417) in(418) the(419) legislature(420) a(421) right(422) inestimable(423) to(424) them(425) and(426) formidable(427) to(428) tyrants(429) only(430) he(431) has(432) called(433) together(434) legislative(435) bodies(436) at(437) places(438) unusual(439) uncomfortable(440) and(441) distant(442) from(443) the(444) depository(445) of(446) their(447) public(448) records(449) for(450) the(451) sole(452) purpose(453) of(454) fatiguing(455) them(456) into(457) compliance(458) with(459) his(460) measures(461) he(462) has(463) dissolved(464) representative(465) houses(466) repeatedly(467) for(468) opposing(469) with(470) manly(471) firmness(472) his(473) invasions(474) on(475) the(476) rights(477) of(478) the(479) people(480) he(481) has(482) refused(483) for(484) a(485) long(486) time(487) after(488) such(489) dissolutions(490) to(491) cause(492) others(493) to(494) be(495) elected(496) whereby(497) the(498) legislative(499) powers(500) incapable(501) of(502) annihilation(503) have(504) returned(505) to(506) the(507) people(508) at(509) large(510) for(511) their(512) exercise(513) the(514) state(515) remaining(516) in(517) the(518) meantime(519) exposed(520) to(521) all(522) the(523) dangers(524) of(525) invasion(526) from(527) without(528) and(529) convulsions(530) within(531) he(532) has(533) endeavored(534) to(535) prevent(536) the(537) population(538) of(539) these(540) states(541) for(542) that(543) purpose(544) obstructing(545) the(546) laws(547) for(548) naturalization(549) of(550) foreigners(551) refusing(552) to(553) pass(554) others(555) to(556) encourage(557) their(558) migration(559) hither(560) and(561) raising(562) the(563) conditions(564) of(565) new(566) appropriations(567) of(568) lands(569) he(570) has(571) obstructed(572) the(573) administration(574) of(575) justice(576) by(577) refusing(578) his(579) assent(580) to(581) laws(582) for(583) establishing(584) judiciary(585) powers(586) he(587) has(588) made(589) judges(590) dependent(591) on(592) his(593) will(594) alone(595) for(596) the(597) tenure(598) of(599) their(600) offices(601) and(602) the(603) amount(604) and(605) payment(606) of(607) their(608) salaries(609) he(610) has(611) erected(612) a(613) multitude(614) of(615) new(616) offices(617) and(618) sent(619) hither(620) swarms(621) of(622) officers(623) to(624) harass(625) our(626) people(627) and(628) eat(629) out(630) their(631) substance(632) he(633) has(634) kept(635) among(636) us(637) in(638) times(639) of(640) peace(641) standing(642) armies(643) without(644) the(645) consent(646) of(647) our(648) legislatures(649) he(650) has(651) affected(652) to(653) render(654) the(655) military(656) independent(657) of(658) and(659) superior(660) to(661) the(662) civil(663) power(664) he(665) has(666) combined(667) with(668) others(669) to(670) subject(671) us(672) to(673) a(674) jurisdiction(675) foreign(676) to(677) our(678) constitution(679) and(680) unacknowledged(681) by(682) our(683) laws(684) giving(685) his(686) assent(687) to(688) their(689) acts(690) of(691) pretended(692) legislation(693) for(694) quartering(695) large(696) bodies(697) of(698) armed(699) troops(700) among(701) us(702) for(703) protecting(704) them(705) by(706) a(707) mock(708) trial(709) from(710) punishment(711) for(712) any(713) murders(714) which(715) they(716) should(717) commit(718) on(719) the(720) inhabitants(721) of(722) these(723) states(724) for(725) cutting(726) off(727) our(728) trade(729) with(730) all(731) parts(732) of(733) the(734) world(735) for(736) imposing(737) taxes(738) on(739) us(740) without(741) our(742) consent(743) for(744) depriving(745) us(746) in(747) many(748) cases(749) of(750) the(751) benefits(752) of(753) trial(754) by(755) jury(756) for(757) transporting(758) us(759) beyond(760) seas(761) to(762) be(763) tried(764) for(765) pretended(766) offenses(767) for(768) abolishing(769) the(770) free(771) system(772) of(773) English(774) laws(775) in(776) a(777) neighboring(778) province(779) establishing(780) therein(781) an(782) arbitrary(783) government(784) and(785) enlarging(786) its(787) boundaries(788) so(789) as(790) to(791) render(792) it(793) at(794) once(795) an(796) example(797) and(798) fit(799) instrument(800) for(801) introducing(802) the(803) same(804) absolute(805) rule(806) into(807) these(808) colonies(809) for(810) taking(811) away(812) our(813) charters(814) abolishing(815) our(816) most(817) valuable(818) laws(819) and(820) altering(821) fundamentally(822) the(823) forms(824) of(825) our(826) governments(827) for(828) suspending(829) our(830) own(831) legislature(832) and(833) declaring(834) themselves(835) invested(836) with(837) power(838) to(839) legislate(840) for(841) us(842) in(843) all(844) cases(845) whatsoever(846) he(847) has(848) abdicated(849) government(850) here(851) by(852) declaring(853) us(854) out(855) of(856) his(857) protection(858) and(859) waging(860) war(861) against(862) us(863) he(864) has(865) plundered(866) our(867) seas(868) ravaged(869) our(870) coasts(871) burnt(872) our(873) towns(874) and(875) destroyed(876) the(877) lives(878) of(879) our(880) people(881) he(882) is(883) at(884) this(885) time(886) transporting(887) large(888) armies(889) of(890) foreign(891) mercenaries(892) to(893) complete(894) the(895) works(896) of(897) death(898) desolation(899) and(900) tyranny(901) already(902) begun(903) with(904) circumstances(905) of(906) cruelty(907) and(&)(908) perfidy(909) scarcely(910) paralleled(911) in(912) the(913) most(914) barbarous(915) ages(916) and(917) totally(918) unworthy(919) the(920) head(921) of(922) a(923) civilized(924) nation(925) he(926) has(927) constrained(928)

our(929) fellow(930) citizens(931) taken(932) captive(933)
on(934) the(935) high(936) seas(937) to(938) bear(939)
arms(940) against(941) their(942) country(943) to(944)
become(945) the(946) executioners(947) of(948) their(949)
friends(950) and(951) brethren(952) or(953) to(954) fall(955)
themselves(956) by(957) their(958) hands(959) he(960)
has(961) excited(962) domestic(963) insurrections(964)
amongst(965) us(966) and(967) has(968) endeavored(969)
to(970) bring(971) on(972) the(973) inhabitants(974) of(975)
our(976) frontiers(977) the(978) merciless(979) Indian(980)
savages(981) whose(982) known(983) rule(984) of(985)
warfare(986) is(987) an(988) undistinguished(989)
destruction(990) of(991) all(992) ages(993) sexes(994)
and(995) conditions(996) in(997) every(998) stage(999)
of(1000) these(1001) oppressions(1002) we(1003) have(1004)
petitioned(1005) for(1006) redress(1007) in(1008) the(1009)
most(1010) humble(1011) terms(1012) our(1013)
repeated(1014) petitions(1015) have(1016) been(1017)
answered(1018) only(1019) by(1020) repeated(1021)
injury(1022) a(1023) prince(1024) whose(1025)
character(1026) is(1027) thus(1028) marked(1029) by(1030)
every(1031) act(1032) which(1033) may(1034) define(1035)
a(1036) tyrant(1037) is(1038) unfit(1039) to(1040) be(1041)
the(1042) ruler(1043) of(1044) a(1045) free(1046)
people(1047) nor(1048) have(1049) we(1050) been(1051)
wanting(1052) in(1053) attention(1054) to(1055) our(1056)
British(1057) brethren(1058) we(1059) have(1060)
warned(1061) them(1062) from(1063) time(1064) to(1065)
time(1066) of(1067) attempts(1068) by(1069) their(1070)
legislature(1071) to(1072) extend(1073) an(1074)
unwarrantable(1075) jurisdiction(1076) over(1077) us(1078)
we(1079) have(1080) reminded(1081) them(1082) of(1083)
the(1084) circumstances(1085) of(1086) our(1087)
emigration(1088) and(1089) settlement(1090) here(1091)
we(1092) have(1093) appealed(1094) to(1095) their(1096)
native(1097) justice(1098) and(1099) magnanimity(1100)

and(1101) we(1102) have(1103) conjured(1104) them(1105) by(1106) the(1107) ties(1108) of(1109) our(1110) common(1111) kindred(1112) to(1113) disavow(1114) these(1115) usurpations(1116) which(1117) would(1118) inevitably(1119) interrupt(1120) our(1121) connections(1122) and(1123) correspondence(1124) they(1125) too(1126) have(1127) been(1128) deaf(1129) to(1130) the(1131) voice(1132) of(1133) justice(1134) and(1135) of(1136) consanguinity(1137) we(1138) must(1139) therefore(1140) acquiesce(1141) in(1142) the(1143) necessity(1144) which(1145) denounces(1146) our(1147) separation(1148) and(1149) hold(1150) them(1151) as(1152) we(1153) hold(1154) the(1155) rest(1156) of(1157) mankind(1158) enemies(1159) in(1160) war(1161) in(1162) peace(1163) friends(1164) we(1165) therefore(1166) the(1167) representatives(1168) of(1169) the(1170) united(1171) states(1172) of(1173) America(1174) in(1175) general(1176) congress(1177) assembled(1178) appealing(1179) to(1180) the(1181) supreme(1182) judge(1183) of(1184) the(1185) world(1186) for(1187) the(1188) rectitude(1189) of(1190) our(1191) intentions(1192) do(1193) in(1194) the(1195) name(1196) and(1197) by(1198) authority(1199) of(1200) the(1201) good(1202) people(1203) of(1204) these(1205) colonies(1206) solemnly(1207) publish(1208) and(1209) declare(1210) that(1211) these(1212) united(1213) colonies(1214) are(1215) and(1216) of(1217) right(1218) ought(1219) to(1220) be(1221) free(1222) and(1223) independent(1224) states(1225) that(1226) they(1227) are(1228) absolved(1229) from(1230) all(1231) allegiance(1232) to(1233) the(1234) British(1235) crown(1236) and(1237) that(1238) all(1239) political(1240) connection(1241) between(1242) them(1243) and(1244) the(1245) state(1246) of(1247) great(1248) Britain(1249) is(1250) and(1251) ought(1252) to(1253) be(1254) totally(1255) dissolved(1256) and(1257) that(1258) as(1259) free(1260) and(1261) independent(1262) states(1263) they(1264) have(1265) full(1266) power(1267) to(1268) levy(1269) war(1270) conclude(1271) peace(1272) contract(1273) alliances(1274) establish(1275) commerce(1276) and(1277) to(1278) do(1279) all(1280) other(1281) acts(1282) and(1283) things(1284) which(1285) independent(1286) states(1287) may(1288) of(1289) right(1290) do(1291) and(1292) for(1293) the(1294) support(1295) of(1296) this(1297) declaration(1298) with(1299) a(1300) firm(1301) reliance(1302) on(1303) the(1304) protection(1305) of(1306) divine(1307) providence(1308) we(1309) mutually(1310) pledge(1311) to(1312) each(1313) other(1314) our(1315) lives(1316) our(1317) fortunes(1318) and(1319) our(1320) sacred(1321) honor(1322).

The Internet version of cipher three reads:

317, 8, 92, 73, 112, 89, 67, 318, 28, 96,107, 41, 631, 78, 146, 397, 118, 98, 114, 246, 348, 116, 74, 88, 12, 65, 32, 14, 81, 19, 76, 121, 216, 85, 33, 66, 15, 108, 68, 77, 43, 24, 122, 96, 117, 36, 211, 301, 15, 44, 11, 46, 89, 18, 136, 68, 317, 28, 90, 82, 304, 71, 43, 221, 198, 176, 310, 319, 81, 99, 264, 380, 56, 37, 319, 2, 44, 53, 28, 44, 75, 98, 102, 37, 85, 107, 117, 64, 88, 136, 48, 151, 99, 175, 89, 315, 326, 78, 96, 214, 218, 311, 43, 89, 51, 90, 75, 128, 96, 33, 28, 103, 84, 65, 26, 41, 246, 84, 270, 98, 116, 32, 59, 74, 66, 69, 240, 15, 8, 121, 20, 77, 89, 31, 11, 106, 81, 191, 224, 328, 18, 75, 52, 82, 117, 201, 39, 23, 217, 27, 21, 84, 35, 54, 109, 128, 49, 77, 88, 1, 81, 217, 64, 55, 83, 116, 251, 269, 311, 96, 54, 32, 120, 18, 132, 102, 219, 211, 84, 150, 219, 275, 312, 64, 10, 106, 87, 75, 47, 21, 29, 37, 81, 44, 18, 126, 115, 132, 160, 181, 203, 76, 81, 299, 314, 337, 351, 96, 11, 28, 97, 318, 238, 106, 24, 93, 3, 19, 17, 26, 60, 73, 88, 14, 126, 138, 234, 286, 297, 321, 365, 264, 19, 22, 84, 56, 107, 98, 123, 111, 214, 136, 7, 33, 45, 40, 13, 28, 46, 42, 107, 196, 227, 344, 198, 203, 247, 116, 19, 8, 212, 230, 31, 6, 328, 65, 48, 52, 59, 41, 122, 33, 117, 11, 18, 25, 71, 36, 45, 83, 76, 89, 92, 31, 65, 70, 83, 96, 27, 33, 44, 50, 61, 24, 112, 136, 149, 176, 180, 194, 143,

171, 205, 296, 87, 12, 44, 51, 89, 98, 34, 41, 208, 173, 66, 9, 35,
16, 95, 8, 113, 175, 90, 56, 203, 19, 177, 183, 206, 157, 200,
218, 260, 291, 305, 618, 951, 320, 18, 124, 78, 65, 19, 32, 124,
48, 53, 57, 84, 96, 207, 244, 66, 82, 119, 71, 11, 86, 77, 213, 54,
82, 316, 245, 303, 86, 97, 106, 212, 18, 37, 15, 81, 89, 16, 7, 81,
39, 96, 14, 43, 216, 118, 29, 55, 109, 136, 172, 213, 64, 8, 227,
304, 611, 221, 364, 819, 375, 128, 296, 1, 18, 53, 76, 10, 15, 23,
19, 71, 84, 120, 134, 66, 73, 89, 96, 230, 48, 77, 26, 101, 127,
936, 218, 439, 178, 171, 61, 226, 313, 215, 102, 18, 167, 262,
114, 218, 66, 59, 48, 27, 19, 13, 82, 48, 162, 119, 34, 127, 139,
34, 128, 129, 74, 63, 120, 11, 54, 61, 73, 92, 180, 66, 75, 101,
124, 265, 89, 96, 126, 274, 896, 917, 434, 461, 235, 890, 312,
413, 328, 381, 96, 105, 217, 66, 118, 22, 77, 64, 42, 12, 7, 55,
24, 83, 67, 97, 109, 121, 135, 181, 203, 219, 228, 256, 21, 34,
77, 319, 374, 382, 675, 684, 717, 864, 203, 4, 18, 92, 16, 63, 82,
22, 46, 55, 69, 74, 112, 134, 186, 175, 119, 213, 416, 312, 343,
264, 119, 186, 218, 343, 417, 845, 951, 124, 209, 49, 617, 856,
921, 936, 72, 19, 28, 11, 35, 42, 40, 66, 85, 94, 112, 65, 82, 115,
119, 236, 244, 186, 172, 112, 85, 6, 56, 38, 44, 85, 72, 32, 47,
63, 96, 124, 217, 314, 319, 221, 644, 817, 821, 934, 922, 416,
975, 10, 22, 18, 46, 137, 181, 101, 39, 86, 103, 116, 138, 164,
212, 218, 296, 815, 380, 412, 460, 495, 675, 820, 952

Notes

Introduction

1. *The Hitchhiker's Guide to the Galaxy* also contains the following exchange between Marvin and the mattress otherwise known as Zem: "I am, at a rough estimate, thirty billion times more intelligent than you. Let me give you an example. Think of a number, any number." "Er, five," said the mattress. Wrong," said Marvin. "You see?"

2. Who wins and who loses can be measured by the debt everyone is carrying at the end of the war. In 1914 prices, the deficits are: Germany $253 million, Austria-Hungary $111 million, the UK $85 million, France $50 million, Italy $38 million and the Balkans $16 million. The beneficiaries are: the U.S. $563 million, Japan $370 million, Spain $170 million, Argentina $100 million, Holland $82 million, Switzerland $24 million, Sweden and Uruguay $20 million and Norway $8 million. This left Europe crippled with debt, as they had spent their gold reserves and borrowed heavily to pay for this most futile of wars.

3. Rudolph Kippenhahn, *Code Breaking* (New York, 1999), p. 59.

4. Initially, the British protest about the Germans putting encrypted material down "neutral" telegraph wires, regarding this as a hostile act, but once they realize the value of the intelligence "take," they let it drop.

5. De Grey's working papers are at the National Archives in Kew, southwest London. The catalog reference is "HW3/187." They have been scanned and can be seen on the Internet at the National Archives website, www.nationalarchives.gov.uk. His account of how it was done is also there.

6. msnbc.com, "Your Bank Account Could Be Emptying Without Your Knowledge," July 11, 2007.

7. Werther's story is told in *Hitler's Traitor* by Lou Kilzer (Presidio Press, California, 2000).

8. The act was condemned by all shades of opinion in the British press, the *Financial Times*, the *Guardian* and the *Daily Telegraph* all being at their vituperative best. The *FT* spoke for them all, writing simply, "Scrap this bill in its entirety."

9. This section of the act, Part III Investigation of Electronic Data Protected by Encryption, etc., is the precursor to any Big Brother state. The grounds for disclosure are:

(3) A disclosure requirement in respect of any protected information is necessary on grounds falling within this subsection if it is necessary—

(a) in the interests of national security;

(b) for the purpose of preventing or detecting crime; or

(c) in the interests of the economic well-being of the United Kingdom.

The defenses are limited:

(4) In proceedings against any person for an offense under this section it shall be a defense for that person to show—

(a) that it was not reasonably practicable for him to make the disclosure required by virtue of the giving of the section 49 notice before the time by which he was required, in accordance with that notice, to make it; but

(b) that he did make that disclosure as soon after that time as it was reasonably practicable for him to do so.

The punishment is severe:

(5) A person guilty of an offense under this section shall be liable—

(a) on conviction on indictment, to imprisonment for a term not exceeding two years or to a fine, or to both;

(b) on summary conviction, to imprisonment for a term not exceeding six months or to a fine not exceeding the statutory maximum, or to both.

Chapter 1: *Kryptos: "There's Another Deeper Mystery"*

1. The British High Court judge in the alleged plagiarism case, Peter Smith, got bitten with the whole idea of encrypted messages and included one in his judgment. The clue was in the letters that he had written in italics, the first ten of which read, "SMITHY CODE." The following thirty-two letters read, "JAEIEXTOSTGPSAC-GREAMQWFKADPMQZVZ," which decrypts as "Jackie Fisher, who are you? Dreadnought." The judge is a fan of John "Jackie" Fisher, a nineteenth-century British admiral who developed the Navy's first modern warship, *Dreadnought*. The cipher system he used is based on the Fibonacci series of numbers, which features in *The Da Vinci Code*.

In this, each number is added to the previous one to make the next one—0, 1, 1, 2, 3, 5, 8, 13, 21, 34, 55, 89, 144 and so on—and the letters are moved on accordingly.

2. The CIA statement says:

> People are the principal resource of the Central Intelligence Agency. It is their intellectual and physical energies that ultimately provide the national policymakers with superior information and analyses—the basis to formulate policies necessary to maintain this country's position in the world. An aesthetically pleasing work environment at its headquarters is an important stimulus to the efforts of those officers assigned here.

3. Code name "MK Ultra."

4. The Church Committee in 1975 investigated this, but there is a mass of other material as well.

5. He left the CIA in 1990 and then set up a local computer-security company, TecSec, in Vienna, Maryland, near his former employers. He is chief scientist there and is "deeply involved in the company's product development and expanding application solutions." Their website is www.tecsec.com.

6. Yuri Shvets, *Washington Station: My Life as a KGB Spy in America* (Simon & Schuster, 1994).

7. www.danbrown.com. Click on "Secrets."

8. www.elonka.com/kryptos/CyrillicProjectorAnnouncement.html.

9. There are the CIA's own pictures, which can be viewed at www.cia.gov/cia/information/tour/krypt.html. Jim Gillogly, who was the second person to break the first three-quarters of the cipher with computers, took some photographs when he visited the CIA headquarters, which can be viewed at www.voynich.net/Kryptos, as did Elonka Dunin, executive producer and general manager of online community at Simutronics Corporation (www.play.net), a leading company for multiplayer games. She runs one of the very best *Kryptos* sites: www.elonka.com/kryptos/pics/images1.html.

10. There are two sites carrying satellite images: www.elonka.com/kryptos/KryptosAerial.html and http://kryptos.arcticus.com/coords.html. At the latter site, there is a detailed breakdown of the exact locations of the various parts of the sculptures, using software that equates each pixel to a square foot.

11. www.elonka.com/kryptos/mirrors/daw/MorseCode.txt.

12. Aerial photographs are available on the web at www.elonka.com/Kryptos/KryptosAerial.html.

13. www.cia.gov/cia/information/tour/kryptos˜code.html.

14. Open letter to curious CIA employees, December 15, 1989.

15. www.wired.com/news/business/0,1367,66333-3,00.html. The interviewer is Kim Zetter.
16. www.cia.gov/cia/information/tour/kryptos˜code.html.
17. Below is the CIA version (taken from the CIA website, www.cia.gov/cia/information/tour/kryptos˜code.html), though it contains some mistakes. The cipher text reads:

```
EMUFPHZLRFAXYUSDJKZLDKRNSHGNFIVJ
YQTQUXQBQVYUVLLTREVJYQTMKYRDMFD
VFPJUDEEHZWETZYVGWHKKQETGFQJNCE
GGWHKK?DQMCPFQZDQMMIAGPFXHQRLG
TIMVMZJANQLVKQEDAGDVFRPJUNGEUNA
QZGZLECGYUXUEENJTBJLBQCRTBJDFHRR
YIZETKZEMVDUFKSJHKFWHKUWQLSZFTI
HHDDDUVH?DWKBFUFPWNTDFIYCUQZERE
EVLDKFEZMOQQJLTTUGSYQPFEUNLAVIDX
FLGGTEZ?FKZBSFDQVGOGIPUFXHHDRKF
FHQNTGPUAECNUVPDJMQCLQUMUNEDFQ
ELZZVRRGKFFVOEEXBDMVPNFQXEZLGRE
DNQFMPNZGLFLPMRJQYALMGNUVPDXVKP
DQUMEBEDMHDAFMJGZNUPLGEWJLLAETG
ENDYAHROHNLSRHEOCPTEOIBIDYSHNAIA
CHTNREYULDSLLSLLNOHSNOSMRWXMNE
TPRNGATIHNRARPESLNNELEBLPIIACAE
WMTWNDITEENRAHCTENEUDRETNHAEOE
TFOLSEDTIWENHAEIOYTEYQHEENCTAYCR
EIFTBRSPAMHNEWENATAMATEGYEERLB
TEEFOASFIOTUETUAEOTOARMAEERTNRTI
BSEDDNIAAHTTMSTEWPIEROAGRIEWFEB
AECTDDHILCEIHSITEGOEAOSDDRYDLORIT
RKLMLEHAGTDHARDPNEOHMGFMFEUHE
ECDMRIPFEIMEHNLSSTTRTVDOHW?OBKR
UOXOGHULBSOLIFBBWFLRVQQPRNGKSSO
TWTQSJQSSEKZZWATJKLUDIAWINFBNYP
VTTMZFPKWGDKZXTJCDIGKUHUAUEKCAR
```

The companion text reads:

```
ABCDEFGHIJKLMNOPQRSTUVWXYZABCD
AKRYPTOSABCDEFGHIJLMNQUVWXZKRYP
BRYPTOSABCDEFGHIJLMNQUVWXZKRYPT
CYPTOSABCDEFGHIJLMNQUVWXZKRYPTO
DPTOSABCDEFGHIJLMNQUVWXZKRYPTOS
ETOSABCDEFGHIJLMNQUVWXZKRYPTOSA
```

```
F O S A B C D E F G H I J L M N Q U V W X Z K R Y P T O S A B
G S A B C D E F G H I J L M N Q U V W X Z K R Y P T O S A B C
H A B C D E F G H I J L M N Q U V W X Z K R Y P T O S A B C D
I B C D E F G H I J L M N Q U V W X Z K R Y P T O S A B C D E
J C D E F G H I J L M N Q U V W X Z K R Y P T O S A B C D E F
K D E F G H I J L M N Q U V W X Z K R Y P T O S A B C D E F G
L E F G H I J L M N Q U V W X Z K R Y P T O S A B C D E F G H
M F G H I J L M N Q U V W X Z K R Y P T O S A B C D E F G H I
N G H I J L M N Q U V W X Z K R Y P T O S A B C D E F G H I J
O H I J L M N Q U V W X Z K R Y P T O S A B C D E F G H I J L
P I J L M N Q U V W X Z K R Y P T O S A B C D E F G H I J L M
Q J L M N Q U V W X Z K R Y P T O S A B C D E F G H I J L M N
R L M N Q U V W X Z K R Y P T O S A B C D E F G H I J L M N Q
S M N Q U V W X Z K R Y P T O S A B C D E F G H I J L M N Q U
T N Q U V W X Z K R Y P T O S A B C D E F G H I J L M N Q U V
U Q U V W X Z K R Y P T O S A B C D E F G H I J L M N Q U V W
V U V W X Z K R Y P T O S A B C D E F G H I J L M N Q U V W X
W V W X Z K R Y P T O S A B C D E F G H I J L M N Q U V W X Z
X W X Z K R Y P T O S A B C D E F G H I J L M N Q U V W X Z K
Y X Z K R Y P T O S A B C D E F G H I J L M N Q U V W X Z K R
Z Z K R Y P T O S A B C D E F G H I J L M N Q U V W X Z K R Y
A B C D E F G H I J K L M N O P Q R S T U V W X Y Z A B C D
```

18. He wrote a detailed account of how he cracked the first three parts of the *Kryptos* code and has published it on the web. www.elonka.com/kryptos/mirrors/daw/steinarticle.html.

19. There is a very clever software analysis of this at http://kryptos. articus.com/coords.html.

20. They are at 7200 Wisconsin Avenue, Bethesda, and 2580 Clarendon Boulevard, Arlington.

Chapter 2: *In the Beginning Was the Code ...*

1. James Henry Breasted, *Ancient Records of Egypt*, Vol. One (1922), p. 622.

2. CIA debriefing of Félix Rodríguez, June 3, 1975, a Cuban-American who used the code name "Félix Ramos" and posed as a Bolivian military officer.

3. Suetonius describes Julius Caesar's simple cipher in his *Life of Julius Caesar*:

> There are also letters of his to Cicero, as well as to his intimates on private affairs, and in the latter, if he had anything confidential to say, he wrote it in cipher, that is, by so changing the order of

the letters of the alphabet, that not a word could be made out. If anyone wishes to decipher these, and get at their meaning, he must substitute the fourth letter of the alphabet, namely D, for A, and so with the others.

4. For an explanation of the theory that he in fact allowed himself to be killed, effectively committing suicide, see *Terminate With Extreme Prejudice* by the same author.

5. Plutarch gives a clear description of it in his *Life of Lysander*, John Dryden (trans.):

> When the Ephors send an admiral or general on his way, they take two round pieces of wood, both exactly of a length and thickness, and cut even to one another; they keep one themselves, and the other they give to the person they send forth; and these pieces of wood they call Skytale. When, therefore, they have occasion to communicate any secret or important matter, making a scroll of parchment long and narrow like a leathern thong, they roll it about their own staff of wood, leaving no space void between, but covering the surface of the staff with the scroll all over. When they have done this, they write what they please on the scroll, as it is wrapped about the staff; and when they have written, they take off the scroll, and send it to the general without the wood. He, when he has received it, can read nothing of the writing, because the words and letters are not connected, but all broken up; but taking his own staff, he winds the slip of the scroll about it, so that this folding, restoring all the parts into the same order that they were in before, and putting what comes first into connection with what follows, brings the whole consecutive contents to view round the outside.

6. Roger Bacon, "Epistle on the Nullity of Magic."

7. The title was bestowed on him by David Kahn, who might himself be dubbed the "Father of Modern Cryptographic History," being easily the best and most influential writer on the subject.

8. Sometimes called Clifford.

9. On very similar philosophical grounds, which the clerics used to sign the death warrants against Yitzhak Rabin of Israel and Sadat of Egypt.

10. Plutarch, *The Lives of the Noble Grecians and Romans*, Arthur Hugh Clough (ed.), John Dryden (trans.), (Modern Library, New York, 1932), p. 542.

11. It was decrypted by Dr. Thomas Ernst, a professor of German at La Roche College, in Pittsburgh, and Dr. Jim Reeds, a mathematician at AT&T Labs in Florham Park, New Jersey.

12. So significant is this as a breakthrough that there has been a German campaign to give him top billing as the "Father of Modern Cryptography."

Chapter 3: The Voynich Manuscript: Let Your Indulgence Set Me Free

1. http://mcs.open.ac.uk/gr768/thingsinprogress/voynich.shtm.
2. Lieutenant Colonel H. W. L. Hime, *Gunpowder and Ammunition* (1904).
3. "An Unpublished Fragment of a work by Roger Bacon, discovered and published by Cardinal Gasquet," *English Historical Review* (July 1897), p. 501, quoted by William Newbold.
4. Letter from Sir Thomas Browne to Elias Ashmole, quoted in the Voynich Manuscript by M. E. d'Imperio.
5. Roger Bacon, *Epistola de Secretis Operibus Artis et Naturae*.
6. Including the John Dee Society, www.johndee.org.
7. The claimant is Roger Brumbaugh, and the clock is on folio 85r.
8. The claim was made by an American botanist, Hugh O'Neill, about the flower on folio 93r, but at best, it is clearly only a crude representation of a plant with a very large head.
9. Folio 100r.
10. The plant was discovered by Dr. Erik Lattman of Aston University, Birmingham, England, and featured in a documentary, *Inside King Cobra*, made for BSkyB by Fulcrum TV.
11. Folio 89r1.
12. Folio 70v1.
13. Folio 68r3.
14. Folio 68v2.
15. Folio 86r2.
16. Initially, a friend of Newbold's called Professor John Manly, an English professor from Chicago, followed by the "grandfather" of American code-breakers, William Friedman.
17. This theory is beautifully expounded by Mary d'Imperio in her monograph *The Voynich Manuscript*, an Elegant Enigma (Aegean Park Press, June 1981).
18. They are sometimes called Vernam ciphers, after Gilbert Vernam, one of the inventors.

Chapter 4: Shugborough: The Shepherd's Monument

1. Josiah Wedgwood was born in 1730 and died in 1795.
2. I have written the main measurements first in inches, as this was the system used by the monument's designers.

3. Tennyson wrote about the contradictory symbolism of the yew tree in his poem "*In Memoriam A.H.H.*"—"with fruitful cloud and living smoke." What he did not know was that the yew is a key source for the active ingredient in the highly effective anticancer drug Taxol.

4. The first Earl of Lichfield, Thomas William Anson, was created on September 15, 1831. He became the postmaster general when the Uniform Penny Post was started in 1840 by Rowland Hill. The key thing about this was that the sender prepaid the cost of sending a letter by attaching a specially designed adhesive label (a stamp). Letters up to half an ounce cost 4 pence to deliver anywhere in Britain. It was a huge success. On the first day, 112,000 letters were posted.

5. www.shugborough.org.uk. A visit is mandatory for anyone seriously interested in cracking this code.

6. Charles Dickens, *Bleak House*, Chapter 6.

7. Copies are available in the Rare Books section of the British Library in King's Cross, London.

8. This was confirmed by Professor David Watkin, professor of history of art at Cambridge and expert on James "Athenian" Stuart and Georgian architecture. In an email exchange, he promptly and very kindly confirmed that Stuart only ever used V for both U and V when writing in Latin. I am eternally grateful to him for providing this crucial piece of evidence, without which the key would not have turned.

9. The original is in the Louvre in Paris.

10. Honoré d'Urfé, Marquis de Valromey and Comte de Châteauneuf (1568–1625), French novelist and writer.

11. There is no obvious source for this line of poetry. As she says, this is her "own translation."

12. In a letter to Paul Smith on May 18, 1987. Quoted at http://priory-of-sion.com/psp/id16.html.

13. Samuel Scott's painting *The Capture of the Nuestra Señora* de Covadonga *by HMS Centurion, 20 June 1743* is on display in the National Maritime Museum, London.

14. The North Carolina State Capitol Building was designed by David Paton (1802–82), a Scottish architect who had been trained by Sir John Soane. Much of the building was inspired by Greek architectural and design principles. In the finest traditions of all large construction works, it came in hideously over budget. Finished in 1840, the final cost was $532,682.34—more than three times the annual income of the State at that time.

Paton wrote:

The State Capitol is 160 feet in length from north to south by 140 feet from east to west. The whole height is 97½ feet in the center. The apex of pediment is 64 feet in height. The stylobate is 18 feet in height. The columns of the east and west porticoes are 5 feet 2½ inches in diameter. An entablature, including blocking course, is continued around the building 12 feet high. The columns and entablature are Grecian Doric, and copied from the Temple of Minerva, commonly called the Parthenon, which was erected in Athens about 500 years before Christ. An octagon tower surrounds the rotunda, which is ornamented with Grecian cornices, etc., and its dome is decorated at top with a similar ornament to that of the Choragic Monument of Lysicrates, commonly called the Lanthorn of Demosthenes.

15. Thomas Pennant, *The Journey From Chester to London* (1782).

16. For a brilliant demolition of the Marco Polo myth, see Frances Wood, *Did Marco Polo Go to China?* (Secker & Warburg, London, 1995).

17. English losses were somewhere between a hundred and five hundred, with the lower figure probably being the most accurate. The French lost between seven thousand and ten thousand men as well as much of the cream of French nobility.

18. I am very grateful to Robert Noel, the Lancaster Herald at the College of Arms, for providing this information.

19. This was Bill Shankley, the bullet-headed manager of Liverpool Football Club.

20. George Anson's will is at the Public Records Office, Kew, London. The reference number is "Prob 11/876," and it is available online.

Chapter 5: *The Beale Papers: Accursed Thirst for Gold ...*

1. Virgil, *The Aeneid* (III, 56). The original Latin reads, "*Quid non mortalia pectora cogis, Auri sacra fames?*"

2. *Lynchburg Virginian*, April 10, 1885.

3. The full text is widely available on the Internet. http://smd173.tripod.com/Beale/BealePapers.htm gives the page breaks as well, for any who might think this is important. The pamphlet itself is no longer in the Library of Congress.

4. A copy of *The Beale Papers* was provided for me by a wonderfully helpful librarian at the Library of Congress, Ms: Christine Beauregard.

5. This is taken from the Albany Library version and I have checked it. It does fit the cipher-text numbers, with a few wrinkles.

6. It appeared in Hartford, Connecticut, in 1805.

7. This number exists in the Internet version of *The Beale Papers* (see Appendix on page 242), not in the version that comes from Albany Library, New York, where the number is 296.

8. *Cryptologia*, April 1980, Vol. 4, No. 2.

9. Many writers call him Thomas Jefferson Beale, but this is one of those "facts" that creep into the record, get endlessly repeated and acquire the status of truth. In some versions of the pamphlet, he is just Thos J. Beale and there is no reference to Jefferson. In the Albany Library version he is Thos Jeffn Beale, the assumption being that "Jeffn" stands for "Jefferson," as he was the president who helped draft the Declaration of Independence, which is the key text for cipher two. This is only an assumption, though probably a safe one.

10. A detailed claim has been made that this person is John William Sherman, a playwright and author of dime novels. He was the editor and then owner of one of the local newspapers, the *Lynchburg Virginian*. He was directly related to the personalities of the story— Ward, the Bufords and Morriss.

   In detail, he was the great-grandnephew of Paschal Buford, the owner of Buford's Tavern, the first cousin once removed of Harriet E. Otey, James B. Ward's wife. Harriet was also the grandniece of Sarah Mitchell, Robert Morriss's wife. Sherman came from a prosperous and well-connected family. His grandfather John T. Murrill was a successful merchant. His father, Henry H. Sherman, was also a successful businessman with his father-in-law. His sister, Harriet Otey Sherman, married Henry Madison Ford, a successful attorney. Julia H. Ward, James's daughter, married William D. Johns in 1881. W. D. Johns is listed in the Lynchburg City Directory of 1884 as a clerk at Adams Bros & Payne. The significance of this comes from an announcement that appeared in the *Lynchburg Virginian* on August 2, 1883: "Mr. Wm. D. Johns is now in charge of the feed store of Adams Bros. & Paynes on Twelfth Street, where he will receive orders for wood and coal." The link is that James Ward used this company's letterhead in 1884 to apply to the Library of Congress for copyright for *The Beale Papers*.

   The sequence of events is regarded as significant. In 1882, Frances Buford, the last possible direct witness to the events of the story, died. The following year, 1883, a fire destroyed some buildings in the town center and funds were set up to help the families of the victims. The argument is that Sherman wrote the novel anonymously (shamelessly plagiarizing Edgar Allan Poe) with the help of his cousin, James B. Ward, who used the Adams Bros & Payne letterhead from his son in law to apply for copyright for *The Beale Papers*.

Sherman—even more shamelessly—then writes two book reviews to promote the pamphlet, which appear on the front page of the *Virginian*. Later that year, he and his brother buy the paper for $5,000 cash and $10,000 on credit. A year later, the paper was in financial difficulty and so they dropped the price of *The Beale Papers* to a dime in a desperate attempt to bring some cash in. A year later, the paper folded.

It is an interesting theory but full of holes. There is no significance to the fact that many of these people were related. Lynchburg was a small town, and like everywhere else on the planet, people tend to marry within their class and everyone here is a member of the town's small entrepreneurial middle class. The surprising thing would be if they were not related. More important, there is not a shred of evidence that Sherman actually wrote *The Beale Papers*, other than the fact that he had means and opportunity.

11. Louis Kruh, "A Basic Probe of the Beale Cipher as a Bamboozlement," *Cryptologia*, Vol. 6, No. 4 (October 1982), pp. 378—82. Louis Kruh is a cryptology researcher of forty years and is coauthor, with Dr. C. A. Deavours, of *Machine Cryptography and Modern Cryptanalysis* (Artech House, Inc., 1985). Louis Kruh is also a cofounder of *Cryptologia* and its book-review editor.

12. Dr. Peter Millican is a fellow and tutor in philosophy at Hertford College, Oxford University. As a philosopher, he is best known for his research on the eighteenth-century philosopher David Hume, and is currently editor of the journal "Hume Studies." From 1985 until 2006, he lectured in computing and philosophy at Leeds University and set up the Leeds Electronic Text Centre, where he is still Director. Signature is one of four user-friendly computer systems that he created to enable students to explore computing and its textual applications in novel ways (the others being Elizabeth, an educational chatbot designed to teach Artifical Intelligence concepts and textual processing, and two visual programming systems based on a common virtual machine, Turtle Pascal and Turtle Java). He is now planning to extend Signature further, to develop its power as a tool for textual research. He is also a Grandmaster of correspondence chess.

13. When Peter Millican ran the chi-square tests on the same figures as shown in these graphs, the results were very different. As before, he took the Beale document as the reference text and the letters purportedly written by Thomas Beale as the sample text and compared them. The results were interesting but not conclusive. As a visual guide, those with asterisks are significant, those without are not:

Word length*	The difference is significant at the 5 percent level. Chi-square 5 percent value = 12.59; 2 percent value = 15.03.
Sentence length	Insufficient data for test.
Usage of letters	The difference is very highly significant at the 0.1 percent level.
Punctuation	The difference is highly significant at the 1 percent level.
Common words	The difference is very highly significant at the 0.1 percent level.

He then swapped them round so that Beale's letters were the reference text and *The Beale Papers* were the sample. The results were as follows:

Word length*	The difference is very highly significant at the 1 percent level.
Sentence length	Insufficient data for test.
Usage of letters	The difference is very highly significant at the 0.1 percent level.
Punctuation**	The difference is NOT significant even at the 20 percent level. Chi-square 20 percent value = 3.22.
Common words**	The difference is NOT significant even at the 20 percent level. Chi-square 20 percent value = 4.64.

14. Millican adds:

> Stylometric results have to be interpreted with great caution, and I'd suggest that to assess the significance of the comparisons you want to make, you should test them not only on your target texts, but also on a number of others—e.g. other writings by the "suspects," AND other comparable writings from "non-suspects." Then you can look at a battery of results, and get a reasonable impression of what is significant in the context and what is not. To be frank, I suspect that on texts of the length you're dealing with (i.e., very short texts), only Signature's word-list test is likely to be of much use.

> However, there is hope for those who wish to pursue Poe as the clandestine author: "Eventually I hope to put more sophisticated tests into the system, because things like word length, sentence length and letter frequency are pretty crude, and tend not to discriminate authors

very reliably (though sentence length gives very interesting results if texts are long enough, e.g. novels)."

15. For a much fuller account of this, see *The Last Haunting of Edgar Allan Poe: an Identification of "Poe Preferences" Contained in* The Beale Papers by Robert Ward, *www.bealepapers.com*.

16. Peter Millican's detailed results are as follows:

Word length	The difference is very highly significant at the 0.1 percent level.
Sentence length**	The difference is NOT significant even at the 20 percent level. Chi-square 20 percent value = 1.64.
Usage of letters	The difference is very highly significant at the 0.1 percent level.
Punctuation	The difference is very highly significant at the 0.1 percent level.
Common words	The difference is very highly significant at the 0.1 percent level.

17. http://bealesolved.tripod.com.

18. All spelling and punctuation is what was supplied by the group who produced the solution and is taken from their website.

Chapter 6: *Dorabella: "Ah, That Is Telling!" Number 36*

1. Dora Penny, Edward Elgar: Memories of a Variation (OUP, 1937).

2. *A Tenderfoot in Colorado, A Tenderfoot in New Mexico* and *Last Memories of a Tenderfoot*, all published in the 1920s. He also wrote a book entitled *Inspired Golf*.

Chapter 7: *"This Is the Zodiac Speaking"*

1. Subsequently increased by a further 152½ years—as pointless a piece of judicial nonsense as any ever committed by a judge, sober or drunk.

2. As he was under the age of eighteen, his identity was not released by the court. He was released on parole in 2004 and located in a different area of Japan. He disappeared a few months later. His current whereabouts are unknown.

3. The film was very close to the original Zodiac in many details. Both used the Zodiac circle and cross icon, both wore the same military-type shoes and had the *San Francisco Chronicle* as the newspaper of choice for communication. In the film, Inspector Callahan tracks Zodiac through a park near the real-life Stine killing. Interestingly, Paul Newman is reported to have turned the part down as he did not like the

right-wing retributive politics of the script and suggested Eastwood instead.

4. The *San Francisco Chronicle* suspected that the killer may have come from their own print room as the killer used similar narrow fan-fold paper. They looked closely at two employees, who were regarded as suspicious. Both vanished, one disappearing during the night shift and leaving behind a sick note, the other never bothering to collect his wages. Source: Robert Graysmith, *Zodiac Unmasked*, pp. 89-90 (paperback edition).

5. Though of course it would also be known to the senior police officers who had worked on the case.

6. He was interviewed at length at the Queen of the Valley Hospital on September 28, 1969. The interview was taped and transcribed.

7. Hartnell was not sure whether he said Colorado or Montana, but there were no escapes from prisons in either state.

8. Hartnell interview with KGO, Channel 7, October 17, 1969.

9. This was smudged by a nervous scene-of-the-crime officer, rendering it valueless.

10. He had attempted to tie his very first victims (Domingos and Edwards), though he had then shot them, even though he was carrying a knife.

11. San Francisco Police Department Incident Report, October 11, 1969, 9:58 p.m.

12. San Francisco Police Department "wanted" poster, October 13, 1969, No. 87-69.

13. Donald A. Fouke, patrolman, Star 847.

14. Michael D. Kelleher and David Van Nuys, *This Is the Zodiac Speaking* (Westport, Connecticut, 2002), p. 93.

15. The full text reads:

> This is the Zodiac speaking up to the end of Oct I have killed 7 people. I have grown rather angry with the police for their telling lies about me. So I shall change the way the collecting of slaves. I shall no longer announce to anyone. When I committ my murders, they shall look like routine robberies, killings of anger, + a few fake accidents, etc.
>
> The police shall never catch me, because I have been too clever for them.
>
> 1. I look like the description passed out only when I do my thing, the rest of the time I look entirle different. I shall not tell you what my descise consists of when I kill
>
> 2. As of yet I have left no fingerprints behind me contrary to what the police say in my killings I wear transparent fingertip

guards. All it is is 2 coats of airplane cement coated on my finger-tips—quite unnoticible + very effective

3. my killing tools have been boughten through the mail order outfits before the ban went into efect. Except one & it was bought out of the state. So as you can see the police don't have much to work on. If you wonder why I was wipeing the cab down I was leaving fake clews for the police to run all over town with, as one might say, I gave the cops som bussy work to do to keep them happy. I enjoy needling the blue pigs. Hey blue pig I was in the park—you were useing fire trucks to mask the sound of your cruzeing prowl cars. The dogs never came with in 2 blocks of me + they were to the west + there was only 2 groups of parking about 10 min apart then the motor cicles went by about 150 ft away going from south to north west

p.s. 2 cops pulled a goof abot 3 min after I left the cab. I was walking down the hill to the park when this cop car pulled up + one of them called me over + asked if I saw anyone acting suspi-cious or strange in the last 5 to 10 min + I said yes there was this man who was runnig by waveing a gun & the cops peeled rubber + went around the corner as I directed them + I disappeared into the park a block + a half away never to be seen again. [This section has been marked off with the note "must print in paper."]

Hey pig doesnt it rile you up to have your noze rubed in your booboos?

If you cops think I'm going to take on a bus the way I stated I was, you deserve to have holes in your heads. Take one bag of ammonium nitrate fertilizer + 1 gal of stove oil & dump a few bags of gravel on top + then set the shit off + will positivily ventalate any thing that should be in the way of the blast.

The death machine is all ready made. I would have sent you pictures but you would be nasty enough to trace them back to developer + then to me, so I shall describe my masterpiece to you. The nice part of it is all the parts can be bought on the open mar-ket with no questions asked.

1 bat. Pow clock—will run for aprox 1 year

1 photoelectric switch

2 copper leaf springs

2 6V car bat

1 flash light bulb + reflector

1 mirror

2 18" cardboard tubes black with shoe polish inside + oute

the system checks out from one end to the other in my tests. What you do not know is whether the death machine is at the sight or whether it is being stored in my basement for future use. I think you do not have the manpower to stop this one by continually searching the road sides looking for this thing. + it wont do to re roat + re schedule the busses because the bomb can be adapted to new conditions. [Here, the Zodiac's crossed-circle has been modified with five Xs drawn along the symbol's left side.]

Have fun!! By the way it could be rather messy if you try to bluff me.

P.S. Be shure to print the part I marked out on page 3 or I shall do my thing.

To prove that I am the Zodiac, Ask the Vallejo cop about my electric gun sight which I used to start my collecting of slaves.

16. The case against Allen is made at greatest length in Robert Graysmith's book *Zodiac Unmasked* and elsewhere on numerous websites. Though very strong, the evidence is only circumstantial. However, many in the U.S. have gone to the electric chair on far less than the circumstantial evidence from the search, plus the positive identification from one of his victims, Mike Mageau.

Index

Other Ulysses Press Books

Atheist Universe: The Thinking Person's Answer to Christian Fundamentalism
David Mills, $14.95
Foreword by Dorion Sagan
Clear, concise and persuasive, *Atheist Universe* details exactly why God is unnecessary to explain the universe and life's diversity, organization and beauty.

Complete Krav Maga: The Ultimate Guide to Over 230 Self-Defense and Combative Techniques
Darren Levine & John Whitman, $21.95
Developed for the Israel military forces, Krav Maga has gained an international reputation as an easy-to-learn yet highly effective art of self-defense. Clearly written and extensively illustrated, *Complete Krav Maga* details every aspect of the system including hand-to-hand combat moves and weapons defense techniques.

Courage After Fire: Coping Strategies for Troops Returning from Iraq and Afghanistan and Their Families
Keith Armstrong, LCSW, Paula Domenici, PhD & Suzanne Best, PhD, $14.95
Foreword by Senator Bob Dole
Deals with the repercussions of combat duty, including posttraumatic stress symptoms, and outlines specific ways to reintegrate into families, workplaces and communities.

The Lost Sutras of Jesus: Unlocking the Ancient Wisdom of the Xian Monks
Edited by Ray Riegert & Thomas Moore, $11.95
Combines the amazing story and remarkable text of the Xian monks into a fascinating historical journey and spiritual quest.

Serial Killers: Up Close and Personal: Inside the World of Torturers, Psychopaths and Mass Murderers
Christopher Barry Dee, $13.95
World-renowned investigative criminologist Christopher Berry-Dee goes deep into the bowels of the world's toughest prisons to face serial killers and hear their stories.

Solomon's Builders: Freemasons, Founding Fathers and the Secrets of Washington, D.C.
Christopher Hodapp, $14.95
Solomon's Builders guides readers on a Freemason's tour of Washington, D.C. as it separates fact from myth and reveals the background of the sequel to *The Da Vinci Code*.

Total Heart Rate Training: Customize and Maximize Your Workout Using a Heart Rate Monitor
Joe Friel, $14.95
Shows anyone participating in aerobic sports, from novice to expert, how to increase the effectiveness of his or her workout by utilizing a heart rate monitor.

To order these books call 800-377-2542 or 510-601-8301, fax 510-601-8307, e-mail ulysses@ulyssespress.com, or write to Ulysses Press, P.O. Box 3440, Berkeley, CA 94703. All retail orders are shipped free of charge. California residents must include sales tax. Allow two to three weeks for delivery.

About the Author

Richard Belfield is an award-winning television producer and writer. Currently a Joint Managing Director of Fulcrum TV in London, he revealed the first human case of mad cow disease and many disturbing aspects of the Paris crash that killed Princess Diana. He is author of *Terminate with Extreme Prejudice*, the definitive modern account of assassination, and two books on Rupert Murdoch. Belfield has three children and lives in south London.